"It's ^{Not} Adam's Fault!"

The Real Sin in Original Sin

Charles Garner

It's NOT Adam's Fault!
The Real Sin in Original Sin

ISBN: 979-8-9924408-4-3

Acknowledgements:

Scripture references are from the English Standard Version, the New American Standard Version (1977), the King James Version, and the Latin *Vulgate*. Any others are noted in the text.

Contributors:

Over a lifetime of grappling with this subject, many individuals have contributed to my understanding and growth. While there are too many to mention, a few deserve special recognition—both those still with us and those who now dwell in the highest plane: Dr. Ivan Parke, Tony Martin, Dr. Brian Brewer, Dr. Frank Stagg, Dr. Ray Robbins, Dr. Fisher Humphreys, Dr. J.W. MacGorman, Dr. Herschel Hobbs, a student who struggled with the sinlessness of Jesus, and an unnamed woman in a conference who asked one of the more pertinent and clarifying questions I ever received on the nature of Jesus.

Just as iron sharpens iron,
friends sharpen the minds of each other.
Proverbs 27:17 Contemporary English Version

About the Author:

Charles Garner is an author, curriculum designer, and teacher to the church. His B.A. is in Biblical Studies and Social Science. He holds a Master of Religious Education with emphasis in Biblical Exegesis and Theology.

He has authored, edited, or designed over fifty resources and books for use in the Christian community. His works include *Gifts of Grace*, *Reclaiming the Real Jesus* co-authored with Dr. Ivan Parke, *Thinking of Leaving*, *A Canary in a Coal Mine* co-authored with Dr. John Powers, *Beyond Expectations*, *Profiles from* Paul, and *It's NOT Adam's Fault!*.

He and his wife, Nancy, live in the Northern Rockies of Montana.

Editor's Note:

This book is more than a theological critique. It is a necessary excavation of the foundations of inherited guilt. With the precision of a detective and the conviction of a reformer, *It's NOT Adam's Fault!* uncovers how a single mistranslation became a dogmatic cornerstone that misrepresented the nature of sin, distorted the character of God, and burdened generations with unnecessary shame. What unfolds is not merely an argument against inherited guilt, but a clear, redemptive call to reclaim a faith anchored in God's word, not tradition.

Bold, balanced, grounded in Scripture and historical fact—it doesn't just ask us to think differently, it dares us to believe differently. This is a work of courage and clarity. It speaks to the mind, heals the heart, and liberates the soul. For anyone brave enough to question what they've been told about sin and bold enough to follow the evidence, this book will change everything.

Contents

Section 3: A Time of Turbulence

Introduction

"It's not the things I don't know that bother me, it's the things I know for sure that just ain't so."
—Mark Twain

"But in your hearts honor Christ the Lord as holy, always being prepared to make a defense to anyone who asks you for a reason for the hope that is in you; yet do it with gentleness and respect."
—1 Peter 3:15

Both Mark Twain and the Apostle Peter offer insights that will guide our investigation into the dogma of *original* sin—a belief that has shaped Christian thought for centuries. Twain's quote challenges us not only to question what we don't know, but also to reconsider what we *think* we know for certain.

In this book, we will take that challenge seriously. Is the dogma of *original* sin truly rooted in Scripture, or is it the result of centuries of ecclesiastical interpretation and tradition?

As Peter instructs, we must always be ready to give an answer—not merely parroting what we've been taught but examining our beliefs with intellectual honesty and spiritual passion. Testing our beliefs produces confidence and commitment. Our faith should be grounded in truth, not just in tradition alone.

Twain and Peter provide the starting point for our investigation of *original* sin—a dogma widely accepted, but which might not be as biblically sound as it's often made out to be. As Twain said, it's not the questions that challenge us, but the certainties we've been taught to accept without scrutiny. This book challenges what we don't know and what we think we know for sure. Together, we'll uncover whether this dogma is truly rooted in Scripture or the result of centuries of ecclesiastical constructs.

Our journey requires both intellectual and spiritual harmony.

Our faith should be reasoned and grounded, not shaped solely by tradition or assumed dogma. This is what Peter was urging: to have a faith that stands on facts.

This book will be both a confessional and personal journey. It is not an academic treatise, but it is a serious investigation. You can expect a conversational tone, but one that challenges both your thinking and your heart. We will examine the biblical text, theology, and history, all while remaining engaged with the larger implications of our beliefs.

Now, imagine yourself as a detective—a theological detective. Think of the great fictional investigator Hercule Poirot, created by Agatha Christie, whose sharp mind and attention to detail helped him solve many seemingly unsolvable cases. Poirot always carried a small notebook, a place to jot down clues, thoughts, observations, and questions as he worked through a case. He knew that solving a mystery wasn't just about looking at the obvious evidence—it was about finding that one detail that doesn't quite fit, the small clue that might reveal a bigger truth.

As you read this book, I encourage you to do the same. Throughout the book, you'll find sections entitled "Notes and Observations." These spaces are for you to reflect, jot down questions, and track your thoughts as you piece together the case. Just like Poirot, pay attention to those seemingly insignificant details—the things that don't quite line up. This is where your investigation begins.

In detective work, sometimes a case seems to have an obvious solution—everything points to a particular suspect, the facts line up, and the case appears open and shut. But a true detective knows better. They understand that the truth often lies in the things that don't fit the accepted narrative. What might seem like an unimportant detail could be the key that unlocks the whole mystery.

In our case, the "crime" is the belief in *original* or inherited sin—a dogma that has been accepted by many without question. But just as Poirot would, we must examine the facts, question assump-

8

tions, and follow the clues wherever they might lead. Is this dogma truly biblical? Or is it the result of centuries of theological interpretation that has obscured the truth?

In this case, you will become a theological detective. Dr. Fisher Humphreys called theology, "thinking about God." All of us think about God. We just want to think clearly about Him and what He has revealed to us through His word. We'll walk through the Scriptures, explore historical context, and analyze theological positions. Along the way, we'll pick up clues—insights from the Bible, church history, and key figures who have shaped our understanding of sin. Expect to encounter unfamiliar terms, original language, events, and persons. Essential information and explanations are provided. But if additional information is needed, today it is just a click away.

The book serves as a guide in this investigation, but the real work will come from you. Together, we become *forensic theological detectives*. Expect to struggle, to question, and to think deeply about the assumptions that have shaped your beliefs. Like Poirot tracing each clue through the web of relationships and events that led to the crime, we must now examine the factors that led to the development of *original* sin—uncovering the subtle and sometimes hidden forces at play in shaping a dogma that would have profound consequences.

The truth can be elusive. The path might be uncomfortable. But it is worth the effort, for the truth we uncover will lead to clarity in our understanding of salvation, grace, and the gospel.

Let's get started. As we dig into Scripture, theology, and history, keep track of your observations in the *"Notes and Observations"* sections. These will be your tools in solving the mystery of *original* sin. And as you work through the material, pray for guidance from the Spirit of Truth, who will lead you into all truth (John 16:13). Together, let's launch our investigation—and discover a truth that is far more liberating and powerful than we've been led to believe.

9

Notes and Observations

Investigative journal entry: Date: _____ / _____ / _____

Hercule Poirot, our model for a detective, carried a small notebook where he recorded clues, thoughts, and questions. This habit helped him organize his thoughts and piece together evidence. Like Poirot, you must engage your intellect and attention to detail as you critically examine how this dogma of inherited sin developed.

You'll find dedicated pages throughout the book to record your own observations. These notes will be crucial as you piece together your conclusions.

I once asked an outstanding preacher—known for his creative, masterful sermons without notes—how he did it. He replied that handwriting each sermon in full was the key. For him, there was a direct link between writing and speaking the words.

Science supports this: Research shows that handwriting activates brain regions tied to motor and visual processing, improving memory and retention. Handwriting also requires more cognitive effort than typing, promoting deeper understanding. Writing on paper has been shown to strengthen brain activity when recalling information, likely due to its complex, tactile nature.

Keep track of your observations in the *"Notes and Observations"* sections as you work toward your own brilliant conclusions. Date them as you work through the questions and responses. This will allow you to track the progress of your case. May the Spirit of Truth illumine our path. Write your own prayer for direction here:

Executive Summary

It's NOT Adam's Fault clears away centuries of theological baggage to offer a more accurate, biblical understanding of sin. We are born into a state of innocence, not guilt. Sin is not inherited; it is a conscious choice we make to place self-rule (egocentrism) above God's rule (theocentrism). Our first sin is making self, not God, the center.

This isn't a hopeless narrative. The good news of Jesus shines brighter in this light. His life, death, and resurrection offer reconciliation, forgiveness, and liberation from the self-centeredness that leads to sin. The gospel is about God's forgiveness, accessible through repentance and faith. Just as we chose rebellion, we can choose faith and live in the freedom Christ offers.

As we explore Scripture and the history of this dogma, we'll uncover how the traditional view of *original* sin is unbiblical. We'll engage with key figures like Jerome, Augustine, and Pelagius, whose debates still influence modern theology. And we'll wrestle with tough questions like:

- What does the Bible really say about the origin of sin?
- How have traditions distorted the message of Scripture?
- What does the virgin birth have to do with *original* sin?
- What does it mean for us that Jesus was sinless?

This book is more than an academic critique; it's a challenge to how we live and relate to God. If we're born into innocence, sin is not something we inherit but something we choose. This shift redefines how we view our struggles, our relationship with God, and our role in His redemptive plan. We move from a fatalistic belief in inherited guilt—that we are doomed by Adam's sin—to a direct, personal relationship with God, empowered to choose His rule.

By the end of this book, you will not only question the idea that

11

we're born guilty because of Adam, but understand that we are accountable for our individual choices. The traditional belief in inherited sin has obscured the true freedom and restoration available in Christ. Jesus doesn't just fix what we have committed; He liberates us from a life of self-centeredness.

This book isn't just about challenging old ideas—it's about embracing a more hopeful, personal, and liberating vision of humanity's relationship with God. It's time to stop blaming Adam and start celebrating the freedom found in Christ's victory. The gospel is more radical, personal, and liberating than you've imagined.

The Cringe of Christmas Sermons
I often cringe at Christmas sermons. The theology in them can be sloppy, sentimental, and, at times, downright wrong.

One Christmas, I found myself enduring a particularly frustrating sermon. The preacher, trying to engage the congregation, led them down a theological path using a passage from Philippians. He was discussing the dual nature of Christ—how Jesus was both fully divine and fully human. He began by stating, "Jesus was born, and He retained all the attributes of God," a claim that the congregation enthusiastically affirmed. Then he continued, "When Jesus assumed human form, He had all the aspects of a human being," to which the congregation again heartily agreed. But then came the twist: "No," the preacher declared, "He did not have our sin!"

In that moment, my cringe reflex kicked in. What the preacher implied was this: babies are born with inherited sin, but Jesus was not. It's a statement that sounds good in the moment and seems to make sense, especially when framed so clearly. The congregation, swept up in the preacher's fervor, responded with enthusiastic agreement. But one question can bring the logic to a halt: if Jesus was fully human, how could He not have inherited sin, like all humans?

This is exactly what this book is about—the questioning of that unquestioned dogma of inherited sin.

12

The Dogma of Inherited Sin

Let me clarify: I'm not denying the reality of sin. Sin is real, and it's the source of spiritual death and the suffering that pervades our world. What I am challenging is the traditional belief in inherited sin. This theological construct, known as *original* sin, has been built over the centuries from verses taken out of context and interpreted with little attention to the broader sweep of Scripture. Many denominations have been shaped by this belief, but it often disregards the full counsel of the Bible on human nature and sin.

Eisegesis—the practice of reading one's own ideas into Scripture—is rampant. In fact, a whole dogma can rest upon just one verse. And that's exactly what happened with the dogma of *original* or *inherited* sin.

Augustine of Hippo, whose theology has shaped much of Western Christianity, based his entire system on a single verse: Romans 5:12. This verse, however, was taken from Jerome's *Vulgate* translation, which, in this case, was a poor translation. It was the only verse referenced by the Council of Carthage in AD 418 when the dogma of *original* sin was officially entered into the canons of the church. Yet, that single verse, used erroneously, became the shaky foundation for an almost universally accepted dogma.

This dogma became a key element to the power the Catholic Church, specifically, has held over people's lives. It was, after all, an eternally fatal condition whose only solution (baptism) could only be wielded by the Church. A single verse is an unreliable foundation for building such a vast and consequential belief system.

The Legacy of Inherited Sin

The belief in inherited sin has persisted for centuries. Dr. M. R. DeHann, for example, claimed, "It was in the blood." For him, this was the only explanation for inherited sin—sin was passed down through the bloodline—and the father's bloodline at that. But the question remains: Do babies really die and go to hell?

13

Augustine believed the answer was "Yes," that even infants who hadn't sinned personally were still tainted by Adam's sin and deserved eternal punishment. This harsh logic led the Catholic Church to develop the concept of *limbo*—an attempt to soften the fate of unbaptized infants. Such theological contortions are required when building a dogma on a shaky foundation.

Final Thoughts

This book is not about denying the reality of sin, but about examining whether the traditional dogma of inherited sin is based on a solid biblical foundation or the product of human speculation, ego, and conflict; poor translations; and faulty reasoning. It's time to take a closer look at what Scripture truly teaches.

Section 1
Authority: Basis for Belief

The authority of Scripture has been a central tenet of Christian theology since the beginning. While various Christian traditions recognize the Bible's primacy, there are differing views on its role in guiding faith and practice. Similarly, the doctrine of sin has been a focal point of theological reflection, especially concerning humanity's inherent nature and its need for redemption.

Since the Reformation, the question of who or what constitutes highest authority in matters of salvation, doctrine, and practice has remained central to the church's self-understanding. For a theological detective, this is the question: What is ultimate "chain of custody" for truth—Scripture, tradition, or a mix of both?

Traditional Views on the Authority of Scripture and Sin
Before we can inspect the crime scene, we must inventory the official statements—*the sworn affidavits*, if you will—issued by the major traditions. Traditional Christian thought on authority and sin is articulated through theological confessions.

For example, the Roman Catholic Church, in its *Catechism*, defines the dogma of *original* sin as a state of deprivation transmitted through human generation, leaving humanity in need of divine grace for salvation (*Catechism of the Catholic Church*, 404). The Catholic Church places authority in both Scripture and Sacred Tradition, with the Magisterium—the Church's teaching authority—serving as ultimate interpreter.

Likewise, the United Methodist Church, as outlined in its *Book of Discipline*, acknowledges *original* sin as a condition of separation from God inherited from Adam's "fall", emphasizing the transformative power of grace through Christ (*Book of Discipline*, ¶ 161). The Methodist tradition, like the Catholic Church, recognizes both Scripture and the church as sources of authority.

The <u>Anglican tradition</u>, expressed in the *Thirty-Nine Articles of Religion*, upholds *original* sin as the corruption of human nature resulting from Adam's "fall", leaving all individuals deserving of God's judgment and in need of grace (*Thirty-Nine Articles*, Article 9). Similarly, the <u>Reformed tradition</u>, as articulated in the *Westminster Confession of Faith*, asserts that humanity's "fall" through Adam's sin left all people spiritually dead and morally corrupt, necessitating divine intervention (*Westminster Confession*, Chapter 6, Article 2).

The <u>Lutheran Church</u>, through the *Augsburg Confession*, echoes this understanding, reinforcing that *original* sin has corrupted human nature, making reconciliation with God impossible apart from divine grace (*Augsburg Confession*, Article II).

In each tradition, Scripture is held as authoritative, though each emphasizes different interpretive structures—whether through the church, sacraments, or personal engagement.

Scripture Alone—and the Rejection of Inherited Sin
While these traditional views on sin and authority have shaped Christian thought for centuries, this section challenges certain key aspects of these doctrines. In particular, we will examine the dogma of inherited sin (explicitly in its Augustinian formulation, based on Romans 5:12, *Vulgate*) and question whether it truly reflects the full sweep of the biblical narrative.

As we focus on *sola Scriptura*, the authority of Scripture alone, you are invited to reconsider the role of tradition and ecclesiastical authority in shaping theological convictions. We will not shy away from the tensions between tradition and Scripture but will let the full counsel of God's word shape our faith.

16

1

The Word of Truth

"The truth lies where the evidence points." —unknown

Have you ever found yourself unexpectedly in deep water? You know that sense of panic that comes when you are expecting the water to be rather shallow and then, suddenly, there's no bottom.

In 1976, I unexpectedly found myself in deep water. With a newly minted seminary degree, I arrived at my first place of service. The church was part of an association of churches that cooperated together to achieve purposes they could not achieve individually. They held a set of beliefs in common. And the basis of their authority that helped facilitate and cement their fellowship was the Bible as a guide "in all matters of faith and practice."

Each year, a study of a specific book of the Bible was promoted. That year, the study was the book of Romans. Various ministers in the association were enlisted or assigned to do a study of certain chapters of Romans and present them to the ministers' conference in preparation for the group leading their congregations through the study. As Providence would have it (I do mean that God had a hand in guiding that assignment), I was assigned chapter 5. Talk about the deep end of the pool—I didn't know how deep it was.

Thirty-five years after leading that study for the group of ministers, I came across a copy of the study resource that had been published to help guide those who would be teaching the study of Romans in their churches in 1976. The book was entitled, *Romans: Everyman's Gospel*, by Dr. J.W. MacGorman, legendary Professor of New Testament at Southwestern Baptist Theological Seminary.

I did not have access to a copy of Dr. MacGorman's book when

17

I prepared to lead the study to the group of ministers in that east Mississippi county. And it was probably best that I didn't. I had to do my own work of exegesis of the text. When you do the work yourself, you own it and have it for a lifetime. And that lends an authority that does not come by quoting other authors or scholars.

I was privileged to hear Dr. MacGorman teach only once, but his power and authority in dealing with the text of the Bible left a lasting impression. When his book came into my possession, I was extremely interested to see Dr. MacGorman's take on the passage that had created my consternation in 1976. He wrote of the critical section from chapter 5 of Romans: *No passage in this letter is more difficult to understand than Romans 5:12-21. No passage has suffered a greater distortion at the hands of its interpreters.*

This passage is the primary basis for the dogma of inherited sin. I could not find that dogma in the text. As I presented the results of my study of chapter 5 to the ministers that October morning in 1976, I posed the proposition that *original* sin appeared to be from the choice of each person's rebellion at a point in time, not an inherited sin nature, guilt, or sin from Adam. Have you ever encountered a doctrine that seemed to conflict with what you believed Scripture taught or what your traditions held? That was me on that day.

The format was designed for give-and-take—questions or observations—from the group. After I posed the concept, I heard a brother clear his throat as he prepared to address the issue. It was Pastor Smith, dressed in his black suit, white shirt, and obligatory black tie. He was the "bishop" of the pastors of the area because he was a long-tenured, respected pastor—and he had the gray hair to give him the necessary aura of wisdom and acumen. He said, "Young man, does a skunk stink because of his choice or because of his nature?" What was I to say, I was ill-prepared to discuss zoology and the defense mechanisms of skunks. So as the young newcomer, I stumbled on and left the image hanging out there.

People often have the correct response long after the moment has come and gone. And the proper response came after a few days of reflection. Brother Smith was actually blaming the skunk's scent glands and their horrific odor on the One who had created the skunk—God! That was no different than Adam blaming God for creating the woman who had offered him the forbidden fruit: *And the man answered, The woman whom **You** gave me, she gave me fruit from the tree, and I ate it* (Genesis 3:12). When you look at Adam's response, it appears that he was blaming Eve. But closer reading will show that he was in reality blaming God.

That seems to be the default position—pass the buck—blame someone else—anyone but ourselves.

That early experience of studying Romans 5 set the stage for a deeper journey into questioning one of the most ingrained dogmas in Christian theology: *original* sin. As I reflected on that passage, I found myself wrestling with a theological construct that, upon closer examination, might not be as biblically supported as claimed.

Maybe God has said something about this.

The Standard of God's Word

To begin our investigation, we must first establish the standard by which all truth is measured. The Bible is our plumb line, the unshakable measure of what is true. In John 17:17, Jesus affirms, *Thy word is truth*. Truth, as a central theme in Jesus' ministry, was not just a concept but a person—*I am the way, the truth, and the life*, He declared to His disciples in the upper room (John 14:6). Jesus, The Word (The *Logos*), as revealed in Scripture (John 5:39), is the fixed point by which we align everything we believe and practice.

This plumb line is made even clearer in the conversation between Jesus and the Jews in John 8. He rebukes them for rejecting the truth, accusing them of trying to kill Him (John 8:40). Their rejection of truth leads to a confrontation that escalates to violence, with the Jews picking up stones to throw at Jesus (John 8:59).

Why this violent response? Because, as in the case of many

19

who challenge established dogma, the truth does not always align with what we are accustomed to believing.

The image of a plumb line, as used by the prophet Amos, further illustrates the unwavering nature of God's truth. Just as a builder uses a plumb line to measure the integrity of a wall, the Bible, interpreted through the lens of Jesus, is the measure of all our beliefs and practices. Scripture hangs straight and unmoving beside every doctrine we construct. It does not bend to human tradition or opinion but is the fixed, unshakable standard by which all things must be aligned. If something leans away from that line—no matter how venerable the tradition—we must rebuild, not bend the plumb line.

Biblical Revelation

During a heated exchange with the Pharisees (John 8:12-59), Jesus emphasized, *"The truth will make you free* (v. 32).*"* Jesus opposed traditions that trumped Truth.

Traditions are not all bad. In fact, many are good. They foster a sense of continuity and commonality in the community of faith.

Erroneous traditions give rise to traditionalisms which, at least, should be resisted and, at most, removed. We should oppose error whenever…

(1) tradition supplants truth;

(2) tradition suppresses truth;

(3) tradition claims to be synonym for truth.

While traditions can be beneficial in maintaining continuity and shared understanding, the danger arises when they either suppress or supplant biblical truth. The call to pursue truth means resisting traditions that, knowingly or unknowingly, twist Scripture to fit man-made systems. This is why we must insist on the authority of Scripture alone—because only Scripture holds the truth that guides us in every aspect of faith and practice.

Believers should be engaged in the pursuit of truth rather than tradition. Where truth leads, we must follow. To quote an earlier confession of faith, *the sole authority for faith and practice...is the Scriptures of the Old and New Testaments*. A fundamental assumption for us should be the authority of Scripture.

Tradition gives rise to dogma and Scripture (truth) gives rise to doctrine—the teachings of God's revealed truth.

Dogma (as I choose to make the distinction in the use of the term) is a creation of man, rather than a revelation of God. The thought processes of human beings give rise to dogma, opinion. *Dogma* is a direct transliteration from the Greek word, *dogma*, and is translated as *decree* (Lk. 2:1; Acts 16:4; 17:7). A related word, *dogmatizō*, is translated as *regulations* in Colossians 2:20. Often *dogma* comes from inappropriate **use** of Scripture. A verse (or even a phrase) is sometimes taken out of context and given the weight of doctrine. It is applied as a principle in ways God never intended. When Scripture is misused, it results in <u>dogma</u>, not <u>doctrine</u>.

Doctrine originates with God. He reveals truth to us through the Scripture that informs our beliefs and behaviors. But, that Scripture must be used properly--being interpreted, using solid principles of hermeneutics (a big word meaning the science and methodology of interpretation).

Read 1 Timothy 1:3-8; 2 Timothy 2:15; 2 Peter 3:14-18.

Each of these passages addresses the right **use** of Scripture. Doctrine comes from the correct interpretation and use of Scripture. To misuse the Scripture is to abuse the Scripture. It is not enough merely to quote a text.

It has been stated that *a text out of its context is a pretext for a proof text*. A proof text is a passage taken out of its context and used to support a teaching that it would not support if taken in context. A proof text is used to "prove" a point. Context is crucial to *handling accurately/rightly dividing the word of truth* (2 Timothy 2:15). Only by understanding a verse in its context can

21

we hope to interpret it accurately.

Here's a quick, simple way to illustrate this—Psalm 14:1 declares, *"There is no God."* That is all some people need to bolster their argument that you can't trust the Bible or if you do, the book unequivocally states that God does not exist. I know this is simplistic and you already know the truth. We must ask, "What is the context of that declaration?" Because the preliminary phrase is crucial to the true meaning— *"The fool says in his heart…"*

When the phrase is put in its context with initial intent, the argument evaporates like spilled water in the Arizona desert. And while this is a simple illustration, other abuses are more subtle.

Two words help us understand the essence of using the Scripture correctly. *Eisegesis* means to read <u>into</u> the text of Scripture that which is not there. *Exegesis* means to <u>draw out</u> from the text of Scripture the meaning of the text. The difference—from *eisegesis*, **we get dogma**; **from** *exegesis*, **we get doctrine**. *Exegesis* draws from the text its meaning and import to our lives.

Eisegesis or Exegesis?

Eisegesis gives rise to traditionalisms. Recall the Christmas plays you have seen. Around the birth event some of these traditionalisms have arisen. Here's three…

(1) *Three* wise men came to visit Jesus.

(2) They came to visit the *infant* Jesus.

(3) They came to the *stable* shortly after the shepherds leave.

Read Matthew 2:1-15 and do some exegesis.

(1) How many wise men actually came to visit Jesus?

(2) How does Matthew refer to Jesus?

(3) Where did the wise men visit Jesus and His parents?

While traditions can be beneficial in maintaining continuity and shared understanding, the danger arises when they either suppress or

22

supplant biblical truth. It is a minor matter whether our Christmas plays get the order and set right for the shepherds and the Magi. But it is a simple illustration of how something can enter the collective mind. It becomes "truth" to many who see but do not know.

The call to pursue truth means resisting traditions that are often the product of eisegesis—reading into the text something that is not there. This is why we must insist on the authority of Scripture alone. Only Scripture holds the truth to guide us in our faith and practice.

Scripture must be used correctly (*handling accurately/rightly divided*— 2 Tim. 2:15 KJV), being interpreted according to proper principles of interpretation. This means knowing the type of literature a passage is from, knowing the language and how the words are used, understanding the historical context, and placing each verse or passage in its proper context. All of these will help us use the Scripture with integrity.

For a period of time, I taught a class, "Introduction to the New Testament," as an adjunct professor in college. It was a state college and the students came from all kinds of backgrounds. To get everyone on the same footing to approach the subject, an overview of the principles of biblical interpretation was useful. I developed a simple overview of the disciplines of biblical interpretation for them. Take a few minutes and review these principles of interpretation. They will assist in your investigation as it unfolds in this book.

Principles of Interpretation

A variety of methods can be used to study and interpret the Bible. For example, some persons use the ***allegorical*** method. In the allegorical method each specific aspect of a text is used to represent some tenet of teaching. This approach is highly figurative, seeing in the text something other than the literal meaning. This method can lead to some highly unusual interpretations. Meaning is not exegeted from the text, but rather, imposed upon it by the interpreter.

An example of this method comes from an exchange that took place early in American history. At issue, the separation of church and state. John Leland spent sixty-seven years as a Baptist evangelist. He became known as a courageous and witty opponent of state-run churches such as the Anglican Church. The following exchange has been reported between Leland and a state clergyman who challenged Leland's denouncement of state support for churches:

The clergyman argued that "The minister should get tax support so he will not have such a hard time preparing his sermons."

Leland replied that he could "expound the Scriptures without any special preparation."

"Let's see if you can," answered the clergyman. "What, for instance would you do with Numbers 22:21, 'And Balaam…saddled his ass?'" Leland proceeded with three points:

(1) Balaam, as a false prophet, represents a state-hired clergy.

(2) The saddle represents the enormous tax burden of their salaries.

(3) The dumb ass represents the people who bear such a tax burden."

This humorous exchange illustrates the allegorical method. Words like <u>represents</u>, <u>means</u>, <u>symbolizes</u> are often indicators of an allegorical approach. This method gives extreme latitude to the interpreter to overlay the text with such meaning as he or she wishes.

This method is suspect because we can easily be subjected to shaky processes of interpretation. If the foundation is off, the building will not be right. If our interpretation is wrong, can the doctrine be right?

Oddly, some of the more influential shapers of Christian beliefs have used this method—for example, the early Church Fathers like Origen and Augustine. This is a scary thought. We can easily be subjected to shaky processes of interpretation. The better approach is the **Grammatical, Historical, Critical, Application** method of interpretation.

24

Critical is the discipline of Biblical Criticism—the detailed investigation of the origin and history of biblical documents. The study of the ancient texts is crucial to an accurate biblical text from which we make modern translations. Because the discipline requires such scholarly preparation, it is far beyond the scope of this study and will not be covered here. We appreciate those members of the Christian community who feel called to this field of investigation. The majority of us are in debt to those who undertake this rigorous, life-long discipline. Their labor has given us reliable translations.

In the **Grammatical, Historical, Critical, Application** method of interpretation, several principles are used to interpret accurately the text of the Bible. The following outline provides an overview of the principles recommended to interpret Scripture with integrity.

1. **Linguistic Principle**: The Bible is written in a variety of languages. Language is intended to be understood. If the words' usage can be discerned, their meaning can be understood.

    Primary languages: Hebrew, Greek
    Secondary languages: Latin, Assyrian, Egyptian,
        Babylonian, Persian, Aramaic

    A. Literary forms: The languages of the Bible employ a variety of literary forms. The Bible is not *a* book; it is a *library* of books. As in any library, it contains a variety of types of literature. A determination needs to be made of the nature of the form of literature because each has unique aspects that must be considered in its interpretation. These forms include:
    - historical narratives: history in story form—Genesis
    - law: civil and ceremonial—Exodus, Leviticus
    - poetry: Job, Proverbs, Song of Solomon, Ecclesiastes
    - songs: poetry set to music—Psalms
    - prophetic sermons: the messages of the prophets—Isaiah
    - gospels: biographical accounts of the life of Jesus
    - letters: communications to specific churches, individuals,

or groups of persons by a specific writer often dealing with moral or theological problems—Romans, Hebrews
• apocalyptic writings: symbolic writings, written in coded language, usually making use of numerology—Revelation

(This resonates with the intent behind Dr. W. A. Criswell's book, *Why I Preach That the Bible Is Literally True*. While the title emphasizes a literal approach, a more precise title might be *Why I Preach That the Bible Is **Literarily** True*, highlighting the importance of recognizing the Bible's literary genres in interpretation. It's important to note that this observation is not a critique of Dr. Criswell; I had the privilege of meeting him over coffee several years ago. He was a brilliant preacher and scholar, advocating for a disciplined approach to scriptural interpretation.

Both Dr. Criswell and the Apostle Paul, who admonished believers to handle the word of truth accurately (2 Tim. 2:15), emphasize the necessity of diligence in studying and interpreting Scripture. Accuracy in scriptural usage was their shared goal.)

B. Figures of speech: Literary devices used in a non-literal way to achieve an effect beyond normal language. Examples are:
• Hyperbole- an extreme exaggeration like *a camel through the eye of a needle*
• Simile- a comparison using like or as such as *the kingdom of heaven is like a pearl of great price*
• Metaphor- a comparison without the use of like of as such as *you are the salt of the earth*
• Parable- an earthly story with a heavenly meaning, usually a short, simple story teaching a moral lesson
• Allegory- a story in which people, things, and happenings usually have another meaning such as the parable of the sower and the seed

26

C. Word meaning/usage: The specific meaning or usage of the words used by the original authors must be determined.

D. Tense of verbs: In English, we have three primary tenses—past, present, and future. Biblical languages, especially *Koine* Greek, use tenses to convey aspect as well as chronological sense or sequence. Know the verb tenses.

E. Literal and figurative language: To arrive at a proper interpretation of biblical literature, attention must be paid to whether the language is used to represent concrete or abstract concepts. For instance, the use of numbers in the text often has representative features rather than concrete applications.

For example, take the numbers 6 and 7. Six is the number of sinister significance—it symbolizes the inability to reach the height of perfection of the number 7. Seven is the perfect number, earth crowned with heaven—the combination of 4 (number of earth: 4 winds, 4 points of the compass, etc.) and 3 (the divine number—heaven or God/the Trinity)—represents the totality of heaven and earth.

In the Revelation, the mark of the Beast is the number 666. Is it an actual number that will be tattooed on the forehead or hand? Or, does the use of this number mean something more? Does its use point to the particular failure to achieve the divine? Does it represent evil raised to the Nth power? Is its use literal or figurative? Probably the latter.

While figurative language is symbolic, this does not mean "unreal"—just "figurative with theological intent."

2. **Historical Principle**: The Bible is history—a different type of history. It is redemption history—the story of God's actions in order to redeem us. The events and people detailed in it were a part of the larger movement of nations and world-wide historical events. Each biblical book must be placed in its historical set-

27

ting. To understand the writings, know the circumstances of the time, who wrote, when, where, what, to whom.

3. **Contextual principle**: It has been stated—*a text out of its context is a pretext for a proof text*. A proof text is a passage taken out of its context and used to support a teaching that it would not support if taken in context. A proof text is used to "prove" a point. Context is crucial to *handling accurately/ rightly dividing the word*. Only by understanding a verse in its context can we hope to interpret it accurately. Scripture has five contexts:
    (1) immediate verses around the passage
    (2) the book in which passage occurs
    (3) other passages on same subject by same author
    (4) other passages on the same subject by other authors in Old Testament or New Testament
    (5) the whole Bible

4. **Application principle**: Dr. Kevin Peacock, Professor of Old Testament at the Canadian Southern Baptist Seminary, offers insight into this principle. He outlines this principle like this: "We call the Bible 'God's word,' and by that we mean that God has something to say. We believe that God wants people to understand His word and is not trying to be obscure. He spoke to people in the past and He wants to speak to people today through His word. Therefore, we can study the Bible with the knowledge and hope that God wants to speak to us. In fact, any person of normal intelligence under the illumination of the Holy Spirit can understand and apply God's word.

    A common sense approach to biblical interpretation assumes the primary meaning of any passage is the meaning the biblical author intended. This "historical meaning" should control all other meanings. The Scripture cannot mean what it did not mean. So, we seek to answer three questions of any passage:

28

(1) *What did it mean to the original author and audience?* Reading the passage in its context, Bible reference notes, commentaries, and dictionaries will help you find this information.

(2) *What does it mean?* (i.e. What timeless truths are found here? Bible cross references, study notes, and commentaries will help you find some of this, but prayer and openness to God's Spirit is your main resource here.

(3) *What does it mean today?* Getting to know yourself and your people will allow the Holy Spirit to draw a connection between people's needs and this passage.

A very important principle is necessary to note here—this last question should not be answered until the previous two have been answered. Once you have found the lasting truth in the passage, then you can apply the truth to today's setting.

These foundational principles of interpretation will not only guide us through understanding God's word but will also shed light on how we approach some of the most debated doctrines, like the nature of sin and human choice. As you face your own deep waters of faith, these principles will help keep you afloat.

After the next two chapters, you will have opportunity to use these principles as you explore some of the larger framework of the Bible's teaching on the nature of sin and how personal choice demands personal accountability. But as an immediate exercise—

Use the principles of interpretation we have outlined to examine Psalm 51. Answer these few questions:

- *Who wrote the book?*
- *Why?*
- *What were the conditions of the author?*
- *What type of literature is it?*
- *What is the central message of the psalm?*

29

Notes and Observations

Investigative journal entry: Date: _____ / _____ / _____

As a detective, imagine you're investigating a case where the evidence has multiple possible interpretations. How can you avoid imposing your own assumptions on the evidence and instead let it speak for itself? How can you ensure Scripture remains the reliable witness, free from personal biases?

When investigating a case, you must understand the who, what, when, where, and why. How does this apply to interpreting Scripture? Why is grasping the historical context and original language essential?

In an investigation, identifying the nature of each piece of evidence is key. How does recognizing different literary forms in Scripture—law, poetry, history, prophecy—shape your understanding? What happens if you confuse a poem with legal text or treat a metaphor as literal history or fact?

Taking evidence out of context often leads to error. How does the principle of context apply to interpreting Scripture? What are the risks of isolating a verse from its surrounding passages or broader biblical context?

Detectives encounter symbols that require special interpretation. When studying Scripture, how do you decide when a passage should be taken literally or figuratively? How can misinterpreting figurative language lead you astray?

2

Reformation Fires

"I am bound by the Scriptures I have quoted and my conscience is captive to the word of God."   —Martin Luther

Some have suggested that we owe the zealous, expansive ministry of the Apostle Paul to the death of the deacon and first martyr of the church, Stephen (Acts 7:58-60). Our influence lives on after we die. In some ways, the life of Jan Hus lived on in the most effective voice of the Protestant Reformation, Martin Luther.

Early in his monastic studies, Luther was rummaging through the stacks of a library. He stumbled upon a volume of sermons by Jan Hus, the Bohemian (Czech) who was burned at the stake as a heretic. Later, Luther wrote, "I was overwhelmed with astonishment. I could not understand for what cause they had burnt so great a man, who explained the Scriptures with so much gravity and skill."

The Czech martyr passed the torch to a young German monk. Luther took the torch and set alight the whole world.

By 1516, Martin Luther was lecturing on the Bible at the University of Wittenberg. As an Augustinian monk, Luther had been instructed in the use of the *Quadriga*, the standard four-fold approach to interpreting Scripture in the Catholic Church. This system of interpretation was rooted in the teachings of Origen, Augustine, and other early Church Fathers—especially in North Africa—who relied heavily on the allegorical method of interpretation.

The allegorical method of interpretation, as used by Origen, Augustine, and others, had a significant influence on the early church. This method did not seek to interpret the text based on its

31

plain, historical, or grammatical meaning (as we would expect with modern exegesis). Instead, it focused on uncovering deeper, "hidden" meanings within the text—meanings that were not necessarily reflected by the text itself, but that the interpreter believed could be drawn from the passage.

Roots in Africa

The early church father, **Origen**, was part of the influential Christian intellectual community based in Alexandria. In his work on Scripture, he promoted the idea that the Bible had multiple layers of meaning. He categorized these into the **literal**, **moral**, and **spiritual** (or **anagogical**) senses, with the **spiritual** or **hidden** meanings often being the most significant. This interpretive model influenced an influencer who would leave an indelible mark on the church.

For **Augustine**, this allegorical method was especially important because it allowed him to make Scripture speak to the broader theological issues of his day, particularly with regard to *original* sin, human will, grace, and salvation. Augustine's interpretative framework gave him the freedom to take verses and passages and stretch their meaning beyond their immediate historical context to make them align with his theological system.

For instance, **Romans 5:12**—often cited by Augustine to support his dogma of *original* sin—was interpreted not just as a historical event but as a passage that applied universally to all humanity. While the text refers to Adam's sin and its impact on humanity, Augustine's allegorical interpretation expanded it into a framework that argued that all humans inherit sin from Adam's "fall", even before they could commit personal sin. This is an example of **eisegesis** (reading one's own ideas into the text) rather than **exegesis** (drawing meaning out of the text). Augustine's interpretation goes beyond the text's plain meaning to serve a pre-existing theological agenda.

By the time Martin Luther was teaching Bible in Wittenberg, the aspects of biblical interpretation used by Origen and Augustine

32

were formalized as the *Quadriga*. A quadriga was a Roman term for a four-horse team that pulled a chariot. In the Catholic Church, the system of biblical interpretation called the Quadriga, had four specific dimensions required to determine the meaning of a text.

The Quadriga was developed in medieval Christianity—which continued the allegorical approach of the Alexandria school but introduced an even more structured method. The Quadriga consisted of four layers of meaning:

1. **Literal**: The plain meaning of the text.
2. **Allegorical**: The deeper, symbolic meanings related to Christ and salvation.
3. **Tropological**: The moral lessons or ethical applications.
4. **Anagogical**: The eschatological or future implications.

The Quadriga allowed for a form of interpretative flexibility that could be used to support a wide range of theological ideas—even those that might not be rooted in the historical and grammatical context of the original biblical text. This opened the door for eisegesis, as individual theologians could make the text say what they needed it to say to support their theological conclusions.

Codified in Paris

This approach was used by Church authorities to interpret Scripture in a way that supported the teachings of the Church. Particularly in a time when the Church of Rome was working to consolidate power and establish doctrinal unity, this method of interpretation was used to bolster the Church's authority.

The Quadriga, as a formalized method of biblical interpretation, became the standard in the Catholic Church during the medieval period. Its roots can be traced back to the Alexandrian school of interpretation, especially the works of Origen and Augustine. However, it was in the early medieval period—specifically around the 12th and 13th centuries—that the Quadriga began to take shape as a recognized and codified method within the Western Church.

A key figure in this development was Peter Lombard, a 12th-century theologian whose *Sentences* (published around 1150) became one of the most influential theological texts of the Middle Ages. In his work, Lombard outlined a method of scriptural interpretation that would become the Quadriga. His work helped to formalize the approach of allegory, moral interpretation, and anagogical readings, which were part of the Quadriga.

While the Quadriga's fourfold system was used in various forms prior to Lombard, his work contributed to its widespread adoption and institutionalization as the standard for interpreting Scripture within the Catholic Church during the High Middle Ages.

The method was eventually codified in Paris through the 13th century figures like Thomas Aquinas and Hugh of St. Victor. These men built on Lombard's ideas and used the Quadriga extensively in their theological writings. So, while the Quadriga had earlier roots in the early church, notably through Origen and Alexandrian theology, it was in Paris that the Quadriga became codified as a standard method of biblical interpretation in the Catholic Church during the medieval period. It reinforced the idea that the interpretation of Scripture was a matter that needed to be mediated through the institutional Church and its teachings, rather than being accessible directly to the individual believer.

The Pivot

During 1516-1517, Luther rejected the dogmatic authority the Church placed on the Quadriga's fourfold interpretation of Scripture. He began to interpret the Scriptures according to their literal meaning.

This was pivotal. The transition severed one of the significant bonds that tied him to the traditional past. The turn to **literal interpretation of Scripture** not only caused a theological shift for Luther, it also led him to question the authority of the Church in guiding the interpretation. Luther's break with past interpretation ap-

34

proaches signaled a growing challenge to the very foundation of papal authority, a foundation that had held for centuries. The struggle was not just academic, but deeply rooted in ecclesial authority.

This shift marked a turning point not just in Luther's life, but in the history of the church. Where tradition had once held sway, dictating how Scripture could be understood, Luther was now charting a course that would place the word of God alone as the authority. The *sola Scriptura* principle, which means "Scripture alone," stood in direct contrast to the Church's reliance on tradition, papal decrees, and the allegorical interpretations of the past.

How we approach the interpretation of Scripture is essential. When Luther made the step to abandon the straitjacket of formulaic interpretation that was prescribed by the Catholic Church, he set his foot on a path that could only lead to conflict. Freed from allegory, Luther now needed a purer text—and Erasmus delivered it.

Erasmus' Greek New Testament

A new tool was added to Luther's interpretation toolbox. On March 1, 1516, Desiderius Erasmus, a Dutch priest and scholar, published the Greek New Testament's first-ever "critical edition." This work drew from all available Greek manuscripts to compile a text with wording as close as possible to that of the original inspired authors. That work, which went through four revisions, was the first published Greek text available to the public. It is credited with changing Bible translation, preaching, and even the course of church history.

Luther was lecturing on Romans 9 when he obtained a copy of Erasmus' Greek New Testament. It was a tool that revealed the text of Scripture as never before because it put the original language of the Bible in the hands of interpreters. This would be a key tool that Luther would use to translate the Bible into the German language. Armed with this new tool for interpreting Scripture, Luther began to challenge not just theological points but the authority structures that upheld Catholic tradition.

35

When Luther began interpreting the Scripture more accurately, his whole perspective changed. It changed his view of traditions, of salvation, of Law and grace, and more importantly, his view on authority. Luther had already been questioning the authority of the Church, but Erasmus' Greek New Testament provided him with the textual clarity that made the Scriptures come alive for him. It was as though Luther was holding a mirror to the Church's teachings and realized they didn't reflect the original Christian message.

His lecture series could not have fit more perfectly. He lectured on Psalms, then Romans, followed by Galatians, and Hebrews. Psalms is a subjective expression and in teaching it, Luther fell into deeper despair at his own condition as never being able to attain his own standing in righteousness.

In Romans, he found the righteousness of God is a standing that God gave by grace. In Galatians, he found that we attain the righteousness of God through faith and through faith alone. In Hebrews, he found the Perfect Sacrifice and High Priest in Christ who ushered in a New Covenant that provided forgiveness and cleansing from all our sin. We can say: Psalms drove him to despair, Romans opened the door of grace, Galatians nailed that door open, and Hebrews showed him the once-for-all sacrifice that secured it.

While the fire of reformation was beginning to burn in Luther, that flame began to burn intensely through his teaching with the flames being stoked by Erasmus' volume of the Greek text.

The power of Scripture, when allowed to speak on its own terms, transformed Luther's understanding of salvation, grace, and authority. With the light of the Greek New Testament illuminating the true meaning of the biblical text, Luther could no longer ignore the stark contrast between what he saw in Scripture and the practices of the Church. No longer shackled by the weight of tradition and allegorical interpretation, Luther stood at the precipice of a revolution—one that would forever alter the course of Christian history.

The fires of reform had ignited, and there was no turning back.

36

3

Scripture Alone

"A simple man with Scripture has more authority than the Pope or a council."   —Martin Luther

In a time when podcasts and streaming services were not available, debates were a form of entertainment and (occasionally) enlightenment. In a college town filled with professors and students, debates were always in supply. On September 4-5, 1517, Luther posted his *97 Theses* (not to be confused with the *95 Theses* posted a month later) as debate topics to the college.

These 97 Theses were a proposal for a debate on the whole system of Catholic theology, including the concept of free will. Free will was denied by Augustine and became a major part of formulating the dogma of inherited sin. Luther is getting closer to the edge.

A month later, on October 31, 1517, Luther posts his famous *95 Theses* of proposed debate topics on the Wittenberg Castle Church door. Primary focus: authority of the pope to offer indulgences.

Indulgences were first offered as enticements to go on crusades. The earliest record of plenary indulgences being offered was by Pope Urban II in a declaration at the Council of Clermont in 1095. At this Council, held in the Duchy of Aquitaine, Urban issued a call to arms that resulted in the First Crusade. He promised absolution to all who die either on the journey or in battle against the infidels possessing and ravaging the Holy Land.

Opportunity Knocks

The Church leadership recognized an opportunity when they saw one. Indulgences weren't just about securing forgiveness for sins.

37

They became a way to raise money for the Church. If it worked for the crusades, what else could be brought under this venue? Indulgences turned into a pay-to-play system, with the Pope offering a way out of purgatory for those who could afford the price.

It went like this: let's say you had committed a particular sin of some kind. Or, maybe there was a sin you were going to commit like a crusade warrior who was going to kill someone and loot their possessions in the future. Or, maybe your father or your mother, or a favorite uncle twice removed had died with unconfessed sin and they were parked in a place in the afterlife for an unspecified period of time, unable to go to heaven because unconfessed sin had to be atoned for and expiated. Let's call that place purgatory.

Then, let's say that someone, maybe the pope, had access to a "Treasury of Merit." This Treasury of Merit had been built up over the centuries by various contributors—Jesus (a definite), and Mary (because she was a wonderful woman, mother of all mothers), and then we can add the various martyrs (let's call them saints—with a capital "S") because they had been killed, or maybe they were just good, godly people, and then let's add the popes (after all chair of Peter, red shoes, miter, and all that and miracles—don't forget the miracles).

And only one person had the key to all that merit. And let's say for the right price. Doesn't have to be money. Can be prayers, pilgrimages, good deeds, property. But money is always good here at the Merit Store and we do take charge cards and a special offer if you use your Vatican card and the special offer code: "Get Out of Purgatory".

People were lining up to get in on this deal. Looked like a Black Friday sale.

Leading up to the Reformation under Martin Luther, indulgences were sold to finance a building project. Here's a brief refresher on the ignition point for Luther: Saint Peter's Basilica was being refurbished. The renovation was first planned by Pope Nicholas V (1447-

38

1455). Then, Pope Julius II launched the renovation during his papacy (1503-1513). The construction began on 18 April 1506.

When Pope Leo X ascended to the Chair in 1513, he inherited a partially completed building project. And it is important to note, Leo was a Medici. Money was their game. They had it, loved to flash it and splash it around. And Leo knew how to do it. A spendthrift, he blew through one seventh of the papal treasury for his inaugural bash and kept a pet elephant named Hanno. Couldn't get a Chihuahua, had to have an elephant. (Granted, it was a gift from King Manuel of Portugal. But even the ostentatiousness spoke volumes.)

Leo saw a great opportunity to fleece the flock for cash through selling indulgences. And Opportunity came knocking in the form of a greedy German archbishop named Albrecht.

At this moment in time, all the players and circumstances came together to ignite what would be called the Protestant Reformation.

The Tinder and the Spark

Archbishop Albrecht of Mainz wanted to expand his territory. But it was going to cost Albrecht. An arrangement was made with the pope (after all, only the pope had the key to the Treasury of Merit). Leo made a deal with Albrecht so he could sell indulgences. After the fee to Johann Tetzel (the German Dominican salesman whose line, "As soon as the coin in the coffer rings, The soul from purgatory springs," had people lining up), the proceeds from the sale of indulgences would be split 50/50. Half of the sale would go to Pope Leo and the other half would go to Jacob Fugger.

Oh, you might not have heard of Jacob Fugger. He was a banker. Wealthiest man in Europe at the time. This is the man that kings went to when they wanted to finance a war. His backing could change the names of the men who sat upon the thrones of the continent. (And, if he made you a loan, you were in his pocket.)

Albrecht wanted more territory to increase his revenues. But the territory came at a price. Simony (essentially a bribe) was just part

39

of the deal. Another pay-to-play scheme that the papacy cooked up.

But Albrecht didn't have the cash. So the German archbishop went to the wealthiest man in Europe, the German banker, Jacob Fugger to float a loan. And that became an issue. Because to repay the loan, Albrecht wanted to sell indulgences. To do this would require cutting a deal with Pope Leo. But Leo was a Medici and this was right down his alley. So Leo agreed to the sale of indulgences on that 50/50 split. As long as he got his cut, Albrecht could do whatever he wanted with the rest. That, of course, was going to repay the loan to Fugger. (Still with me?)

Now all of this rubbed the local priest and Bible professor at the local University, the German monk named Martin Luther, the wrong way. The professor proposed a debate. Didn't have Netflix. A debate could be informative and entertaining.

All Hallows' Eve—1517

On All Hallows' Eve, October 31, 1517, Martin Luther nailed his *95 Theses* to the Wittenberg Castle Church door—a customary place for academic postings. These theses, simply a list of topics intended for scholarly debate, challenged the sale of indulgences, a practice that had become a lucrative enterprise for the Church.

When he nailed the list to the door, all heaven broke loose. The reaction was swift and severe. Money was at stake, and Luther's challenge could not be tolerated.

At the heart of the controversy lay a fundamental question of authority: Who had the final say—the pope or Scripture? Luther, appalled by the blatant exploitation of faith, saw indulgences as a grievous distortion of grace and a moral affront that preyed on the fears of the faithful.

His propositions shook the very foundation of the Papal system. What began as an invitation to debate became a direct threat to the Church of Rome's power. Luther had to be stopped—at all costs. The powers in Rome didn't know it, but it was too late.

Destroying Luther

A series of events were intended to destroy Luther and silence his voice:

June/July 1519: The Leipzig Debate between Luther and Johannes Eck took place at Pleissenburg Castle in Leipzig, Germany. Eck was Professor of Theology at the University of Ingolstadt and the leading Catholic theologian in Germany. He was a brilliant defender of the dogma of the Church of Rome and of papal and Church councils' authority. In this debate, Luther took a public stand against papal authority and several of the ecclesiastical constructs that gave the Church of Rome power over the adherents to the faith and that were so lucrative to the papal treasury.

June 15, 1520: Pope Leo X issues Papal Bull, *Exsurge Domine*, threatening excommunication if Luther did not recant 41 statements drawn from his writings.

April 17, 1521: Luther appeared before the Diet of Worms (a 'diet" was a formal assembly of religious and political leaders in the Holy Roman Empire) to stand trial for heresy. The Diet had been called by the Holy Roman Emperor, Charles V, who presided himself. Luther might have thought the Diet would be an opportunity to present and defend his ideas, theology, and ecclesiology. However, that was not the case.

Luther was cautioned by the Imperial Marshal that he should speak only in answer to direct questions from the presiding officer. The presiding officer, or prosecutor of the Diet was none other than Johann von der Ecken (often called Johannes Eck). On a table in the room was a collection of 25 of Luther's books and writings. Eck asked Luther basically two questions: 1) Is the collection of books and writings his? and 2) Was he ready to revoke their heresies?

After the titles were read, Luther stated that they were his. He asked for time to consider how he might answer the second question. The next day, April 18, would be a pivotal day in Western Christianity. Here is the account of what occurred:

When the counselor put the same questions to him, Luther first apologized that he lacked the etiquette of the court. Then he answered, "They are all mine, but as for the second question, they are not all of one sort." Luther went on to place the writings into three categories: (1) Works which were well received even by his enemies: those he would not reject. (2) Books which attacked the abuses, lies and desolation of the Christian world and the papacy: those, Luther believed, could not safely be rejected without encouraging abuses to continue. To retract them would be to open the door to further oppression. "If I now recant these, then, I would be doing nothing but strengthening tyranny." (3) Attacks on individuals: he apologized for the harsh tone of these writings but did not reject the substance of what he taught in them; if he could be shown by Scripture that his writings were in error, Luther continued, he would reject them. (Oberman, Heiko, *Luther: Man Between God and the Devil*, New Haven: Yale University Press, 2006.)

Luther concluded by saying: "Unless I am convinced by the testimony of the Scriptures or by clear reason (for I do not trust either in the pope or in councils alone, since it is well known that they have often erred and contradicted themselves), ***I am bound by the Scriptures I have quoted and my conscience is captive to the word of God.*** I cannot and will not recant anything, since it is neither safe nor right to go against conscience. May God help me. Amen."

The die was cast. Luther's fate sealed. He would be excommunicated as a heretic. His life was forfeit. But God had other plans. The fire that was ignited in Luther when he cast off the Quadriga as an enforced grid through which the Bible had to be read, set all of Europe aflame. The revolutionary nature of Luther's action would go on to fracture the unity of the Church over Europe and the world.

Luther went on to translate the Bible into the German language so it could be read and studied by all. The recent invention of the printing press with moveable type became the tool of mass production. Copies of the Bible were produced affordably and distributed all over the country. The watchword of the Reformation became *sola Scriptura*—Scripture alone. Scripture alone would be the sole authority for faith and practice.

Papal Authority and the Magisterium

The Catholic Church's claim to be the exclusive interpreter of Scripture was closely tied to the role of the **Magisterium**, which refers to the teaching authority of the Church. According to Catholic doctrine, the Magisterium (comprising the Pope and the bishops in communion with him) holds the responsibility and authority to interpret the Bible correctly.

This teaching was rooted in the Church's belief that it had been granted by Christ the responsibility to safeguard the truth of Scripture and apply it to contemporary issues. The **Council of Trent (1545-1563)**, which was held in response to the Protestant Reformation, made this position more explicit by declaring that only the Church, in its official capacity, had the correct understanding of Scripture. Here is the statement of the Church:

Council of Trent (Session IV, 1546)

"Moreover, it [the Church] is the supreme judge of the true sense and interpretation of Holy Scripture... Therefore, it is not permissible for anyone to interpret the Sacred Scriptures contrary to that sense which holy mother Church has held and holds."

The Catholic Church, at this time, upheld the idea of **Sacred Tradition** alongside Sacred Scripture. The Church argued that Scripture could not be fully understood without the accompanying Tradition, which was passed down through the Church's teachings and practices. This reinforced the idea that private interpretation was not only dangerous but impossible to get right without the Church's guidance.

Pope Leo XIII (*Providentissimus Deus*, 1893), though later than Luther, articulated this view in the following way: "The task of giving the true meaning of the Holy Scriptures belongs solely to the Church...and no one is permitted to interpret the Bible in any way contrary to the sense which the Church has held and continues to hold."

Luther's Declaration—Ours

The Diet of Worms was Luther's point of no return. Refusing to recant, declaring himself bound by Scripture alone, he defied both Pope and Emperor—shattering the unity of Christendom.

His excommunication led to his "kidnapping" by Frederick the Wise, who hid him in Wartburg Castle. There, Luther translated the Bible into German, breaking Rome's hold on biblical interpretation. Meanwhile, the printing press spread his writings rapidly, fueling reform across Europe.

The Reformation wasn't just theological—it was political. Princes embraced Protestantism to assert independence from Rome, leading to religious wars and the 1555 Peace of Augsburg, which allowed rulers to choose their territories' faith.

Luther's defiance fractured the Church, giving rise to Lutheran, Reformed, and Anabaptist movements. His declaration of *sola Scriptura* struck at the heart of the Church's claim to be the final arbiter of truth. The Reformation permanently reshaped Western Christianity, shifting authority from the Church to Scripture and individual conscience.

Asserting the authority of Scripture was a direct challenge to the tradition that had held sway for centuries. In a world where the Church's voice was considered final, Luther's insistence on the authority of Scripture alone was as scandalous as it was radical. He reminds us that Scripture—free from tradition's constraints—is our sole authority. This word is our guide: *Scripture alone!*

4

Gathering Evidence
Sin and Responsibility

In the previous chapters, we established that the Bible alone is our rule and guide in matters of faith and practice. We emphasized that tradition, while valuable in certain contexts, cannot hold equal authority to the Scriptures. As we turn now to explore personal responsibility, free will, and the nature of sin, it is essential that we continue to ground our understanding in the truth of God's word.

The exercise in this chapter invites you to apply the principles of Grammatical-Historical Interpretation to passages that challenge us to reflect on our personal accountability before God. By doing so, we reinforce the biblical truth that each person must stand before God and give an account for their own actions (Romans 14:12).

This exercise is shaped not by human tradition or opinion, but by the clear teaching of Scripture itself, which continues to be our only source of authority. Through careful reflection on God's word, we align our hearts and minds with His will, ensuring that our faith and practice are rooted in the truth of the Bible alone.

You'll find some texts from the Old and New Testaments along with thoughtful questions for each passage to guide reflection and response. Take the time to work through these. They are evidence. There's no time limit. Advance at your own pace. Put into practice the Principles of Biblical Interpretation introduced in Chapter 1.

1. Isaiah 53:6
"All we like sheep have gone astray; we have turned, every one, to his own way; and the Lord has laid on him the iniquity of us all."
Reflection:
How do you understand the personal nature of sin in this passage?

45

What does it mean that "every one" has gone astray in their own way? In what ways does this verse challenge the idea that we can blame others for our sin or choices?

_____

_____

2. Romans 3:10-12

"As it is written: 'None is righteous, no, not one; no one understands; no one seeks for God. All have turned aside; together they have become worthless; no one does good, not even one.'"

Reflection:

How does Paul's declaration of the universal failure to seek God challenge our assumptions about human goodness and righteousness? What does this say about our own personal accountability before God?

_____

_____

3. Romans 3:23

"For all have sinned and fall short of the glory of God."

Reflection:

What does *fall short of the glory of God* mean to you? How does this verse stress the need for personal responsibility in our relationship with God, and how does it contrast with the idea of inherited sin?

_____

_____

4. Romans 14:12

"So then each of us will give an account of himself to God."

Reflection:

In what ways does the idea of standing before God and giving an account of our actions shape your view of personal responsibility? How does this verse make you think differently about the choices you make each day?

_____

_____

5. Ezekiel 18:20

"The soul who sins shall die. The son shall not suffer for the iniquity of the father, nor the father suffer for the iniquity of the son. The righteousness of the righteous shall be upon himself, and the wickedness of the wicked shall be upon himself."

Reflection:

What is the significance of personal accountability emphasized in this verse? How does this challenge or confirm your understanding of sin and responsibility, especially regarding the impact of others' actions on us?

_____

_____

6. Galatians 6:7-8

"Do not be deceived: God is not mocked, for whatever one sows, that will he also reap. For the one who sows to his own flesh will from the flesh reap corruption, but the one who sows to the Spirit will from the Spirit reap eternal life."

Reflection Question:

How do you interpret the connection between choices and consequences in this passage? How can you apply the idea of sowing to the Spirit in your daily life to avoid the corruption that comes from selfish choices?

47

_____

_____

7. Matthew 12:36-37

"I tell you, on the day of judgment people will give account for every careless word they speak, for by your words you will be justified, and by your words you will be condemned."

Reflection Question:

What does this passage teach you about the power of words in shaping your spiritual accountability? How can understanding the weight of our words influence the way we communicate with others?

_____

_____

8. 2 Corinthians 5:10

"For we must all appear before the judgment seat of Christ, so that each one may receive what is due for what he has done in the body, whether good or evil."

Reflection Question:

How does this passage shape your view of the final judgment? What does to receive *"what is due"* for your actions? How does this underscore personal accountability in the way you live now?

_____

_____

9. Jeremiah 31:30

"But everyone shall die for his own sin. Each man who eats sour grapes, his teeth shall be set on edge."

Reflection Question:

What do you think this passage is trying to convey about individual responsibility and the consequences of personal choices? How does this affect your understanding of sin's personal nature and the importance of personal repentance?

_____

_____

10. Revelation 20:12

"And I saw the dead, great and small, standing before the throne, and books were opened. Then another book was opened, which is the book of life. And the dead were judged by what was written in the books, according to what they had done."

Reflection Question:

What does this scene of judgment in Revelation reveal about the personal nature of judgment and accountability? How does it impact your thoughts on how we live our lives now, knowing we will be judged for what we've done?

_____

_____

11. Matthew 16:27

"For the Son of Man is going to come with his angels in the glory of his Father, and then he will repay each person according to what he has done."

Reflection:

How do you interpret the idea of *"repaying each person according to what he has done"*? What does this suggest about how God sees our actions, and how should this influence our approach to our daily choices?

_____

_____

12. Luke 12:47-48

"And that servant who knew his master's will but did not get ready or act according to his will, will receive a severe beating. But the one who did not know, and did what deserved a beating, will receive a light beating. Everyone to whom much was given, of him much will be required, and from him to whom they entrusted much, they will demand the more."

Reflection Question:

How do you reconcile the idea that those who know more are held to a higher standard with the overall message of individual responsibility? What does this passage reveal about the relationship between knowledge, accountability, and consequences?

_____

_____

13. John 5:29

"Do not marvel at this, for an hour is coming when all who are in the tombs will hear his voice and come out, those who have done good to the resurrection of life, and those who have done evil to the resurrection of judgment."

Reflection Question:

How does this verse reinforce the idea of personal responsibility in the context of eternal outcomes? What do you think it means to be judged based on what one has "*done*," and how does this affect your view of salvation and judgment?

_____

_____

14. Hosea 14:9

"Whoever is wise, let him understand these things; whoever is discerning, let him know them. For the ways of the Lord are right, and the upright walk in them, but transgressors stumble in them."

Reflection Question:

What does this passage suggest about the consequences of choosing either wisdom or folly? How do you see the individual responsibility in making choices that align with God's ways versus those that lead to stumbling?

---

15. Proverbs 24:12

"If you say, 'Behold, we did not know this,' does not he who weighs the heart perceive it? Does not he who keeps watch over your soul know it, and will he not repay man according to his work?"

Reflection Question:

What does this passage say about the accountability that exists even for what is hidden from others? How does it change your perspective on the internal thoughts and motives behind your actions?

---

16. Romans 2:6-8

"He will render to each one according to his works: to those who by patience in well-doing seek for glory and honor and immortality, he will give eternal life; but for those who are self-seeking and do not obey the truth, but obey unrighteousness, there will be wrath and fury."

Reflection Question:

How does this passage illustrate the connection between one's actions and eternal outcomes? What does it teach about the importance of perseverance in doing good and the personal responsibility of seeking God's truth?

_____

_____

17. James 1:14-15

"But each person is tempted when he is lured and enticed by his own desire. Then desire when it has conceived gives birth to sin, and sin when it is fully grown brings forth death."

Reflection Question:

How does this passage explain the process of temptation and sin? What insights do you gain from this about personal accountability in resisting temptation and the consequences of unchecked desires?

_____

_____

18. 1 Corinthians 3:13-15

"Each one's work will become manifest, for the Day will disclose it, because it will be revealed by fire, and the fire will test what sort of work each one has done. If the work that anyone has built on the foundation survives, he will receive a reward. If anyone's work is burned up, he will suffer loss, though he himself will be saved, but only as through fire."

Reflection Question:

What does this passage teach you about how our actions and choices will be evaluated at the judgment seat of Christ? How does it emphasize personal responsibility and the lasting impact of our works, both good and bad?

These reflections should guide you as you think further about the individual nature of sin and accountability before a holy God. When confronted by the vison of God high and lifted up, with the seraphim encircling the throne crying, *Holy, holy, holy is the Lord of hosts*—Isaiah had one response, *Woe is me, for I am ruined! Because I am a man of unclean lips, And I live among a people of unclean lips; For my eyes have seen the King, the LORD of hosts.* We might well feel that same way. But, praise God, He made a way and in our helpless state:

For while we were still weak, at the right time Christ died for the ungodly. For one will scarcely die for a righteous person—though perhaps for a good person one would dare even to die—but God shows his love for us in that while we were still sinners, Christ died for us. Since, therefore, we have now been justified by his blood, much more shall we be saved by him from the wrath of God. For if while we were enemies we were reconciled to God by the death of his Son, much more, now that we are reconciled, shall we be saved by his life. More than that, we also rejoice in God through our Lord Jesus Christ, through whom we have now received reconciliation (Romans 5:6-11).

Notes and Observations

Investigative journal entry: Date: _____ / _____ / _____

If you were given a magnifying glass to aid your investigation, how might viewing Scripture through the lens of *sola Scriptura*—as the ultimate authority for faith and practice—change the way you study the Bible and shape your understanding of doctrine?

As you sift through the evidence of Scripture, how can you tell the difference between faithfully interpreting the text and reading your own ideas into it (eisegesis)? What tools or steps would help you stay true to the text and avoid twisting it to fit your preconceptions, just as a detective carefully piecing together evidence without jumping to conclusions?

As a detective investigating a case, what would you do if you found that a certain teaching or tradition did not align with the solid evidence of Scripture? How would you respond, and what would it look like for you to uphold *sola Scriptura* as the definitive authority amidst competing ideas and voices?

When a detective uncovers new evidence, it often sheds light on the case in ways previously unseen. How might learning about the Bible's original languages—or choosing trustworthy translations—serve as new tools in your investigation? How might you deepen your engagement with the biblical text in ways that reveal details previously unseen, much like a detective using a new piece of technology or insight?

5

Ecclesiastical Constructs

Because they believed in the authority of Scripture for their faith and practice, the reformers rejected what they saw as ecclesiastical constructs—additions to the system of dogmas that were not supported by Scripture. Such additions included: indulgences (1095), transubstantiation (1215), auricular confession (1215), purgatory (1274), penance and so forth. ***Ecclesiastical Constructs*** are additional dogmas, practices, structures, and traditions that the institutional Church developed over the centuries removed from the New Testament era. Another description for ecclesiastical constructs is ***"make-it-up-as-you-go."*** These are additions to church lore and law that do not appear in Scripture.

The Catholic Church was able to use Christianity and particular *doctrinal innovations* as weapons to receive benefits in its dealings with both Church adherents and the secular political world.

One of the clearest examples of a dogma that evolved over time without solid biblical grounding is the Catholic practice of indulgences. The dogma of indulgences allows individuals to reduce the punishment for their sins through certain actions, such as giving money to the church or performing specific acts of penance—prayers, pilgrimages.

(The system of penance grew out of persecutions that occurred in North Africa in the mid-200s. Bishop Cyprian of Carthage required that

INDULGENCES

The Faithful who spend at least a quarter of an hour in reading Holy Scripture with the great reverence due to the Word of God and after the manner of spiritual reading, may gain an indulgence of 300 days (S. C. Ind., Dec. 13, 1898; S. P. Ap., March 22, 1932).

The Raccolta (Preces et Pie Opera) No. 645.

From the flyleaf of The Holy Bible translated from the Latin *Vulgate*, The Douay Bible House, New York, 1932

55

Christians who had denied the faith during persecution perform acts of penance before being restored to full fellowship in the church. Indulgences grew out of that historic event. More on this later.)

While the church's goal in offering indulgences, which formally began as a system in 1095, was to offer a form of spiritual release or purification—and raise significant funds or, in the case of 1095, an army—indulgences have no biblical basis whatsoever. The practice evolved into a complex system of penance in the Middle Ages, where the church claimed authority to grant these reductions in punishment in the afterlife. Nowhere in Scripture is the church given such authority, nor is there any precedent for the idea that sins can be atoned for by monetary offerings or prescribed acts beyond personal repentance before God.

Similarly, auricular confession (the practice of confessing sins to a priest) was formalized in 1215 at the Fourth Lateran Council, yet it cannot be found as a specific command or practice in the New Testament. While the Bible teaches the importance of confessing sins (James 5:16; 1 John 1:9), it doesn't prescribe confession to a priest or offer backing that absolution from a priest cleanses sins on behalf of God. The church added this practice over time, using its authority to shape how believers sought God's forgiveness.

The doctrine of transubstantiation, formally declared in 1215 at the Fourth Lateran Council, asserts that during the Mass, the bread and wine literally transform into the body and blood of Christ. While the symbolic nature of the Eucharist is firmly rooted in Scripture (Luke 22:19-20), the teaching that the bread and wine become Christ's literal body and blood is not clearly supported in the New Testament. This dogma evolved over time and became central to the Catholic sacramental system, though it finds no explicit support in the teachings of Jesus, His apostles, or the New Testament letters.

Lastly, at the Second Council of Lyon in 1274, the Catholic Church defined, for the first time, its teaching on purgatory, in summary two points:

56

(1) some saved souls need to be purified after death;

(2) such souls benefit from the prayers and pious duties that the living do for them.

The Council declared:

> [I]f they die truly repentant in charity before they have made satisfaction by worthy fruits of penance for (sins) committed and omitted, their souls are cleansed after death by purgatorical or purifying punishments, … And to relieve punishments of this kind, the offerings of the living faithful are of advantage to these, namely, the sacrifices of Masses, prayers, alms, and other duties of piety, which have customarily been performed by the faithful for the other faithful according to the regulations of the Church.

Each of these practices—indulgences, auricular confession, transubstantiation, and purgatory—originated not from Scripture but from the Catholic Church's evolving traditions and authority claims. They were layered onto the faith over centuries, codified by councils and popes rather than by Christ or the apostles. Nowhere in Scripture do we find these constructs commanded, taught, or practiced in the early church. Their development was driven by theological speculation, institutional power, and, in some cases, financial and political interests—not by divine revelation.

This pattern should give every believer pause. If we accept doctrines merely because they have been handed down, rather than because they are rooted in the word of God, then we risk elevating human tradition above divine truth. This is precisely what the Reformers saw and what they sought to correct. And it is the same critical lens we must apply to the dogma of inherited sin—does it originate in the inspired words of Scripture, or was it constructed over time by councils, theologians, and church institutions?

Over the centuries many ecclesiastical constructs have been layered upon the simple, once-for-all-delivered faith of the Bible. It is not unlike the original farm house of four small rooms that has been added to over the years as the family and needs demanded enlargement.

Some additions might have enriched the structure; others might have compromised its integrity. Some church expressions have added or changed one item. Other churches added others. Some developed whole systems that are "other than" New Testament teachings. These added beliefs and practices often have no basis or only a tangential connection in Scripture. Some are, on their face, against the teachings of the New Testament. Like Belshazzar of ancient Babylon, they have been *weighed and found wanting*.

If we are to think clearly about moving forward in faith, a biblical vocabulary will be required. Charting a new course requires a return to the language God inspired (2 Tim. 3:14-17). The words of the biblical authors are the words we want to use to evaluate the condition of the church and to shape our faith.

These doctrinal innovations became part of the Catholic Church's identity, often carried out with the authority of the Church and framed as necessary for salvation or spiritual benefit. But, as the Reformers argued, they were not simply "unbiblical"—they were, at worst, misleading and harmful, creating a gap between the true teachings of Scripture and the religious practices of the time.

Indulgences, for instance, not only obscured the sufficiency of Christ's sacrifice on the cross, but they also led to the exploitation of the poor and vulnerable, as people were encouraged to "buy" their way out of sin's consequences. It was one of these "make-it-up-as-you-go" developments that helped spark the Reformation.

In the same way that these man-made traditions evolved within the context of a particular religious system, we can see how *original* sin might have similarly evolved as an ecclesiastical construct. The doctrine of *original* sin was codified over time through theological debates, and it became central to many Christian traditions—even though its foundation in Scripture is not as clear as many assume.

58

Eisegesis and Romans 5:12

This same pattern of doctrinal development applies to *original* sin. To see this, simply examine Romans 5:12-21. It's not immediately apparent that the passage teaches inherited sin, guilt, or a "sin nature" passed down from Adam. This, too, represents a doctrinal innovation—centered on *original* sin. But much like indulgences or auricular confession, it took on a life of its own over time.

Augustine's influence, for instance, heavily shaped Western Christianity's view of *original* sin, but his interpretations might not have fully reflected the intent or clarity of Scripture. The same critical examination that we apply to doctrines like indulgences and transubstantiation can be and should be applied to *original* sin. By doing so, we create space for a deeper, more biblically faithful understanding that resists human-made traditions or interpretations that might have veiled the true meaning of God's word.

We must avoid dogma in favor of doctrine based on careful biblical interpretation. These examples show how traditions and practices, while sometimes well-intentioned, can evolve beyond their scriptural basis and require scrutiny to ensure they align with the truth of God's word.

Notes and Observations

Investigative journal entry: Date: _____ / _____ / _____

In what ways has your own faith tradition developed or added doctrines over time that might not be explicitly grounded in Scripture? Are there practices or teachings in your church that need closer biblical examination?

Think about how your faith perceptions have been shaped. What roles have pastors, teachers, parents played? How do the hymns and songs we sing impact our beliefs? How does the particular Bible translation you use shade your faith concepts? What role does your personal faith exploration and expressions such as mission volunteerism mold your belief system?

Do you find any similarities between the historical development of indulgences, auricular confession, or transubstantiation and the development of the dogma of *original* sin? Why or why not?

How can a return to the language and authority of Scripture (2 Timothy 3:14-17) help you clarify your understanding of faith and doctrine? What steps can you take to deepen your study of the Bible with this commitment in mind?

6

Heresy
Church Authority or Biblical Authority

The label *"heretic"* gets thrown about in various circles. And often the word becomes a term of derision for enemies of orthodoxy. But we need to understand that **heresy** is simply a **minority position** (remember the definition of heretic is someone who holds a minority view—**orthodoxy** is a majority-rules game, though true orthodoxy should be a *"thus saith the Lord"* dictate).

The label *"heretic"* was often used to delegitimize voices of dissent within the church. But we must remember that heresy doesn't always reflect a position that is contrary to Scripture—it simply refers to a view held by a **minority**, a view that challenges the accepted majority interpretation. The reformers, though branded as **heretics** by the Roman Catholic Church, were, in fact, advocating for a return to biblical clarity and truth.

Consider the striking example of **Nicolaus Copernicus**, the brilliant astronomer who proposed the **heliocentric theory** of the solar system—that the Earth revolves around the Sun, not the other way around. This view, based on careful observation and evidence, was condemned as **heretical** by the Catholic Church in the 16th century. For centuries, the Church held to the **geocentric** model, which positioned the Earth at the center of the universe—a view supported by Church teachings and ancient interpretations of Scripture. In retrospect, who was the real heretic—Copernicus, who was simply proposing a scientifically sound theory, or the Church, which fought vehemently to maintain a doctrine proven to be false?

This historical irony underscores a critical point: heresy is often determined by power and authority rather than truth. The majority

61

view, especially when institutionalized by a powerful entity like the Catholic Church, does not necessarily represent the truth of God's word. The Reformers were labeled heretics not because their ideas contradicted Scripture, but because they challenged the authority of the Church. Similarly, Copernicus' challenge to the established geocentric view of the universe was not an attack on Scripture itself, but on a man-made system of understanding that had been improperly placed above Scripture.

In both cases, the **minority view**—whether it was the Reformers or Copernicus—was later vindicated by the weight of truth and evidence. This serves as a stark reminder that **true orthodoxy** is not simply a majority opinion, but **a faithful reflection of Scripture and truth**, regardless of how it might be received at the time.

The Shift to Historical-Grammatical Interpretation
The pivotal shift that occurred with Martin Luther and the Reformation was when he rejected the Quadriga, particularly its allegorical and moral layers, and instead embraced a historical-grammatical approach to biblical interpretation. This new method emphasized the importance of understanding the Bible in its original language and context, paying close attention to the historical setting and the grammatical structure of the text.

Luther's breakthrough in interpreting the Bible this way was revolutionary because it shifted the focus back to what the text actually said, in its original context, rather than what the interpreter wanted it to say. Luther's emphasis on *sola Scriptura* (Scripture alone) also directly challenged the authority of the Church in its interpretation of the Bible, arguing that all Christians should have direct access to the text and interpret it according to its natural meaning, not through the lens of ecclesiastical tradition.

Luther's embrace of this method of interpreting Scripture was not without pain. It led him into a direct conflict with the papacy. This was a rejection of **eisegesis** in favor of **exegesis**—a return to the

62

integrity of the text, where the interpreter seeks to draw out its meaning from its original language and context, without imposing outside ideas on it. Luther's change in approach opened the door for future generations of scholars, reformers, and theologians to interpret the Bible in a way that was more consistent with the original meaning and message of the text. It also meant that Augustine's and Jerome's theological constructs, which had been based on allegorical readings, were now subject to scrutiny under a new interpretative methodology.

Eisegesis vs. Exegesis: The Key Distinction
The shift to the **historical-grammatical** method represented a move toward **exegesis**—the careful study and interpretation of the Bible in its original context. **Exegesis** seeks to understand the intent of the author in light of the historical, cultural, and linguistic context in which the text was written. By contrast, **eisegesis** involves reading one's own presuppositions, ideas, or theological commitments into the text.

The shift toward **exegesis** in the Reformation and its subsequent adoption by many modern biblical scholars was crucial in correcting the theological errors that had been built on **eisegetical** interpretations. This is why, when doctrines like *original* **sin** or **infant baptism** are scrutinized under the historical-grammatical lens, they often unravel as being based on misreadings or overly selective interpretations of Scripture.

The Influence of Augustine and Jerome
Despite the reformational shift, the legacy of **Augustine** and **Jerome**—through their theological writings and their interpretative methods—has been profoundly influential in the Western Christian tradition. Their **eisegetical** approach to Scripture was institutionalized by the Roman Catholic Church and continues to affect theological traditions that are rooted in Augustinian thought, even in the pre-

63

sent day. The way they used **allegory**, **symbolism**, and **selective interpretation** to support their dogmas set the stage for an ecclesiastical system that emphasized the authority of the Church as the sole interpreter of Scripture, while sidelining the personal interpretation of the Bible.

However, the rise of **exegesis** as the dominant method of interpretation has allowed for a more biblically faithful understanding of God's word. By focusing on the **historical** and **grammatical context**, theological errors that stemmed from **allegorical excess** can be corrected. This allows for a more direct engagement with the text itself, rather than relying on the interpretative framework of any one individual or ecclesiastical institution.

Conclusion

In conclusion, **Jerome's** and **Augustine's** allegorical and eisegetical readings of Scripture were highly influential in shaping the theological landscape of the Western Church, especially in the development of dogmas like *original* sin and infant baptism. Their methods of interpretation, which often sought hidden meanings rather than the plain sense of the text, were institutionalized within the Church and helped reinforce the authority of the Roman Church.

However, the Reformation marked a significant shift in the approach to Scripture. By embracing the historical-grammatical method, reformers like Luther sought to restore integrity to biblical interpretation, challenging the dominant tradition of eisegesis and advocating for exegesis—allowing the Bible to speak for itself, in its original context, free from ecclesiastical imposition. This shift continues to influence how we interpret the Bible today, emphasizing the need to carefully examine the text and draw out its true meaning rather than imposing our own ideas upon it.

7

Reformation and Challenges to Augustine's Dogma of *Original* Sin

The theological implications of the Reformation, particularly as they relate to the doctrine of *original* sin, are not as clear as many of us were taught. The view remains dominant in western expressions of the church. But dominant is not universal. Various reformers and groups show the diversity of thought on *original* sin. Augustine's view of inherited sin was far from universally accepted in the aftermath of the Reformation.

The Reformation, while a pivotal moment in the history of Christianity, did not simply reaffirm established dogmas. One of its key outcomes was a challenge to the theological authority of the Roman Catholic Church and a reinvigoration of the central role of Scripture in the life of the believer. The cry of *sola Scriptura*—Scripture alone—was the banner under which the reformers rallied, and it would profoundly impact how doctrines were understood, including the dogma of *original* sin.

The Legacy of Augustine and the Reformers' Response

Augustine's dogma of *original* sin, which posited that all human beings inherit the guilt of Adam's sin through procreation, dominated the Western Christian tradition. This teaching was foundational in the development of doctrines surrounding salvation, grace, and the nature of humanity. Yet, as the Reformation unfolded, the dogma of *original* sin became a topic of renewed scrutiny.

For many of the reformers, Augustine's influence loomed large.

65

They maintained that Scripture must be the final authority on all matters of doctrine, and they often interpreted Augustine's views in light of this principle. However, not all reformers accepted his view of *original* sin without question. In fact, some reformers offered significant deviations, challenging the Augustinian view of inherited guilt.

Martin Luther: Upholding Augustine but Emphasizing Grace
Martin Luther is often associated with an endorsement of Augustine's dogma of *original* sin. In his famous work *The Bondage of the Will* (1525), Luther defended the idea that humanity is so deeply fallen as to be incapable of choosing God without the intervention of divine grace. He wrote:

> "The human will is a mere 'puppet,' dragged this way and that by the power of sin, and it cannot choose good without God's grace."

Luther's embrace of Augustine's view on *original* sin was clear. For him, *original* sin was not only a corruption of the human will but also an inherited guilt passed down from Adam. The extent of this fallenness necessitated divine grace to restore humanity, a grace that, in Luther's view, could only come from God. While Luther's articulation of this doctrine was rooted in Scripture, he did not entirely free himself from Augustine's framework, and his views on the sin nature of humanity were shaped by this understanding.

However, even as Luther upheld Augustine's core view, he still emphasized a personal, intimate connection with Scripture that allowed for his doctrine of salvation—justification by faith alone (*sola fide*)—to emerge. He began to open the door for alternative readings of *original* sin, although he himself did not adopt them fully.

John Calvin: Systematic Development of Augustine's Views
John Calvin, the French Reformer and architect of Reformed theology, was another who largely maintained Augustine's dogma of *orig-*

66

inal sin. Calvin emphasized the total depravity of humanity and the idea that all people are born with a sinful nature inherited from Adam. He wrote in his *Institutes of the Christian Religion* (1536):

> "*By Adam's disobedience, the many were made sinners, so by the obedience of one, the many will be made righteous.*" (Romans 5:19—citing the Apostle Paul)

Calvin followed Augustine in teaching that the "fall" of Adam brought about a hereditary sin nature in all humans. He argued that this inherited corruption extended to every part of human existence, rendering humans incapable of choosing righteousness without God's regenerating grace.

While Calvin was deeply committed to the authority of Scripture and grounded his views on *original* sin in his reading of key texts such as Romans 5 and 1 Corinthians 15, his reliance on Augustine's interpretation of these texts shows the depth of the continuity between Calvinist and Augustinian thought. However, even Calvin's theology was shaped by his broader theological vision of predestination and divine sovereignty, which made room for debate on the nature of sin.

The Anabaptists: A Different View on *Original* Sin

Not all reformers embraced Augustine's dogma of *original* sin. The Anabaptists, a reform movement that emerged during the Reformation, offered a distinctive perspective on *original* sin that diverged significantly from Augustine's dogma. They rejected the notion of inherited guilt, asserting that humans are born morally neutral, without the inherited guilt of Adam's sin. Menno Simons, a prominent Anabaptist leader, encapsulated this view by stating:

> "The soul of man, as it is created by God, is pure, and has no innate sin."

This perspective stands in stark contrast to Augustine's view, which posits that all human beings inherit the guilt of Adam's sin through procreation. The Anabaptists' rejection of *original* sin as an inherited condition emphasized the power of individual choice in salvation. They argued that sin results from personal choices and actions, not from an inherited condition passed down from Adam. For them, baptism was not a means of cleansing inherited sin but a public declaration of one's personal commitment to Christ.

The Anabaptists' stance on *original* sin and their emphasis on adult baptism created significant tension with both Catholic and Protestant reformers. Their ideas about human nature and sin would later influence the development of denominations such as the Mennonites and the Amish. This divergence underscores the diversity of thought on *original* sin during the Reformation and challenges the notion that Augustine's dogma was uniformly accepted.

The Anabaptists' rejection of Augustine's dogma of *original* sin and their emphasis on individual responsibility and adult baptism highlight the theological diversity of the Reformation period. Their views offer a compelling argument against the idea that Augustine's teachings were universally and uniformly accepted, suggesting instead a more nuanced and varied understanding of *original* sin among different reform movements.

The Radical Reformers: A Bridge to Modern Thought
In a similar vein, other **Radical Reformers**, such as **Sebastian Franck** and **Michael Servetus**, moved still farther from the traditional Augustinian view of *original* sin. Franck, for instance, saw human beings as not fully corrupted by sin in the way Augustine had proposed. He believed that, while humans had the capacity for sin, they were also capable of goodness, and that salvation was about returning to a state of harmony with God.

Michael Servetus, whose theological writings later influenced Unitarian thought, argued that *original* sin was not a hereditary condition. He denied that human beings were born with an inherent inclination toward evil. Instead, Servetus held that sin was something that individuals chose freely. He contended that humanity's true na-

68

ture was found in God's original creation, untainted by the "fall", and that human beings were capable of great moral potential.

The Reformation Confessions and the Legacy of *Original* Sin
While figures like Luther and Calvin maintained Augustine's understanding of *original* sin, there were significant theological shifts in how this dogma was presented, especially in the confessional statements of the time. Both the **Augsburg Confession (1530)** and the **Belgic Confession (1561)**, which were central to Lutheran and Reformed traditions respectively, affirmed the dogma of *original* sin, but with nuances that were distinctive to each tradition.

The **Augsburg Confession**, which sought to define the Lutheran position in contrast to Roman Catholicism, states:

> "Since the fall of Adam, all men who are born in the natural way are born with sin. That is, they are without the fear of God, without trust in God, and with concupiscence."

This represents a standard Lutheran understanding of *original* sin, acknowledging both the inherited condition and the need for divine grace for salvation. The Lutheran position emphasizes the corruption of human nature but maintains the possibility of a renewed relationship with God through Christ.

The **Belgic Confession**, which represents the Reformed tradition, elaborates on *original* sin by emphasizing the depth of human depravity:

> "Therefore, we reject the error of the Pelagians, who say that human beings are able to love God with all their heart and to keep the commandments of God, to some extent, through the strength of their free will. We reject that idea and affirm that all people, having inherited their sin from Adam, are born in a state of guilt and corruption."

This reflects the Reformed tradition's adherence to Augustine's understanding of inherited sin, affirming that all of humanity is tainted by the "fall" and in need of divine grace. The Belgic Confession, much like the Augsburg Confession, served as a theological response to Catholic teachings, and its assertions about *original* sin would influence later Reformed and Presbyterian confessions.

The Reformation's Impact on the Dogma of *Original* Sin
The Reformation's emphasis on *sola Scriptura* undoubtedly brought about a renewed engagement with the Scriptures and led to fresh debates about core theological doctrines, including *original* sin. While many of the Reformers, particularly Luther and Calvin, continued to uphold Augustine's dogma of inherited sin, there was a significant diversity of thought. Some reformers, especially within the Anabaptist and Radical Reformer movements, rejected the idea of *original* sin as an inherited condition, offering instead views that allowed for greater human responsibility and moral capacity.

This theological diversity challenges the idea that Augustine's dogma of *original* sin is the only viable interpretation of Scripture. It opens the door for rethinking the inherited nature of sin and offers a basis for reexamining the dogma in light of biblical teachings, free from the constraints of tradition. If the Reformers themselves, who sought to return to Scripture as the final authority, offered a variety of perspectives on *original* sin, then it is certainly worthwhile for modern Christians to revisit this dogma with fresh eyes.

Tradition or Truth
As we conclude this chapter, it becomes clear that the dogma of *original* sin, as taught by Augustine, was not the settled dogma within the Reformers themselves. While figures like Luther and Calvin maintained aspects of Augustine's views, others, such as the **Anabaptists**, **Radical Reformers**, and some dissenting voices in the Reformation, questioned or outright rejected the idea of inherited guilt. The Reformation was not a simple affirmation of previously held teachings—it was a time of scrutiny and reexamination. Scrip-

70

ture alone (*sola Scriptura*) became the final arbiter of truth, challenging the authority of both Catholic Church tradition and centuries of theological teaching.

For those of us looking at this from a modern perspective, the Reformation's theological diversity gives us a crucial insight: the church's authority—Catholic and otherwise—is not infallible. What we have here is a broader debate about the very nature of sin and its transmission. The Reformers themselves were not uniform in their conclusions. This means that Augustine's views on *original* sin were far from universally accepted—and were never beyond question, for the Reformers or for us.

Just as the Reformers set the stage for rethinking doctrinal issues based on Scripture, so too should we approach the question of inherited sin with the same critical mindset. The theological groundwork laid by figures like the Anabaptists—who rejected the inherited nature of sin—gives us permission, as modern Christians and as detectives, to question and reconsider entrenched theological ideas. We, too, are called to evaluate dogmas through the lens of Scripture, not tradition alone.

Imagine, if you will, that you, as the detective, have just uncovered a crucial piece of evidence: even the Reformers, those champions of scriptural authority, did not accept all aspects of Augustine's views on *original* sin. The case was not closed even in their time—it was under investigation. As you continue to peel back the layers of church tradition and historical authority, remember that just as the Reformers were given permission to rethink *original* sin, you too have the freedom to question longstanding theological dogmas. Like any good detective, you examine the evidence—Scripture—and draw your own conclusion, even if that means challenging centuries of thought.

71

Notes and Observations

Investigative journal entry: Date: _____ / _____ / _____

Evidence of Different Perspectives: As a detective, you're uncovering various testimonies. How does the diversity of views on *original* sin among reformers like Luther, Calvin, and the Anabaptists complicate the case for Augustine's dogma of *original* sin? What clues suggest that *original* sin wasn't universally accepted?

Scripture Alone: Reformers embraced *sola Scriptura*—Scripture alone—as the foundation for theology. How does this challenge or reshape the traditional view of inherited sin? What role does *sola Scriptura* play in your investigation? Could Scripture alone lead to a different verdict?

Anabaptists' Divergence: The Anabaptists rejected Augustine's dogma of *original* sin, seeing humans as morally neutral. How does their focus on personal choice affect your investigation? What do you make of their stance that sin is chosen, not inherited?

Luther and Calvin's Alignment with Augustine: Luther and Calvin upheld Augustine's views but with their own twists. Do their adaptations of Augustine's dogma strengthen or weaken the case for inherited guilt? What tensions do you notice in their reasoning? What do their views imply about the nature of sin?

Reformation Confessions as Evidence: Confessions like the Augsburg and Belgic affirm *original* sin with varying nuances. How do these documents shape your understanding of *original* sin in the Reformation? What insights can you draw from their language and interpretations?

72

Section 2

Witnesses to Truth
Toward a Biblical Theology

"He who controls the language controls the masses."
—Saul Alinsky, *Rules for Radicals*

In George Orwell's *1984*, language is the key to determining culture. Michael Brown, Ph.D. in Near Eastern Languages and Literatures, posted the following about *1984*: "By controlling the language, Big Brother controls the way that the people think. With a limited vocabulary, the people are limited in how much they can think, as well as, what they think about." Brown concluded, "Those who control the language control the culture."

You might think language a strange place to begin exploring the underlying issues related to whether inherited or *original* sin is biblical. It is, however, at the very core of the issue. Our difficulty lies partly in finding an accurate vocabulary. We are forced to use words and terms that have become part of the problem—words defined and controlled by leadership in Christianity, specifically the Catholic Church, over centuries. We've become steeped in concepts expressed in language the Bible itself never uses.

Regarding how influence is exercised through language, Amanda Montell writes: "The real answer all comes down to words…from the crafty redefinition of existing words (and the invention of new ones) to euphemisms, secret codes, buzzwords, chants, mantras… even hashtags, language is the key means by which all degrees of influence occur... Words are the medium through which belief systems are manufactured, nurtured, and reinforced."

Montell quotes John E. Joseph, Professor of Applied Linguistics, University of Edinburgh: "Without language, there is no belief, ideology, or religion. These concepts require a language as a condition of their existence." (Cultish: The Language of Fanaticism, Amanda Montell, Harper Wave, 2021)

When New Testament language is altered, we lose the faith "once for all delivered to the saints." Jude warned of the perversion of true faith in his brief but crucial epistle. He urged: *contend for the faith that was once for all delivered to the saints...certain people have crept in...who pervert the grace of our God* (Jude 3-4 ESV).

To move forward in faith, we need a truly biblical vocabulary. Charting a new course requires a return to the language God inspired (2 Tim. 3:14-17). The words of the biblical authors are the words we must use to evaluate the condition of the church and to shape our faith. In our pursuit of truth, God's word will be our guide. The psalmist reminds us: *Your word is a lamp to my feet and a light to my path.* And in another place—*Your word is truth*—a sentiment stated by Jesus before His arrest in the Garden. In His moments of struggle, He relied on the truth of God's word. And so will we.

As forensic theological detectives in this investigation, we now turn our attention to the next step: gathering testimony from key witnesses who will provide crucial perspective on the crime. Before a detective ever questions suspects, he photographs the scene and catalogs every item. In theology, those items are words—grace, flesh, law, sin. If the labels on the evidence bags have been swapped, the verdict will be wrong. In Section 2, we will interview key doctrines—essential witnesses that relate to God, creation, sin, grace, salvation—examining the biblical terms and texts themselves.

These witnesses prepare us to re-enter the crime scene—the Council of Carthage (A.D. 418), where Augustine's case against Pelagius hardened into canon law. Like any good investigator, we will scrutinize their testimony—probing language, facts, and implications in a 1,600-year-old cold case. Let's see what they have to say...

74

8

The Beginning Point: God

Our view of man begins with our view of God. If we have a high view of God, we will generally have a high view of man. If we have a low or no view of God, we will have a low or no view of man. The person who has a high view of God affirms the attributes outlined in *I Believe, Volume 1*. That brief litany of the attributes of God is provided in the following abbreviated form merely to refresh your memory of what God has revealed of Himself. Here's a simple list.

Absolute Attributes:
Immense
Eternal
Immutable
Sufficient
Unity

Relative Attributes:
Omnipotent
Omniscient
Omnipresent

Moral Attributes:
Holiness
Love
Justice
Mercy

Let's explore these attributes briefly…
God is immense. If nothing else, the size of the universe proclaims

the immensity of God. Scripture states that God created the universe and then goes further to help us see the immensity of God. The Psalmist noted that *the heavens declare the glory of God and the firmament shows His handiwork.*

Isaiah's portrait has God measuring the heavens in a span— that's the distance from the tip of your outstretched little finger to the tip of your outstretched thumb. The distance to the nearest star from Earth is four and a half light years away—and that's to the nearest star! Modern instruments like the Hubble telescope and the Keck Interferometers are helping us understand just how large the universe is—and it is immense, beyond description. And yet Isaiah stated that God *measured the heavens in a span* (Is. 40:12). God's pretty big, immense.

God is timeless, eternal. While God is active in time, He also transcends time. He is over and beyond time. While we can voice the idea, we cannot fully understand it because we are creatures of time. We had a beginning, we have a present, and we anticipate a future. He is the ever-present One. When Moses asked God's name for the confrontation with Pharaoh, God gave His name as *I AM THAT I AM* (Ex. 3:13-14). The name in English translates as the present tense form of the verb *to be*. God was telling Moses that He is the One Who Is.

God is also good. The character of God is honest, moral, righteous. He is neither tempted nor tempts. He leads us away from temptation and delivers us from evil. He is no trickster. He doesn't fool us. He is lovingly just and just in His love. He is holy and wants human beings to know His holiness and participate in it. He extends mercy to us and treats us based on His grace.

God is immutable. He doesn't change. He is not capricious— good one day, bad the next. He is not fickle in His character, attitudes, or actions (Mal 3:6; Heb 1:12). The consistency of God that has been revealed allows us to have confidence in Him and in His word. When He says something, we need not doubt the veracity. His

76

truthfulness is never in question; He is eternally truthful.

God is totally sufficient. He doesn't need anything. He created the universe and all in it that we might share in His personhood. It was not out of a sense of need that the world was created.

God is unified in His being. The plurality of His being—Father, Son, Holy Spirit—is totally unified: a tri-unity. This is unity of character, purpose, action.

God is omnipotent, omniscient, and omnipresent. *Omni* means *all*. God is all-powerful, all-knowing, and all-present. We cannot imagine anything God cannot do, cannot know, or a place He is not. (And before we go further, we understand that God cannot lie, sin, nor be untrue to His nature. We know that hell is the place from which God has withheld His presence. These are familiar theological amusements. But they do not diminish what we know of God. He is ALL in ALL.)

The moral attributes of God are holiness, love, justice, and mercy. God is set apart; He is holy. He is totally Other than we are. He has neither sin nor unrighteousness in Himself. One of the three designations, *God is...*, is that God is love. His love is the selfless action for others, *agape*. His holiness demands justice. Because God knows everything from beginning to end, His judgment is true. He knows even the motive, not just the deed. Therefore, His judgment is absolutely true. Every decision is right and just. Yet, His judgment is tempered with mercy. This combination of attributes reveals God to be lovingly just and justly merciful.

Scripture simply assumes the existence of God—doesn't argue it, simply states, *In the beginning **God**....* The revelation that God has given of Himself provides much of the insight presented in this brief description. A number of the attributes of God reflected here are mirrored in our understanding of the doctrine of man.

This high view of God, based on His revelation of Himself, is the basis for our view of man. The inspired account in Genesis provides much insight for our understanding of the doctrine of man.

77

God's Dilemma

God had a problem—at least from a human perspective. A dilemma, a paradox, lying at the very heart of creation itself. His holiness and justice demanded that the rebellion of His creatures be penalized. That rebellion was fueled by the desire for self-rule: Adam and Eve chose to step out of the perfect communion He had designed. The consequence was clear: *"In the day you eat of it, you shall surely die."*

The penalty of sin was spiritual death—separation from the very life of God—and that was a law God could not break.

But this wasn't merely a judicial matter. The God of the Bible is no distant, impersonal force, nor an unfeeling judge tallying infractions. Love is intrinsic to His being; mercy flows from His essence. He longs to relate to His creation not through robotic obedience but through relationship—rooted in freedom, love, and choice.

And herein lay the dilemma: How could He express mercy and love while remaining true to His holiness and justice? It's a tension we may never fully grasp, yet it defines the gospel itself. How does a holy and just God forgive those who have spurned His authority, broken His laws, and walked away from the life He intended? How does a perfect, all-knowing Creator extend mercy without compromising perfect justice?

The solution was something only God could conceive: a sacrifice—the ultimate convergence of mercy, justice, and love. God Himself would pay the price, being just and the justifier (Rom 3:26).

This is where the doctrine of the atonement is revealed. The *Logos*, the eternal Word who was with God and was God (John 1:1), entered our world. He would not remain aloof from His creation's suffering and rebellion. Instead, He came in human form—living as we live, feeling as we feel, and ultimately dying the death we deserve. God's perfect justice demanded a penalty, and that penalty was death. Yet His mercy and love demanded redemption, not destruction.

78

As my beloved professor, Dr. Ray Robbins, put it, *"Forgiveness is absorbing the hurt and pain done to you by another and then treating that person as if they had never done that."* That is precisely what God accomplished for us in Jesus Christ.

The Attributes of God and the Solution to Sin

To understand the magnitude of God's decision, we must return to His attributes—His nature—because the act of redemption is rooted in who He is.

1. God's Holiness: The Demand for Justice

God is holy, set apart, and completely without sin. This means He cannot look on sin with indifference. Sin violates His perfect nature, and His justice demands that it be addressed. The penalty for sin is death—not just physical death, but spiritual separation from God. The very fabric of reality—God's law, His word—requires this. When humanity fell into sin, we broke that fabric, and God's holiness could not overlook it.

Yet, this same holiness is balanced by His love and mercy. God's justice requires payment, but His mercy makes space for reconciliation. His holiness cannot let sin slide, but His love will not let His creatures be abandoned forever.

2. God's Love and Mercy: The Desire for Restoration

It is here, at the intersection of holiness and love, that God's mercy comes into play. God is love (1 John 4:8), and His love is not passive or sentimental. It is active, sacrificial, and redemptive. God could not stand by while His creation—whom He deeply loved—was separated from Him by sin.

His love moved Him to act in the only way that could reconcile the two realities of His holiness and justice. Instead of demanding humanity pay the price for their rebellion, God Himself would absorb the penalty. The sacrifice of Jesus Christ—God in human form—becomes the meeting point between God's holiness (which

79

demands justice) and His love (which seeks to redeem).

This is the essence of forgiveness. God, in His mercy, chooses to absorb the pain and penalty of sin, and, in Christ, He extends forgiveness to all who believe.

3. God's Justice: The Atonement

Justice demanded that someone pay the price for sin. It could not be a mere excuse or an overlooking of the offense. For God to be just, He had to provide a means of satisfying the debt humanity owed. Jesus Christ's sacrifice on the cross is the ultimate demonstration of God's justice—He bore the penalty for our sin, satisfying God's righteous anger toward sin.

Yet, through this same act, God extended mercy to us. The cross is where justice and mercy meet. It is the great exchange: Christ took on Himself the punishment we deserved, and in return, we receive His righteousness, clothed in the perfection of His life and death. This is the glory of the gospel—the mercy and justice of God coming together in the most profound way.

The Apostle Paul's Reflection on Justification

The Apostle Paul encapsulates this glorious exchange in his letter to the Romans: *Now we know that whatever the law says, it says to those who are under the law, so that every mouth may be silenced and the whole world held accountable to God. Therefore no one will be justified in His sight by works of the law. For the law merely brings awareness of sin. But now, apart from the law, the righteousness of God has been revealed, as attested by the Law and the Prophets. This righteousness from God comes through faith in Jesus Christ to all who believe. There is no distinction, for all have sinned and fall short of the glory of God, and are justified freely by His grace through the redemption that is in Christ Jesus.* (Rm. 3:19-24).

Paul's words draw a clear picture. **The law cannot justify us.** It merely reveals our sinfulness. But the righteousness of God, revealed in Christ Jesus, makes justification possible—not through our works, but through faith in Him.

"God presented Him as an atoning sacrifice in His blood through faith, in order to demonstrate His righteousness, because in His forbearance He had passed over the sins committed beforehand. He did this to demonstrate His righteousness at the present time, so as to be just and to justify the one who has faith in Jesus." (Romans 3:25-26)

In Jesus Christ, God was both just in His wrath against sin and merciful in justifying the sinner who believes. In the cross, God's justice was satisfied, and His mercy was extended, all through the same sacrifice. It's no wonder then that Paul concludes: *"Where, then, is boasting? It is excluded. On what principle? On that of works? No, but on that of faith. For we maintain that a man is justified by faith apart from works of the law."* (Romans 3:27-28)

Conclusion: The Dilemma Resolved

In the end, God's dilemma was resolved in the most profound way imaginable. His holiness and justice demanded payment, but His love and mercy provided the solution. Through Jesus Christ, God Himself bore the cost of sin, absorbing its penalty and offering forgiveness. And now, by faith in Him, we can be justified—declared righteous—before a holy God, not by our works, but by His grace.

This is the heart of the gospel: God, in His love and mercy, solving the problem of sin and death through the sacrifice of His Son. A perfect demonstration of how the attributes of God—His holiness, justice, love, and mercy—work together to redeem fallen humanity.

Notes and Observations

Investigative journal entry: Date: _____ / _____ / _____

Sin and Redemption: How does the understanding of God's attributes deepen our view of humanity's sin problem? What does God's perfect nature say about the seriousness of sin and the need for redemption?

God's Holiness: What does God's holiness reveal about the nature of sin? Why is sin such a serious offense in light of God's perfect nature?

The Atonement and Justification: What is the significance of the cross in God's plan of redemption? How does the justification by faith (as mentioned in Romans 3:19-28) impact our understanding of how God deals with sin?

God's Justice and Mercy: How do God's justice and mercy work together in the act of redemption? In what ways does God's justice demand payment for sin, and how does His mercy make space for forgiveness?

God's Love: How does God's love intersect with His holiness and justice? How does His active, sacrificial love make a way for redemption through the cross?

The Dilemma of God: In the divine paradox at the heart of the gospel, how does God remain just while justifying those who rebel against Him and His rule? How does the fact that God Himself absorbed the penalty of sin reshape your understanding of justice, love, and relationship?

9

The Purpose of God
Forming a People for Himself

From the beginning, God's intent was clear: to create a people for Himself. Genesis 1:26-27 reveals this profound truth: *Let us make man in our image, after our likeness….* Humanity was created to reflect God's glory, to share in His divine fellowship, and to enjoy relationship with Him. God didn't need people, but He chose to create them out of His will and desire. In His self-sufficiency, He longed to share His glory with others.

This divine plan for a people began with humanity's creation and placement in the garden prepared by God (Gen. 2:7-8). Yet, humanity's first decisive act was rebellion. Adam and Eve disobeyed God by eating from the forbidden tree, and thus sin entered the world. The choice to disobey would become the tragic pattern repeated by every human being, except for Jesus. However, God did not abandon His purpose. In His infinite mercy, He had already established a plan for redemption through Jesus Christ.

Paul's words in Ephesians 1:3-10 remind us that God predestined a people for Himself before the foundation of the world. His plan of redemption was always through Jesus—the Lamb slain before time began. Even in the face of human rebellion, God's promise remained, and the path to reconciliation would be through the sacrifice of His Son.

The crucifixion of Jesus is the fulfillment of this eternal plan. Jesus, fully God and fully man, perfectly obeyed the Father in every way. His death on the cross was the ultimate act of self-giving love, in which God, in Christ, bore the weight of humanity's sin to reconcile the world to Himself. This act of obedience, even to

83

the point of death, was the completion of God's plan to create a people who would be His own possession (1 Peter 2:9-10). Through Jesus' sacrifice, God reconciled the world to Himself, offering forgiveness to all who would receive it by faith.

The church, the *ekklesia* (from *ek*–out and *kaleo*–to call—to call out), is the *called-out* people, chosen to proclaim the excellencies of God, who called them out of darkness into His marvelous light. The gospel declares that God has always had one plan—to form a people for Himself. The resurrection of Jesus sealed God's Kingdom victory, now unfolding on earth even as we await its ultimate fulfillment.

Through the death and resurrection of Jesus, God is reconciling all things to Himself. The story of creation, rebellion, and redemption culminates in the work of Jesus. As we live as part of God's Kingdom, we are called to partner with Him in sharing this good news, spreading the message of reconciliation to the world.

"The Purpose Fulfilled"

In the beginning, God declared,
"Let us make man, in our image shared."
A people to reflect His light,
To walk in fellowship, pure and bright.
Yet in the garden, sin began,
A choice made by the first of man.
Rebellion marked the human way,
Yet God had planned another day.
For in the fullness of all time,
God sent His Son to heal the crime.
Through Jesus' death upon the tree,
A people would be set free.
The cross, the throne of kingship found,
A sacrificial love unbound.
Now, in Christ, we are made new,

84

A chosen people, born anew.
With faith in Him, we rise and stand,
Redeemed, adopted by His hand.
To share the news, the Kingdom call,
A people gathered, one and all.

Analysis and Application:

The narrative of God's creation of humanity in His image (Gen. 1:26 -27) sets the foundation for understanding the central theme of God's desire for a people who belong to Him. This concept is not new, but rather embedded in the very fabric of Scripture. From the beginning, God intended for humanity to reflect His glory and participate in His divine fellowship.

This divine image, however, was marred by sin. Humanity's rebellion in the garden was not a surprise to God; He had already foreseen it. And within this divine foresight, He initiated a plan for redemption. The Apostles, especially Paul, spoke of this in Ephesians 1, where God's purpose to create a people for Himself, a holy nation, was predestined in Christ. This was not an afterthought, but part of God's eternal design.

At the heart of redemption lies the person and work of Jesus Christ. As a fully divine and fully human figure, Jesus lived a perfect life, obeying the Father's will even unto death (Phil. 2:8). His death on the cross was not only a fulfillment of prophecy but also the ultimate expression of God's love and justice. As Paul explains in Romans 3:21-26, the death of Jesus served to satisfy God's holiness and justice while simultaneously displaying His mercy and grace.

Through Jesus, humanity is offered reconciliation with God. The cross becomes the point at which God's justice and mercy meet. Through His sacrifice, God reconciled the world to Himself, offering forgiveness to all who receive Him by faith (2 Corinthians 5:16-21). By our faith, God reconciles, restores, and recreates.

The church, the *ekklesia*, is the people God has called out of darkness into His marvelous light (1 Peter 2:9-10). This people is not just a future reality but a present one. The Kingdom of God, inaugurated through the death and resurrection of Jesus, is already in motion, and those who are part of it are called to partner with God in spreading the message of reconciliation to the world. The church's mission, then, is to make disciples, sharing the good news of Jesus Christ, and pointing to the fullness of God's Kingdom.

As followers of Jesus, we are part of this grand story of redemption. God has formed a people for Himself, and that includes us. We have been called out of darkness and into the light of His Kingdom.

This truth has profound implications for our lives. First, it compels us to live in light of our new identity as God's chosen people, reflecting His glory in everything we do. Secondly, it calls us to be active participants in God's mission of reconciliation. We are ambassadors for Christ, entrusted with the message of the gospel (2 Cor. 5:18-20).

Our partnership with God in spreading the good news is not optional—it is a fundamental part of being in His Kingdom. The story of creation, rebellion, and redemption is the story that defines us. And our mission is clear: to declare this story to a world in need of the reconciliation that comes through Jesus Christ. As we live out this mission, we are fulfilling God's eternal purpose of creating a people for Himself, a people who will bring glory to His name both now and forever.

Let us, then, boldly proclaim the good news that Jesus has died and risen to reconcile the world to God, and invite others into the same reconciliation we have received. In doing so, we fulfill God's eternal intent and live as part of His Kingdom, now and in the age to come.

86

10

Created in the Image of God

The concept of humanity as being created in the image of God is foundational to our understanding of who we are and what our purpose is. Found in Genesis 1:26, the narrative speaks to God's intention to create humanity in His image, a declaration that resonates deeply with our identity, purpose, and relationships: *Let Us make man in Our image, according to Our likeness*…. This act of creation reflects a divine design that sets humanity apart from the rest of creation, highlighting the spiritual, moral, relational, and creative dimensions of human existence.

From the very first moments of human creation, we are told that we were made not as mere creatures, but as *images* of the Divine. The term *image* here does not refer to a physical resemblance since God is spirit (John 4:24), but it speaks to the moral, spiritual, and relational attributes that humanity bears. As we reflect on this, we begin to see that humanity's likeness to God is revealed in various dimensions of our being. These dimensions are not static but dynamic and interconnected, impacting how we relate to God, to others, and to the world around us.

1. We Are Emotional Beings

The first aspect of humanity's reflection of God's image is seen in our emotional nature. God is not distant or detached; He is intimately involved in His creation. Scripture speaks of God who experiences love, joy, grief, and even wrath. His emotions are not reactions to circumstances, but expressions of His perfect and holy nature. Human beings, created in God's image, share this capacity for emotion.

We too are designed to experience love, joy, grief, anger, and compassion. Our emotional range is an integral part of what it means to be human. Emotions reflect our connection to God, and through them, we are able to engage with the world, form relationships, and express the fullness of who we are. In a world marked by pain, we mourn. In a world in need of hope, we can love. These emotions are not flaws or anomalies—they are reflections of the divine nature we are made to reflect.

2. We Are Relational Beings

From the very beginning of human existence, it was not good for man to be alone (Genesis 2:18). God, in His image, is inherently relational within the Trinity—Father, Son, and Holy Spirit are not solitary beings but are in eternal communion. The creation of humanity in God's image, then, includes the design for relationships. We are made to be in fellowship—with God and with one another.

The creation of Adam and Eve illustrates this relational nature. The formation of Eve from Adam's side emphasizes the equality and complementary roles in relationship. In this design, male and female together reflect the fullness of God's relational image. The relationship between Adam and Eve was not merely a functional arrangement, but a beautiful and intimate union designed to reflect the loving, communal nature of God Himself. This relational aspect of humanity becomes the foundation of society, as family, friendship, and community become arenas where God's image is reflected and made known.

3. We Are Moral Beings

A third aspect of being made in the image of God is our moral nature. We are not only emotional and relational beings; we are also moral beings, possessing the ability to discern right from wrong. When God gave Adam and Eve the command regarding the tree of the knowledge of good and evil (Genesis 2:16-17), He placed before

88

them a choice—one that required moral decision-making. This free will—the ability to choose to obey or disobey—is a key component of our moral nature.

Moral choice is integral to our identity as those made in the image of God. To choose freely, to obey or disobey, is what grants our love for God its significance. A love forced or controlled is not true love. Therefore, the moral landscape of our existence is set against the backdrop of free will. It is in this free will that our decisions reflect our understanding of God's character and His commands. The very presence of the tree of knowledge in the garden (and its prohibition) reveals that human beings are endowed with the capacity for moral discernment and moral action.

4. We Are Creative Beings

Creativity is another powerful aspect of our image-bearing. In the Genesis account, Adam was tasked with naming the animals (Genesis 2:19-20), a job that involved rational thought, creativity, and an exercise of dominion. Naming creatures was not merely an administrative task; it was a creative expression of dominion. Humanity's role in creation is not to dominate destructively but to steward, protect, and creatively shape the world in ways that reflect God's creativity.

We, like our Creator, are endowed with the ability to think, invent, create, and innovate. From art to technology, from literature to architecture, the creative expressions of humanity are a reflection of God's own creativity. The ability to make something new out of raw materials, to bring order and beauty from chaos, is part of what it means to bear God's image. Whether it is the creation of music or the development of solutions to human problems, our creative faculties are a direct extension of the divine nature that made us.

5. We Are Self-Aware Beings

Self-awareness is one of the most profound aspects of the image of

89

God in humanity. In the opening chapters of Genesis, we see the created order being made good, but humanity is described as having a unique awareness of time, place, and purpose. Ecclesiastes speaks to this notion, saying that God has *set eternity in the heart of man* (Ecclesiastes 3:11). We are aware of our mortality and our eternal significance.

This awareness of our existence—our past, present, and future—marks humanity in a way that no other creature experiences. We not only live in the world, but we reflect upon it, question it, and seek meaning from it. This consciousness of time, eternity, and our place in the created order sets us apart as beings who are not only aware of our own identity but also aware of our need for relationship with God, and our accountability to Him.

6. We Are Beings of Intrinsic Value

Intrinsic value is another core component of humanity being made in God's image. From a biblical perspective, humanity is precious to God—not because of what we do, but because of who we are. God created humanity to reflect His glory, and He placed His image upon us as a sign of our value. We are not mere objects or accidents of nature; we are created for purpose and with great worth in God's eyes.

This intrinsic value is not lost because of sin. While sin distorts and corrupts the image of God in us, it does not erase it. We are still made in God's image, and thus, each person retains inherent dignity and worth. Jesus' incarnation, death, and resurrection highlight the value that God places on humanity. Christ did not die for animals, trees, or stars; He died for people—those created in His image. This profound truth shapes our understanding of every person's worth, regardless of their status, sin, or condition.

7. We Are Beings with the Potential for Perfect Union with God

Finally, humanity's creation in the image of God points to our potential for union with the Creator. The very first humans, Adam and Eve, enjoyed perfect fellowship with God. The picture of God walking with Adam in the garden speaks of a closeness, a perfect union between humanity and the Creator. This union was broken by sin, but it is not lost forever.

The doctrine of the restoration of humanity is found in the person of Jesus Christ. Jesus, the *perfect* image of God, reveals the fullness of what it means to be truly human. He is the model of what humanity was always meant to be. In Christ, God is restoring the perfect image of Himself in humanity, as we are being transformed into the image of His Son (Romans 8:29). It is through Christ that we find the potential for perfect union with God once again.

Conclusion: The Image of God in Us

The doctrine of man as the image of God is not just theological abstraction; it is intensely practical. It touches every aspect of our lives—our relationships, our decisions, our creativity, and our purpose in the world. As we reflect on these aspects, we are reminded of the deep and sacred truth that we are made in God's image. We are emotional, relational, moral, creative, self-aware beings of intrinsic value with the potential for perfect union with God.

As we continue to explore the doctrines of sin, salvation, and transformation, we do so in the light of this foundational truth. The reality that we are made in God's image shapes our understanding of every other doctrine, for it is through the lens of the image of God that we see the depth of our need for redemption, and the hope that we can be restored to perfect union with our Creator.

The Exercise of Free Will and the Mercy of God

Yet, as we know from the opening chapters of Genesis, the perfect fellowship between humanity and God was not meant to remain unchallenged. Adam and Eve, while created in innocence and endowed with free will, were faced with the choice to trust God's authority or

91

to rebel against it. In this moment, when they chose to eat the fruit from the tree of the knowledge of good and evil, they exercised their moral agency in a way that would forever alter the course of human history. The result of their disobedience was not merely physical death, but spiritual death—the severing of the intimate relationship with God.

As Genesis 3:22-24 describes, God, in His mercy, blocked access to the Tree of Life, setting an angel with a fiery sword to guard the way. This action symbolized both the tragic reality of humanity's spiritual death and the mercy of God. It is reasonable to infer from God's actions that had they eaten from the Tree of Life in their spiritually dead state, they might have remained in that state of separation from Him forever, without the hope of redemption. But that was not in keeping with God's purpose. What do you think?

God's decision to banish Adam and Eve from the Garden, though painful, was not a punitive act of wrath alone; it was an act of grace. By preventing them from existing forever in spiritual death, He allowed the natural course of physical death to take its place, ensuring that the curse of sin would not be eternal. The imagery of the fiery sword guarding the tree powerfully illustrates the reality of the broken relationship and the separation caused by sin, but it also highlights God's mercy in the face of that brokenness.

The tree's protection stood as a reminder that spiritual death does not have to be the final word for humanity. Redemption and restoration, while hidden in mystery at the time, would eventually be made possible through the sacrificial death of Jesus Christ.

And what's remarkable is that God's plan for redemption was not an afterthought. Ephesians 1:4, Revelation 13:8, and other passages clearly state that before the foundation of the world, God had already set in motion His plan for the salvation of humanity. The fall did not surprise God; He was not caught off guard. The same mercy He showed by barring the way to the Tree of Life was a precursor to the greater mercy that would be revealed through Christ.

Even as Adam and Eve exercised their free will to choose rebellion, God had already prepared a way to restore humanity to Himself. This plan, unfolding throughout Scripture, would ultimately reveal that God's grace was always intended to meet human failure and that in His perfect wisdom, redemption would come through the life, death, and resurrection of the Son. As we consider the implications of Adam and Eve's choice, we are reminded that the exercise of free will—though it led to rebellion—also opens the door for redemption, proving that the gift of choice, even when misused, does not exclude the possibility of grace and restoration.

The Mystery of Redemption: Revealed in Christ
As we reflect on the rebellion and the merciful prevention of eternal spiritual death, we are drawn into a deeper understanding of God's grand narrative of redemption—a *mystery* that was hidden but now made known. In Ephesians 1:4-14, Paul reveals that God's plan of salvation was not a reaction to humanity's sin but was always in the works, conceived before the foundation of the world.

The "mystery" Paul speaks of is not one of confusion or ambiguity, but a divine secret now revealed through the person and work of Jesus Christ. The plan for humanity's salvation was hidden in ages past, but in the fullness of time, it was disclosed to us through Christ's redemptive work. This mystery was God's eternal purpose to unite all things in Christ, both in heaven and on earth (Eph. 1:10).

This idea is consistent with the deeper truths revealed in passages like Galatians 4:4-5, where Paul states that *when the fullness of time had come, God sent forth His Son, born of a woman, born under the law, to redeem those who were under the law, so that we might receive adoption as sons.* God, in His perfect wisdom and timing, sent Jesus at the precise moment in history when He would offer Himself as the once-for-all sacrifice for sin. Jesus' coming was not accidental; it was the fulfillment of God's eternal plan—a plan established even before the world's foundation, as seen in Revela-

93

tion 13:8 and Hebrews 9:23-28.

Hebrews 9:26 tells us that *he has appeared once for all at the end of the ages to put away sin by the sacrifice of himself*. At just the right time, Jesus came, not just as a moral teacher or a prophet, but as the Lamb of God, foreordained to bear the sin of the world. His sacrificial death on the cross bridged the chasm caused by humanity's rebellion, restoring the possibility of reconciliation with God. Through His death and resurrection, Christ became the fulfillment of the promise that redemption and spiritual life would come, not through any human effort, but through God's grace alone.

In this light, the mystery of redemption is revealed as the very heart of God's plan—His plan to bring about the restoration of humanity's broken relationship with Him, which had been severed by sin. It was not an afterthought; it was the culmination of God's eternal purpose, established *before the foundation of the world* (Eph. 1:4). What was hidden in time past was now made clear through Christ: the way of salvation is by grace, through faith, in the finished work of the Lamb slain for our sins. The mercy shown in guarding the Tree of Life was a precursor to the greater mercy that would be revealed in the cross, where death would be defeated and spiritual life made possible for all who believe.

Thus, as we consider the grand story of sin and salvation, we see the continuity of God's eternal plan, from the rebellion in Genesis to the revelation of Christ in the fullness of time. Redemption, which seemed hidden from Adam and Eve in their moment of rebellion, was always God's intention—to redeem, restore, and ultimately reconcile all of creation to Himself through His Son. And now, through Christ, the mystery is no longer concealed, but has been made clear: in Him, we are offered the forgiveness of sins and the gift of eternal life, through grace alone.

The Long Shadow: Christ, the Sinbearer and the Sacrifice
In the ancient worship practices that God established for Israel dur-

94

ing the Exodus, we find a vivid foreshadowing of Christ's ultimate work of atonement. The Day of Atonement, or *Yom Kippur*, was a sacred event meant to roll back the sins of the people, offering them temporary reconciliation with God. On this day, two goats were chosen: one was designated as the *sinbearer*, and the other as the *sacrifice*. The first goat symbolically carried the sins of Israel into the wilderness, a powerful image of sin being removed and taken away from the people. The second goat was sacrificed as a sin offering, its blood poured out as an atoning sacrifice for the sins of the nation. This ritual, deeply embedded in Israel's consciousness, was a shadow—a vivid picture—of what was to come in Christ.

As the writer of Hebrews points out, these images were not just ceremonial rites but prophetic symbols that pointed to the ultimate fulfillment of God's plan in Jesus. In Hebrews 9:24-28, we see that Christ Himself was both the perfect *sinbearer* and the ultimate *sacrifice*. He entered the true, heavenly Tabernacle—not with the blood of goats or bulls, but with His own precious blood, offering Himself as the once-for-all atoning sacrifice for the sins of the world (Heb. 9:12). In this sense, Jesus was not just a moral teacher or prophet, but the fulfillment of the Day of Atonement in its truest form: He bore the sins of humanity and became the sacrifice that makes eternal reconciliation with God possible.

This theme of Christ as the Sinbearer and the Sacrifice brings us back to the imagery of the *Tree of Life*, which we first encounter in the garden. When Adam and Eve chose self-rule over God's rule and were banished from the garden, the Tree of Life was guarded by cherubim with flaming swords (Gen. 3:24). This act of mercy, though it severed the relationship between God and humanity, was also a foreshadowing of a greater mercy to come. Humanity, by nature of their sin, could not be allowed to exist eternally in a state of spiritual death. Thus, the prevention of access to the Tree of Life was, in fact, a merciful act to prevent humanity from existing forever in their state of separation from their Creator.

95

But in a profound turn of divine irony and mercy, the way to the Tree of Life would eventually be opened again—but this time, not through an earthly garden, but through another tree: the cross of Jesus Christ. Just as the first tree in the garden had been the symbol of life and immortality, the cross became the instrument of life and redemption. On the cross, Jesus bore the weight of humanity's sin, and in His sacrificial death, He overcame the spiritual death that had entered the world through Adam's sin. In this way, the cross itself became the fulfillment of the Tree of Life—it was on that tree that the possibility of eternal life, spiritual renewal, and access to God was restored.

As the apostle Paul writes in Romans 5:18-19, *As one trespass led to condemnation for all men, so one act of righteousness leads to justification and life for all men.* Through the sacrifice of Christ, the way to eternal life is once again opened to humanity—not through the preservation of our sinful state, but through the forgiveness and restoration found in the cross. The mercy God showed in preventing access to the Tree of Life after Adam and Eve's rebellion was ultimately a mercy that pointed forward to the cross, where the way to eternal life was made possible through Christ's atonement.

This understanding deepens our view of the cross—not just as a moment of suffering, but as the moment when God's entire redemptive plan came to fruition. The cross is the final fulfillment of the shadow cast by the Day of Atonement, where sin was not merely covered, but completely, forever atoned for. It is the moment when the long shadow of God's promise to redeem and restore humanity reaches its culmination in Jesus Christ, the Lamb of God who takes away the sin of the world. Through His death, the severed relationship between God and humanity is reconciled, and the way to eternal life is opened again, now available to all who believe.

11

Three Terms

In the New Testament, three terms help us understand the Christmas event and, more importantly, the nature of salvation itself: *Logos*, Jesus, and Christ. These terms have all been applied to the same person—the God-Man—but they are not interchangeable. In fact, each one carries a distinctive meaning that helps us understand different aspects of who Jesus is and the significance of His coming.

Unfortunately, over time, these terms have been used interchangeably, often they are conflated without much thought to the theological implications of each. Understanding the nuances of these terms will help us grasp not only the mystery of the incarnation but also the depths of the salvation that Jesus offers.

You might find yourself struggling, even as we do, to express thoughts about one term without referring to it by using one of the other terms. We find ourselves in much the same place as Augustine of Hippo when asked about the trinity. He said, "When one asks: *What three?*, human speech suffers from a great lack of power. Nevertheless, we say: Three persons, not in order that we should say this, but that we should not be silent." He knew the limitations of language when discussing the nature of God. But let us grapple as best we can.

Logos – The Eternal Word

The term *Logos* is the Greek word for "word." John used it to indicate the Son of God, the second person of the Trinity. In John 1:1-4, we read: *In the beginning was the Word, and the Word was with God, and the Word was God. He was in the beginning with God. All things came into being by Him, and apart from Him nothing came*

97

into being that has come into being. In Him was life, and the life was the light of men.

John adds in verse 14, *And the Word became flesh and dwelt among us, and we beheld His glory, glory as of the only begotten from the Father, full of grace and truth.*

The *Logos* is not just a word or a concept; it is a distinct divine being. He is the second person of the Godhead. The ancient Greek philosophers referred to the *Logos* as the principle that gives order to the universe. It was considered to be the force that links mankind to God and the cosmos. However, John introduces us to something far greater: the *Logos* is not a vague principle but a personal being—the pre-incarnate Christ, who was both with God and was God. The *Logos* is the Creator, the source of all life and light.

For our purposes, the *Logos* establishes the divine authority behind the salvation story. The fact that Jesus is the incarnate *Logos* emphasizes His divinity. He is not simply a man born into history but the eternal Word who has existed from the beginning and who entered human history through the incarnation to bring about redemption. The *Logos* coming as a human being is central to understanding salvation. It was the resolution to God's dilemma. Through the incarnation God could be both just and the justifier providing the salvation humanity so desperately needed. The eternal, divine *Logos* entering into creation is the foundation upon which all redemption rests.

Jesus – The Fully Human Savior

The name Jesus is derived from the Hebrew *Yeshua*, meaning "The Lord saves." This is the human name that the divine *Logos* took on in His incarnation. In the Gospels, we see Jesus embrace His full humanity. He was born into a family, grew up in a particular culture, and experienced all the limitations that come with being human.

In Matthew 1:1-17 and Luke 3:23-38, the genealogies of Jesus are presented to show His human heritage. His humanity is not just a

98

superficial appearance; He was born, He grew, He felt, He suffered, and He made choices just like any other human. Philippians 2:5-8 provides insight into the mystery of the incarnation, where the Apostle Paul writes that Jesus, though equal with God as the *Logos*, did not cling to His prerogatives but emptied Himself, taking on the form of a servant and being born as a human being.

The humanity of Jesus is a vital part of understanding salvation. He did not come as a detached, distant deity but as one of us. Jesus experienced the full range of human life, from joy to suffering, temptation to obedience. His sinlessness was not a by-product of divinity alone; it was the fruit of a fully human life lived in perfect surrender to the will of the Father.

If we are to understand sin and salvation, we must first see Jesus as the model human being—one who experienced the struggles of humanity yet lived without sin. This is crucial for us to understand—sin is tied to personal choice and responsibility. Jesus, as a model for humanity, shows us that despite being born into a broken world, we are still responsible for our personal choices.

Christ – The Anointed One, The Messiah
The third term we encounter is Christ, which is derived from the Greek *Christos* and corresponds to the Hebrew *Messiah*, meaning "the Anointed One." Unlike *Logos* and Jesus, which refer to the identity and nature that the *Logos* took on in the incarnation as Jesus, Christ refers to His role and mission. Jesus came to fulfill the promises made in the Old Testament regarding the Messiah. He was the long-awaited Deliverer, the one chosen by God to redeem humanity from sin and restore the broken relationship between God and man.

In the Old Testament, prophecies about the Messiah were clear: He would be born of a virgin (Isaiah 7:14), come from the line of David (Isaiah 11:1; Jeremiah 23:5), and would bear the sins of the people (Isaiah 53:1-12). Jesus fulfills all of these prophecies. His

99

coming as the Christ is not an accident or an afterthought; it is the culmination of God's plan for redemption. The incarnation was in the plan of God from *the foundation of the world* (Ephesians 1:4) or as Paul expressed it to his assistants, *before time began*:

*Therefore do not be ashamed of the testimony about our Lord, nor of me his prisoner, but share in suffering for the gospel by the power of God, who saved us and called us to a holy calling, not because of our works but because of his own purpose and grace, which he gave us in Christ Jesus **before the ages began*** (2 Timothy 1:6-9).

*Paul, a servant of God and an apostle of Jesus Christ, for the sake of the faith of God's elect and their knowledge of the truth, which accords with godliness, in hope of eternal life, which God, who never lies, promised **before the ages began** and **at the proper time** manifested in his word through the preaching with which I have been entrusted by the command of God our Savior;* —Titus 1:1-3

Here's how the Berean Standard Bible rendered the thought: *in the hope of eternal life, which God, who cannot lie, promised **before time began***. —Titus 1:3

The term *Christ* helps us understand the "why" of the incarnation. Why did Jesus come? He came as the Christ, the Anointed One, to fulfill the mission of saving humanity from sin. Jesus, as Christ, is the one who provides the solution to the problem of sin and restores the brokenness of the world. His death on the cross and subsequent resurrection are the ultimate acts of redemption, securing salvation for all who believe.

In understanding Christ in this way, we can see how salvation is not simply a matter of individual choice but is bound up in the divine mission of Jesus to restore humanity to God. As the *Logos*, He reveals the nature of God; as Jesus, He models what it means to live as a human; and as Christ, He provides the means for redemption.

Pulling Terms Together: Understanding Sin and Salvation

When we understand these terms—*Logos*, Jesus, and Christ—we begin to grasp the full depth of salvation. It is not enough to view Jesus as simply a man or as merely a divine figure. He is the *Logos* who became flesh, the eternal Word that entered into human history. He is Jesus, the Savior who came as one of us, fully embracing the human condition. And He is the Christ, the Anointed One who fulfilled the promises and prophecies of God and provided the way for humanity's salvation.

This understanding of Jesus' nature directly impacts how we view sin. If we view Jesus as merely human, we might reduce sin to a failure to follow moral examples rather than seeing it as a deeper separation from God that requires divine restoration. But if we see Jesus as both fully human and fully divine, we understand that sin is more profound—it is a separation from God that requires divine intervention. And if Jesus is the Christ, the one sent to save, then salvation is not something we can achieve on our own. It is a gift from God, granted through faith in Jesus' sacrificial work.

In the chapters that follow, we will explore the debate surrounding *original* sin and the ways in which the early church wrestled with its implications. Before diving into the debate on *original* sin, we must first grasp the necessity of Jesus' divinity, humanity, and His role as the Christ. Only by understanding His full identity can we appreciate the depth of the salvation He offers and our responsibility in responding to His grace.

Notes and Observations

Investigative journal entry: Date: _____ / _____ / _____

Why is the incarnation of the *Logos* essential to salvation?

Why was His full humanity necessary to salvation?

101

How does Jesus' experience as a human, with all its limitations, suffering, and temptations, enable Him to be the perfect mediator between God and humanity? (You might consult Hebrews 2:10.)

What does it mean for our understanding of sin and redemption that Jesus lived a sinless human life?

How does Jesus' humanity challenge or reinforce our understanding of the free will of humans in relation to sin?

In what ways does the model of Jesus, as fully human, provide insight into the role of choice in the moral and spiritual realm?

How does choices Jesus made to live a righteous life inform our understanding of personal responsibility in relation to sin?

In light of the role of Jesus as the Christ (Messiah), how does His mission of redemption redefine our understanding of sin?

How does viewing Jesus as Christ affect our understanding of the purpose behind His death, resurrection, and the forgiveness of sins?

How does the term "Christ" inform our view of salvation as a divine mission rather than just an individual choice?

How do these terms provide a more holistic understanding of who Jesus is and what He came to accomplish?

Why is it insufficient to view the Second Person of the Godhead from only one of perspective in considering His identity and mission?

12

The Mystery of the Incarnate *Logos* —Self-Limitation

The Incarnation was about salvation not sinlessness.

In Philippians 2:5-11, the Apostle Paul paints a profound picture of the *Logos*—the Word of God, who is fully divine, yet voluntarily took on the form of a servant. The passage stands as a theological masterpiece, addressing the union of divinity and humanity in the person of Jesus Christ. Central to this passage is the idea of *kenosis*—the self-emptying of the *Logos*, but not in the sense of losing His divine essence. Rather, He voluntarily laid aside the privileges and prerogatives that came with His divine glory, choosing to live among us as fully human.

This concept, rooted deeply in Scripture, challenges many traditional understandings of the human being named Jesus. To the devout, He is often seen as "God among us," and yet the Bible presents a more subtle and powerful mystery. Jesus, the incarnated *Logos*, refrained from using His divine powers, choosing instead to embrace the human condition—vulnerable, dependent, and fully surrendered to the Father's will.

As we work through this passage, it will be good for you to read this passage from your own Bible. Keep your Bible open for quick reference and for any notes you might want to make.

1. *Kenosis*: Not the Loss of Divinity, But Laying Aside Glory

Theologians have long debated the meaning of *kenosis*, with divergent views often influenced by tradition. Some have suggested that the *Logos* emptied Himself of His divinity in the incarnation. But as

103

Joseph Henry Thayer in his Greek lexicon wisely points out, the term *ekenosen* (from the verb *kenóo*) suggests not a loss but a voluntary laying aside. Jesus did not cease to be divine when He became incarnate; rather, He chose to function within the limitations of human life. In His divine nature, He was, and always remained, fully God. That is the initial statement—the beginning point in the quotation that Paul used in verse 6.

(What many readers miss is that Paul is quoting an early Christian hymn in Philippians 2:6–11. Several modern translations—such as the New Revised Standard, Berean Standard, Christian Standard, and Holman Christian Standard—indent or format the passage as poetry to signal its lyrical structure. The depth of this text is equally instructive: the early church sang their theology, internalized it, and carried it with them.)

The hymn declared that Jesus, the Christ, was in His pre-incarnate state fully God: *who, though he was in the form of God, did not count equality with God a thing to be grasped*.... The word that is translated as "form" is *morphe*, meaning the intrinsic essence of a person or thing. The hymn declares that the pre-incarnate Jesus was in every way truly God.

This is exactly what John 1:1 declares: *In beginning, was the Logos, and the Logos was with God, and the Logos was God*. The *Logos* was eternal, separate, and equal to the Father. In His intrinsic essence, He was all that God was. The attributes of the Father were those of the Son. And vice versa.

But in His incarnation as the human named Jesus, He took on the constraints of time, space, and experience that are part of what it means to be human. The debate for centuries has centered on what this meant. The doctrine that explains this is called the hypostatic union: the coexistence of two natures—divine and human—in one person. How do the two natures (divine/human) interact? And this has direct bearing on the dogma that arose from the conflict between Augustine and Pelagius (AD 400—more about this later).

104

The hymn went further—the *Logos* took upon himself the intrinsic essence (form, *morphe*) of a servant. He emptied Himself (*ekenosen*, v.7)—that does not mean that the *Logos* had one essence inside and poured it out to take in another essence. Because He was God, He could not cease being God. The incarnation was not about subtraction, it was about addition. The *Logos* added something. So how did this work?

J.B. Lightfoot's insight that the *Logos* "stripped Himself of the insignia of majesty" further clarifies. An insignia is a badge or emblem of office or rank. Dr. Lightfoot explained, "He [the *Logos*] divested Himself, not of His Divine nature, for that is impossible, but of the glories, the prerogatives, of Deity. This He did by taking upon Him the form of a servant." (*Saint Paul's Epistle to the Philippians*)

In verses 7 and 8, Paul used *heauton* (ἑαυτον), translated as himself. The word, a reflexive pronoun, connotes **He Himself**: the agent acting and the one acted upon are the same person. The meaning emphasizes that the emptying and humbling by our Lord was sovereign, voluntary, self-imposed. The *Logos* Himself determined how He would come into the world to redeem the world from sin.

Though equal in rank with God the Father, He divested Himself of the rights that came with that rank. This self-emptying coincided with taking upon Himself the form—that is, the intrinsic and essential essence—of a servant. He assumed the outward appearance of a human being, and that human was named Jesus. The *Logos* was eternal, but Jesus had a beginning.

As Jesus, He did not abandon His divine essence but chose to live without the outward marks of divine glory. He did not cling to the prerogatives of His attributes—omniscience, omnipotence, and omnipresence—choosing instead to live as a servant, fully reliant on the Father for His words, actions, and knowledge.

The humility of this decision is staggering: the eternal God, who created all things, subjected Himself to the limitations of a human body, living in complete dependence on His Father.

105

2. The Divine and Human Coexist in a Single Person

The key to understanding the nature of Jesus is not a division of His two natures but the inseparable union of both the divine and the human in one person. J.B. Phillips emphasized in his translation of Philippians 2, that Jesus, *who had always been God by nature*, did not grasp onto His equality with God. But He chose to become a servant, a slave—fully human, and fully reliant on the Father. The *Logos* added humanity to His divinity in a manner that does not diminish the fullness of either nature. (*The New Testament in Modern English*)

This dual nature of Jesus—divine and human—was not a blending or confusing of the two. Rather, it was the seamless coexistence of both natures in the person of Jesus. The fullness of God was present in Jesus, but He did not exercise that fullness. He voluntarily self-limited. While He retained His divinity, He voluntarily laid aside the prerogatives of His divinity and became a human being. He experienced hunger, fatigue, sorrow, and death—all the realities of the human experience. He relied on the Father for everything—what He knew, what He said, what He did.

Yet, He remained fully God. This is the mystery of the incarnation—the *Logos* who was eternal, separate from the Father, and was God became flesh and dwelt among us (John 1:14).

3. Prerogatives and Privileges: The Sovereign Choice to Limit

In the Garden of Gethsemane, when Jesus, faced with the anguish of the coming cross, declared that He could call on twelve legions of angels, He revealed the vast extent of His self-limitation. The Son of God had at His disposal an unimaginable army of angels, yet He chose not to use that power.

Instead, He laid aside the privilege of divine intervention for the sake of fulfilling His redemptive mission. His refusal to act in His own defense was a clear demonstration of His voluntary restraint and the sovereign choice to fulfill the Father's will. This choice was not a failure of power but the ultimate demonstration of sacrificial love and obedience.

106

The restraint Jesus showed in the Gethsemane moment further emphasizes His understanding of His mission and His full submission to the will of the Father. It is a profound mystery that the same hands that created the universe, the same voice that spoke life into existence, would allow Himself to be arrested, mocked, and crucified. Yet this was the path He chose, and He walked it with a voluntary surrender, not out of weakness, but in the exercise of perfect strength.

4. The Transfiguration: A Glimpse of Glory

While Jesus' glory was veiled throughout His earthly ministry, the Transfiguration offers a momentary lifting of that veil. As Matthew records, Jesus' face shone like the sun, and His clothes became dazzling white (Mt. 17:1-8). For a brief moment, the fullness of His divine glory was revealed to a select few. This fleeting glimpse of His divine nature affirms that Jesus, though He lived as a man, was and always remained fully God.

The Transfiguration was not a contradiction to His humanity but a revelation of the truth of His being. His glory was hidden in His life on earth, but it would one day be fully revealed after His resurrection and ascension. The Transfiguration thus becomes a powerful symbol of the reality of His divinity—an essential truth that undergirds the entire narrative of His life and ministry.

5. Theological Implications: A Model for Humanity

Jesus' self-limitation has profound theological implications. He serves as the ultimate model for humanity—not in spite of His limitations, but precisely because of them. Jesus' life demonstrates what it means to live in complete surrender to the Father. He embraced the full human experience, with all its limitations, and lived in total reliance on God. He demonstrated what it means to live in submission, to trust fully in the Father's will, and to model servant leadership.

This understanding of Jesus invites us to reflect on our own relationship with God. Like Jesus, we are called to surrender our own prerogatives, to live with the recognition that our lives are not our own but are given to us for a higher purpose. In our humanity, we are invited to follow the model of Christ, living in reliance on the Father, just as He did.

The Mystery Revealed: a Self-limited Life

In the mystery of the incarnation, the *Logos* chose to take on human limitations without surrendering His divinity. He became fully human, experiencing all the constraints of life, but never once losing His divine essence. This self-limitation was a voluntary choice to experience life as we do, for the sake of our redemption. In Jesus, we find the perfect model of what it means to live in full surrender to the will of the Father, fully dependent on Him for everything.

While discussing the implications of the incarnation in a conference, a lady asked if Jesus shared our "sin nature." (She was coming from the base of inherited sin. We'll explore the nature of Jesus as it relates to sin in a bit.) My response was immediate—and something I had never expressed in just that way before: "No. He didn't share our sin nature; He shared our human nature."

Human nature is simply the physiological and psychological composition every person shares. Jesus was fully human. He shared totally our human nature. He had the appetites we have—hunger, thirst, desire. He had the same psychological needs we have—love, affection, belonging, success, productivity, self-fulfillment. None of which crossed into sin.

Ego is not of itself sinful. Actually, being fully human requires a healthy ego. Jesus in His teaching alluded to this when He stated that we are to love our neighbors as we do ourselves (Mt. 19:19). Unlike us, however, Jesus never crossed the line into *egocentrism* that caused Him to rebel against God's will. The essence of sin is the desire for self-rule. The sin of Adam and Eve was not simply the

108

eating of the fruit. The act of eating the fruit of the tree of the knowledge of good and evil was the outward expression of a rebellion that had already occurred within their spirit.

The desire for self-rule rather than God-rule (theocentrism) was the real sin. Isaiah caught the essence of the sin nature in his prophecy against the king of Babylon: *But you said in your heart, "I will ascend to heaven; I will raise my throne above the stars of God, And I will sit on the mount of assembly In the recesses of the north. I will ascend above the heights of the clouds; I will make myself like the Most High"* (Is. 14:13-14).

When Isaiah put into the king's mouth the words, *I will*, he revealed sin's essential nature. ***Egocentrism* is the essence of sin.**

Jesus lived the fully human life as God intended—balanced, wholly surrendered to the Father's will. Jesus was what God intends every person to be—a fully-functional human being.

The traditional view of inherited sin complicates our beliefs about Jesus. The complication is raised by the incarnation. Christians believe Jesus was the God-man, fully divine and fully human, sharing equally both natures. Most believers have no difficulty accepting His divinity. The rub comes at the point of His humanity because it raises this question: How could Jesus be human and not have inherited sin? This question is not easily answered through dogmatic statements. But it can be answered through a deeper understanding of the divine revelation in the person of Christ.

The Incarnation was about salvation not sinlessness.

Notes and Observations

Investigation Journal Entry: Date: _____ / _____ / _____

Kenosis: Voluntary Self-Limitation
How does Jesus' voluntary self-limitation challenge traditional views of His divinity and deepen our understanding of salvation?

Sin Nature vs. Human Nature
What is the difference between Jesus sharing "our human nature" and sharing "our sin nature"? How does this distinction challenge the doctrine of inherited sin?

Theological Implications for Humanity
How does Jesus' perfect surrender to the Father's will provide a model for humanity and challenge the idea of inherent sin in human nature?

Prerogatives and Privileges: A Sovereign Choice to Limit
What does Jesus' refusal to use His divine power (*e.g.*, in Gethsemane) reveal about His voluntary self-limitation and sacrificial love?

Jesus and the Desire for Self-Rule
How does the essence of sin—egocentrism, the desire for self-rule—contrast with Jesus' perfect submission to God?

The Divine and Human Coexist in a Single Person
How does the seamless union of Jesus' divine and human natures shape our understanding of His redemptive mission—and challenge the concept of inherited sin?

Jesus and Salvation
How does the incarnation of the *Logos*—with its voluntary self-limitation—clarify salvation as something greater than mere sinlessness?

110

13

The Virgin Conception
The Incarnation as God's Redemptive Plan

The Virgin Conception is often viewed as one of the most profound and mysterious events in human history. (Most Christians speak of a "Virgin Birth." But to be more precise: the miracle was in the conception. The birth itself was entirely natural—especially after a 90-mile donkey ride!)

As a Christian doctrine, the Virgin Conception has been the subject of much reflection, debate, and misunderstanding. Many approach it with reverence and devotion, considering it a miraculous intervention in the natural world. Yet, beneath its awe-inspiring surface lies a deep theological significance that stretches far beyond human comprehension.

The Virgin Conception of Christ is often discussed in the context of sinlessness, but this perspective risks missing the deeper reality: the Incarnation was about redemption, not simply a way to side-step inherited guilt. The biblical witness does not suggest that Christ's divine nature required a sinless human birth to protect Him from contamination. Instead, His sinlessness is rooted in His perfect obedience to the Father, not in the mechanics of His conception.

Planned Before the Foundation of the World

The Incarnation was not a reaction to sin but a plan established before the foundation of the world (1 Peter 1:20, Ephesians 1:4-5). This was not a divine pivot in response to humanity's rebellion but the predetermined means by which God would bring about the fullness of redemption. Christ's coming was always the way God in-

111

tended to reconcile creation to Himself—a mystery hidden for ages but revealed in Christ:

The mystery hidden for ages and generations but now revealed to His saints. To them God chose to make known how great among the Gentiles are the riches of the glory of this mystery, which is Christ in you, the hope of glory (Colossians 1:26-27).

Paul uses the word **mystery** to describe what God did through the Incarnation of the *Logos*. This word means something that was once hidden but now has been revealed. Our hope for redemption and the restoration of our relationship with God was concealed for ages, but in Christ, God's plan was unveiled.

God's Redemption: The Virgin Conception in Context

When we view the Virgin Conception as the moment God enters the world to redeem, rather than a necessary method of circumventing *original* sin, we align more closely with the biblical narrative. The Incarnation is God's movement toward humanity—His stepping into time to reconcile, heal, and restore. This was an act of divine mercy and justice intertwined, not a technical requirement to preserve Christ from sin's contamination.

The Gospel writers present the Virgin Conception as a sign of divine initiative—God acting in a way that declares His purposes unmistakably. The miraculous conception is not about isolating Christ from the stain of humanity but about uniting God with humanity in a new and redemptive way.

Redemption, Not Sinlessness: A Plan for Humanity

It is crucial to grasp that the Virgin Conception is primarily about redemption, not an abstract notion of Jesus' sinlessness. While many have placed primary emphasis on Jesus being sinless from the moment of His conception, the deeper truth of the Incarnation lies in the fact that Jesus entered the world to redeem it. The Virgin Conception is not about avoiding inherited sin or escaping the reality of human frailty—it is about God Himself entering into the frailty of humanity to rescue it.

In the economy of salvation, Jesus' sinlessness was the result of His perfect obedience to the Father throughout His life. His sinlessness was not merely the result of His conception but was the result of His daily choices, His resistance to temptation, and His unwavering commitment to fulfill God's will. It was through His obedience to the Father, even to the point of death on the cross, that Jesus became the **Lamb of God who takes away the sin of the world** (Eph. 2:8; John 1:29). The Virgin Conception allowed for this redemptive act to take place by providing the means through which God would enter the world and live among us, sharing in our humanity yet remaining obedient and sinless.

This is the heart of the *hypostatic union*—the mysterious and profound reality that Jesus is both fully God and fully human. In Him, divinity and humanity are united, making possible the full redemption of humanity. Jesus is not only fully God, but He is fully human, experiencing the full range of human emotions, temptations, and struggles. Yet, He remained obedient to the Father, and in doing so, He became the perfect sacrifice for sin.

Christ's Sinlessness: Rooted in Obedience, Not Birth

Throughout His life, Jesus demonstrated perfect obedience to the Father (John 8:29, Hebrews 5:8-9). His sinlessness was not a condition imposed by a special birth to avoid inherited guilt; rather, it was the active reality of His unwavering fidelity to God's will. The temptation accounts in the Gospels (Matthew 4:1-11) highlight that Jesus' sinlessness was tested, yet He remained obedient. His righteousness was not an automatic condition but a fully realized choice, made in perfect harmony with the Father.

This is where the forensic approach to sin, particularly as framed in Augustine's dogma of *original* sin, falters. The biblical narrative does not depict sin as a substance transmitted through birth

113

but as a relational and volitional reality. Christ's victory over sin is not in avoiding a theoretical contamination but in actively defeating sin through His life, death, and resurrection.

The Incarnation: Mercy and Justice in Perfect Harmony
God's justice requires that sin be dealt with, not ignored. His mercy demands reconciliation rather than mere condemnation. In Christ, justice and mercy meet in a way that transcends legalistic frameworks. The Incarnation is not God's reaction to a human dilemma but the very means by which He fulfills His eternal purpose. Paul captures this beautifully in 2 Corinthians 5:19:

God was in Christ reconciling the world to Himself.

One of the more striking aspects of God's redemptive plan is the way in which forgiveness is extended to humanity. Recall Dr. Ray Frank Robbins' description of forgiveness as **"absorbing the hurt and pain done to you by another and then treating that person as if they had never done it."** This profound definition mirrors precisely what God did in Christ.

On the cross, Jesus absorbed the hurt, the pain, the wrath, and the punishment that humanity deserved for sin. He bore the full weight of our disobedience. And through His sacrifice, He transformed that pain into a means of reconciliation. The Incarnation, in this sense, was the beginning of the great act of forgiveness.

Through the Virgin Conception, God took on human flesh so that He could absorb the consequences of sin and then offer us the gift of reconciliation. God, in Christ, treats humanity as though we had never sinned, offering us a new identity in Him.

This understanding of forgiveness is deeply personal. It means that, in Christ, God does not hold our sin against us. Through Jesus' life, death, and resurrection, we are not simply forgiven in the sense of having our sins overlooked. Rather, we are transformed. Jesus' sacrifice is the means by which we are made new (2 Cor. 5:17). It is not just the removal of guilt but the restoration of the relationship

114

between humanity and God. Jesus, through perfect obedience, restored humanity's relationship with God, offering a new life in Him.

A well-known parable, often shared by radio broadcaster Paul Harvey, illustrates this idea beautifully: One winter, as a man sat in his warm home, he noticed a flock of birds outside, struggling in the snowstorm. Wanting to help, he went outside and tried to guide them into his barn, where they would be safe. But each time he approached, they panicked and scattered, unable to understand that he meant them no harm. Frustrated, he thought, *If only I could become one of them—then I could lead them to safety.*

Just as the man would have to become a bird to save them, so too did God take on flesh to reach and redeem humanity. The Incarnation was not merely a theological necessity but the ultimate act of divine love—God stepping into our world so that we might finally understand and follow Him to salvation.

At its core, the Incarnation is the perfect harmony of God's justice and mercy. Through the Virgin Conception, God did not bypass humanity's brokenness or the consequences of sin. Instead, He chose to enter it, to take on human flesh, and to experience the full range of human suffering. But in doing so, He also fulfilled the law's demands for justice—by absorbing the punishment for sin in the body of Jesus on the cross. In this way, Jesus became the propitiation for our sins, satisfying God's justice and offering forgiveness to all who believe in Him (1 John 2:2).

This is the wonder of the Virgin Conception and the Incarnation: through Jesus, God was able to both satisfy the demands of His holiness and extend mercy to the sinner. It is a divine mystery, a cosmic act of reconciliation, in which God makes a way for humanity to be restored to Himself—not through anything we can do, but through what Jesus has done for us (Romans 3:21-26).

The Virgin Conception: Entrance of Redemption
The Virgin Conception stands as a declaration of God's initiative in

115

redemption. It is the moment when eternity enters time, when the Divine takes on flesh to dwell among us. Its significance is not in protecting Jesus from inherited guilt but in signaling the dawn of God's redemptive work. Christ's lifelong obedience, not the mechanism of His birth, is the source of His sinlessness. His obedience, His suffering, His death, and His resurrection accomplish what no birth condition ever could—the salvation of humanity.

The Incarnation is the heart of the gospel. It is God's movement toward us, His willing entrance into our frailty, so that we might be led out of darkness into His marvelous light.

Notes and Observations

Investigative Journal Entry: Date: _____ / _____ / _____

Redemption or Protection? How does viewing the Virgin Conception as the entrance of redemption—rather than a means of avoiding inherited sin—shift our understanding of Christ's mission and nature?

Sinlessness and Obedience: According to Scripture, what is the basis of Jesus' sinlessness? How does His obedience, rather than His birth, reveal the character of true righteousness?

Incarnation as Divine Initiative: What does the Incarnation say about God's desire to be known by and present with humanity? How does this initiative reflect both divine justice and mercy?

Personal Response to Redemption: This chapter challenges us to reflect on the Incarnation as God's personal invitation to reconciliation. How does this truth affect your understanding of forgiveness and your relationship with God?

14

The Annunciation
(Luke 1:26-38)

The Annunciation marks the moment when the angel Gabriel appears to Mary in Nazareth, delivering the incredible news that she will conceive a child by the Holy Spirit—God's Son, the long-awaited Messiah. Mary, a young woman betrothed to Joseph, is perplexed and initially troubled by the angel's greeting and message. The angel reassures her, explaining that this child will be *great* and will *reign over the house of Jacob forever*, fulfilling the promise made to King David.

This announcement is not just about the birth of a child but the fulfillment of prophecies. It speaks of God's active intervention in the world, bringing salvation through His Son, who will rule an eternal Kingdom. This moment is rich with theological and messianic implications, as it places Mary at the center of God's redemptive plan for humanity. Her response, *"I am the Lord's servant. May your word to me be fulfilled,"* demonstrates her obedience and faith, despite the incredible nature of the message.

This event foreshadows the role that Mary will play throughout Jesus' life—not just as His mother, but as a willing participant in God's plan of salvation.

"The Annunciation"
In the quiet town of Nazareth,
A young heart beat in simple faith,
Unknowing that the world would turn,
With a single word, her life to shake.

119

The angel's voice, a call so clear,
"Rejoice, O Mary, favored near!
You will conceive, by Spirit's grace,
The Holy One will take your place."
She questioned, "How can this be so?"
For the power of God, she'd never known.
"Do not fear," the angel said,
"God's hand upon you is laid."
A promise made, a king to come,
The throne of David, His Kingdom won.
Through you, the world will know His name,
His reign, eternal, none shall claim.
She trembled, yet with faith she bowed,
Her heart was pure, her soul was proud.
"I am the servant of the Lord,
Let it be done, by Your Word."
And so it was—God's will proclaimed,
A virgin's heart in faith unchained.
The Savior's call, the world's reply,
In Mary's trust, the world would lie.

Analysis:

- **Messianic Fulfillment:** This scene directly addresses messianic expectations. Gabriel's message to Mary speaks of the fulfillment of God's promises to David and to Israel. The Messiah, who was expected to come as a deliverer, a king in the line of David, is revealed as a humble child. Yet, this child will be *great* and will *reign forever*, embodying the eternal Kingdom that the Jews had longed for. The initial shock and confusion Mary feels are understandable—she was expecting a kingdom of power and military might, but God's Kingdom would come through humility and divine intervention.

- **The Role of Mary:** Mary's response encapsulates the heart of obedience and submission to God's will. Her "Yes" is a key turning point in God's redemptive plan. By accepting her role, she becomes a model of faith for all believers. Her acceptance of God's calling, even though it was an unimaginable and risky proposition, highlights the nature of true discipleship.

- **Theological Implications:** Theologically, this passage introduces the concept of the Incarnation—God becoming man in the person of Jesus Christ. This divine mystery is captured in the angel's words: *The Holy Spirit will come on you, and the power of the Most High will overshadow you.* The idea that the eternal God would take on human flesh in such an intimate and vulnerable way through Mary speaks to the depth of God's love and commitment to His creation.

- **Connection to the Old Testament:** Gabriel's words to Mary echo the promises made to King David, showing that Jesus is the fulfillment of God's covenant with Israel. This is a powerful link between the Old and New Testaments, demonstrating that Jesus is the Messiah they had long awaited, though His arrival is unexpected in its form.

Immaculate Conception: Another Ecclesiastical Construct

The role of Mary is clear in the Annunciation. She is the person God selected as the vessel, the means by which to enter the world. The conception was the miracle. The birth was quite natural. But in church history, the role of Mary would take an interesting twist. And it was connected to the dogma of *original* sin. It was called the "Immaculate Conception."

The *Immaculate Conception* and its timing raise some important theological questions. Particularly about how the Catholic Church sought to protect its understanding of Jesus' sinlessness by introducing the idea of Mary's sinlessness. Since our objective is to explore a broader theological perspective of sin and in particular challenging or engaging with the traditional dogma of inherited sin,

121

it's important to carefully frame what the Catholic Church did with this pronunciation about Mary.

The Annunciation and the Immaculate Conception: An Engaged Theological Reflection

The Annunciation marks the beginning of God's incredible intervention into human history. When the angel Gabriel declared to Mary that she would conceive a child by the Holy Spirit—God's Son, the promised Messiah—Mary's response demonstrated remarkable faith and obedience. Her willingness to cooperate with God's plan of redemption in this pivotal moment reveals the heart of discipleship: a submission to God's will, even in the most bewildering circumstances. Can you imagine being a teen-aged girl hearing this?

However, this event, celebrated as a moment of divine favor, has been the subject of much theological reflection, particularly within the Roman Catholic tradition. In 1854, Pope Pius IX in the papal bull, *Ineffabillis Deus,* proclaimed that Mary was immaculately conceived, meaning that she was born free from *original* sin.

This ecclesiastical construct had been debated off and on over the centuries. It remained in the realm of speculation because there was no biblical basis for the belief. The speculation stemmed from the sinlessness of Jesus. The argument for Mary's sinlessness was that it was seen as essential to preserving the sinlessness of Jesus. It was argued that for Jesus to be sinless, His mother must also be sinless. This notion stems from a larger theological concern: If Mary were not sinless, then Jesus could be seen as inheriting sin, something that would conflict with the belief in His absolute purity and holiness.

The Historical Context of the Immaculate Conception

At the time of the Immaculate Conception's declaration in 1854, there was a growing tension between religious authority and emerging scientific paradigms. As the Enlightenment gave rise to more secular and rationalist thinking, the Church sought to bolster its theological claims by making definitive statements about dogmas that were not directly outlined in Scripture. The Immaculate Conception was introduced as a way to maintain the Church's teachings on the sinlessness of Jesus, making sure that both His divinity and humanity were perfectly aligned with their dogmatic expectations.

In this context, the Immaculate Conception can be understood as a theological safeguard—a way to protect the dogma of inherited sin and the power structures associated with it. The belief that all humans inherit *original* sin has long been a cornerstone of Catholic teaching, and by asserting that Mary herself was free from this sin, the Church could secure the sinlessness of Jesus while maintaining its control over the nature of salvation. This move was not just theological but also an assertion of the Church's power in defining who is pure and who can be redeemed.

Theological Reflections:
A Kingdom in Humility, Not Control

However, while the Immaculate Conception addresses theological concerns around the nature of sin and purity, it arguably does so at the cost of neglecting the humility inherent in God's redemptive work. The gospel presents Jesus' entry into the world not as a claim to power or control, but as a humble act of divine love—a baby born in a manger, not a king born in a palace.

The biblical narrative emphasizes that sinlessness was not an inherent trait of Mary but was embodied in Jesus Himself as it is in every infant. Through His life, death, and resurrection, Jesus demonstrates perfect obedience to the Father, revealing the Kingdom of God not through power or purity based on human merit but through sacrifice and self-giving love.

Jesus' sinlessness is not an inherited trait from His mother but a chosen path. While Mary's faith and obedience are central to her role in

123

God's plan, it is important to note that the sinlessness of Jesus is a result of His perfect relationship with God the Father, rather than a byproduct of Mary's "immaculate" nature. Thus, the theological narrative of God's redemption through Jesus highlights that Jesus alone is the true Lamb without blemish, and His sinlessness is not based on His conception, but on His *perfect obedience* to the will of God.

The Role of Mary: A Model of Faith, Not Sinless Perfection
Mary's role in the Annunciation story, and her willingness to bear the Messiah, shows her deep faith and submission to God's will. She becomes a model of obedience for all believers. The dogma of the Immaculate Conception, while deeply meaningful to Catholic theology, raises important questions about how we view the humility of God's redemptive plan.

In the context of this book, the focus is not on a dogma of inherited perfection but on the faithful participation of humanity in God's plan. Mary, as an obedient servant of God, offers herself to the unfolding of God's redemptive purposes—not because of her sinlessness, but because of her obedience. This is a much more accessible model for believers: God's redemptive plan is not about human perfection or purity, but about faith in the work of Jesus Christ.

The key theological takeaway from the Annunciation, in light of the broader narrative of redemption and reconciliation, is that God's Kingdom is one built not on human merit but on God's grace and mercy. Mary's "immaculate conception," while holding a place in Catholic dogma, is not necessary to protect the sinlessness of Jesus. Instead, we see that Jesus' sinlessness is not about human biology but personal obedience—Jesus chose to live a perfect life, and His obedience is what secures salvation for His people.

Reconceiving Redemption
In conclusion, the Immaculate Conception was an ecclesiastical response to the emerging challenges of modernity and a way to safe-

guard the sinlessness of Jesus. However, it is important to emphasize that true redemption comes through the sacrificial love of God, which was fully revealed in Jesus.

The Annunciation sets the stage for this divine intervention, where Jesus would be born into a broken world not as a prince in power, but as a servant. Thus, the true *sinlessness* of Jesus is not about the lineage of His mother but about His *perfect obedience* to the Father, a humble path of salvation that turns worldly expectations upside down.

The Immaculate Conception, while a valid part of Catholic tradition (but only since 1854), has no basis in Scripture whatsoever. This ecclesiastical construct can be viewed as one response to the mystery of salvation. But it can be argued that this creation by the Catholic Church is just another attempt to maintain the fragile dogma of inherited or *original* sin built upon a shaky and inadequate foundation. It is this dogma that is the source of immense power and control over adherents—and so must be maintained at all costs.

But such a dogma is not the key to unlocking the true nature of God's redemptive work in Jesus Christ. Rather, it is Jesus' sinlessness through His life, death, and resurrection that is the heart of the gospel message, offering a way to reconciliation for all humanity.

The Annunciation is not just a moment to reflect on Mary's obedience, but also on how God's redemptive plan ultimately reconciles all things to Himself through the life and work of Jesus.

Notes and Observations

Investigative Journal Entry: Date: _____ / _____ / _____

Understanding the Virgin Conception
How does the virgin conception relate to Jesus being fully God and fully man?

125

The Virgin Conception and Redemption
How does the virgin conception relate to concepts of sin and redemption? How does it inform our understanding of the dogma of *original* sin?

The Annunciation and Its Message
What does the angel Gabriel's message to Mary reveal about God's plan for salvation? How does this moment in history mark a turning point in God's relationship with humanity?

Mary's Faith and Obedience
What does Mary's final response, *"I am the Lord's servant. May your word to me be fulfilled,"* reveal about her understanding of discipleship and obedience to God?

Messianic Fulfillment in the Annunciation
How does Gabriel's message to Mary connect the Old Testament promises (like those made to David) to the coming of Jesus? What does this say about God's faithfulness and His plan for redemption?

God's Plan of Salvation
How do the concepts of the virgin conception and the Annunciation fit into the larger biblical narrative of God's plan for salvation? How do these two events prepare the world for the coming of the Messiah in a way that is both surprising and profound?

Human Response to Divine Calling
What do the responses of Mary and Joseph teach us about accepting God's will in our own lives?

Theological Reflections on Redemption
How does the Annunciation emphasize the theme of redemption and God's intervention in the world? How does this event set the stage for the ultimate act of salvation through Jesus' life, death, and resurrection?

15

The Sovereign Hand in History

The birth of Jesus stands as the most profound and mysterious event in human history. It is a story of divine orchestration, where God's sovereign plan unfolds in the most unexpected and humble of settings. And yet, it is brought to pass at exactly the right moment: *But when the fullness of time had come, God sent forth His Son, born of woman, born under the law, to redeem those who were under the law, so that we might receive adoption as sons* (Gal. 4:4-5).

God brought all of the events together at the optimum time. Over the course of centuries, conditions were set in place that led to this precise moment for this exact event. From the rise and fall of kingdoms like Babylon, Persia, Greece, and Rome (Daniel 2:21), to the seemingly insignificant details of a taxation decree or the exact moment of conception, God directs all things toward His ultimate purpose. The birth of Jesus is truly the hinge of history.

Not only did the birth of Jesus change the world, but it also revealed God's eternal purpose for humanity—woven through centuries of prophecy, history, and the human heart. Every detail of this moment points to a God who is sovereign over time, yet draws near in the most intimate and unexpected ways.

The Divine Decree: Caesar Augustus and the Census

The birth of Jesus did not happen in isolation; it was the culmination of a divine plan set in motion long before this night in Bethlehem. In the moment that Caesar Augustus, the powerful Roman emperor, issued a decree for a census to be taken across the empire, he believed he was simply exercising his will to count and tax the people. Behind the emperor's command, the hand of God was at work.

127

This was no accident. God moved in the heart of the emperor, shaping events to bring Mary and Joseph to the very place where prophecy had foretold the Messiah would be born. In His sovereignty, God orchestrated even the actions of the greatest rulers, guiding history in ways that humans could never fully understand.

And so, the seemingly mundane act of a Roman census—an order that would send a pregnant Mary on a 90-mile journey—was done to fulfill prophecy. From Bethlehem, the ruler of Israel would come, as the prophet Micah had declared centuries earlier. This was no ordinary event. It was part of the eternal plan of God.

"A king commands from Rome's great throne,
A census called across the lands, alone.
And though the emperor thought his voice held sway,
The hand of God moved the world that day."

Journey of Faith: Destination—Humble Manger

As Mary traveled with Joseph to Bethlehem, her heart must have been filled with wonder and exhaustion. She was nearing the end of her pregnancy, and yet, in God's perfect timing, it was here—in this humble town—that the Savior of the world would be born.

The child she carried was not just any child. He was the promised Messiah, the Son of God. The Creator, who spoke the universe into being, was about to enter His creation, not as a mighty king, but as a helpless infant.

The conception was an undeniable miracle—a sign of God's extraordinary power and love, wrapped in human form. (And again, just to be precise in our language—the miracle was in the Virgin Conception. The birth was entirely natural—especially for a young woman nine-months pregnant riding on a donkey for 90 miles over a three-day journey. But language and terms are difficult to change.)

In the quiet of the night, under the starry sky, Mary would give birth to the King of Kings—not in a royal palace, but in a humble manger, where animals fed.

"A maiden's womb, untouched by man,
Bore the mystery of God's eternal plan.
In the hush of night, upon a beast's back,
Mary rode through the rocky track."

There, in the simplicity of the manger, God would meet humanity—lowly, humble, and wrapped in swaddling cloths. This child, so fragile, would one day break the chains of sin and death, but for now, He lay helpless in the arms of His mother. God had entered the world, not with power, but with humility, to show that His Kingdom would not be built on the world's standards of greatness.

The Chosen Caretaker: Joseph's Role in God's Plan
God's perfect plan also extended to the man who would raise Jesus—Joseph. A simple carpenter, just and righteous in heart, he was chosen to be the earthly father, the chosen caretaker of the Messiah. Though Mary was pregnant, he took her as his wife, obedient to the divine message he received through a dream.

Joseph's role was crucial, not only in protecting and providing for Mary and Jesus but in fulfilling another piece of God's plan. Joseph's heritage traced back to Bethlehem, and so, by fulfilling the emperor's decree, he was positioned to bring Mary to the town where the Savior would be born.

"In quiet strength, a man was called,
To guard the Christ, though all seemed small.
Joseph, obedient to dreams divine,
Took Mary as his wife, by God's design."

This simple man, chosen by God, would provide a stable home for Jesus. Through his quiet obedience and humble faith, Joseph would help rear the One who would one day redeem the world.

Micah's Prophecy: The Promise of a Savior
God had been preparing this moment for centuries. The prophet Mi-

129

cah had spoken of it long ago, declaring that the ruler of Israel would come from the small and seemingly insignificant town of Bethlehem. No one could have predicted that the King of Israel would be born in such a humble place. And yet, God had chosen Bethlehem, so unremarkable, as the birthplace of the Messiah.

"In Bethlehem, so small and low,
A king was born, the world to know.
Though Judah's town was known to few,
A ruler's heart would bring it new."

The prophecy had now come to fruition. The child born in Bethlehem, though small and humble, was the eternal King whose reign would bring salvation to the world. The glory of God's Kingdom was not to be found in earthly grandeur, but in humble surrender.

The Shepherds: First to Hear the Good News
As the Savior lay in the manger, the heavens themselves declared His birth. It was not to royalty or powerful rulers that the first announcement was made, but to a group of humble shepherds—men who lived on the margins of society. As they watched over their flocks in the quiet fields outside Bethlehem, the night sky suddenly exploded with heavenly glory. An angel appeared, proclaiming peace on earth and goodwill toward men.

"Out in the fields, by firelight's glow,
Shepherds kept watch, while cold winds blow .
The night was quiet, the stars above,
Until the sky broke with heavenly love."

The angel's message was clear: the Savior had been born. The shepherds, filled with awe, hurried to the manger to find the child, just as they had been told. In their simplicity, the shepherds were the first to hear the Good News. They would be the first to worship the newborn King, while the rich and powerful slept, unaware of the monu-

130

mental event unfolding. Expectations met, the shepherds rejoiced.

Mary's Heart: Pondering

As the shepherds left, glorifying God for what they had seen, Mary quietly pondered all these things in her heart. What did it mean that this child, her Son, would be the Savior of the world? She held in her arms the One who would one day heal the sick, raise the dead, and bring salvation through His death on the cross.

"In the stillness of that sacred night,
Mary held the child, in soft moonlight.
The angels sang, the shepherds came,
Yet her heart, could not proclaim."

In the mystery of that moment, Mary understood that her Son had come to fulfill a purpose far greater than any of them could have imagined. Though she would not fully understand until later, she knew that this child had been set apart for a divine mission—one that would bring salvation to the world, but would also require great sacrifice. A sacrifice she could not fathom.

Birth of the Savior: Pivot of History

The birth of Jesus marks a definitive turning point in history. This baby, born in a humble manger, was no ordinary child. He was the fulfillment of centuries of prophecy, the Savior of the world. His birth was not just the beginning of a life; it was the start of a journey that would change the course of human history.

From the decree of Caesar Augustus to the humble manger in Bethlehem, every detail of this story speaks of God's sovereign hand at work. His timing was perfect. His plan, unfolding over centuries, reached its pinnacle in the birth of Jesus Christ. Through the humility of the manger and the lowliness of the shepherds, God revealed a Kingdom unlike any the world had ever known—a Kingdom built on love, sacrifice, and grace.

131

As we reflect on this story, we are reminded of the unexpected nature of God's plan. His ways are higher than ours, and His Kingdom is not built on power and pride, but on humility and sacrifice. The birth of Jesus invites us into a Kingdom that upends all our ideas of what greatness and power truly mean. And from that quiet night in Bethlehem, the Savior's reign began, a reign that would span eternity.

Notes and Observations

Investigative Journal Entry: Date: _____ / _____ / _____

How does the timing of Jesus' birth, as described in Galatians 4:4-5, demonstrate God's sovereignty over history? Why is the concept of *"the fullness of time"* significant in understanding the birth of Jesus?

In what ways did Caesar Augustus' decree for a census reveal God's providence in bringing Mary and Joseph to Bethlehem? What does this teach us about God's ability to work through the decisions of even powerful earthly rulers to achieve His purpose?

How does the humility of Jesus' birth in a manger challenge our perceptions of greatness and power? What do you think this tells us about the nature of God's Kingdom?

Micah's prophecy about the Messiah being born in Bethlehem is described in this chapter. Why is it significant that the Savior of the world was born in such a humble, unremarkable town?

16

Becoming a Man

The life of Jesus between the age of twelve and thirty is often referred to as the "silent years." In the Gospels, this is a period where little is recorded. Yet, this silence does not mean passivity. Instead, these years were formative for Jesus, revealing the depth of His humanity. Luke 2:51-52 tells us that during this time, Jesus *"increased in wisdom and in stature and in favor with God and man."* This verse encapsulates the growing process of Jesus as He matured into the man who would later embark on His public ministry.

While the Scriptures offer few specifics, we can imagine the milestones of His life, which reflect His full humanity. Jesus would have learned to walk and talk, grown in understanding, and faced the challenges and trials that come with each developmental stage.

Raised in a Jewish household, He would have been immersed in the customs, traditions, and responsibilities of His faith. He participated in the rhythms of Jewish life—Sabbaths, feasts, prayers, and the study of the Scriptures. His life in Nazareth, a small, tight-knit community, would have offered the normal human experiences of friendship, family, and social interaction.

In the midst of these "ordinary" years, Jesus was not just growing physically and emotionally; He was learning the fullness of obedience to the Father. As the Gospels later show, His will was always in perfect alignment with God's, even in the face of temptation and suffering. This submission to the will of His Father, even in the small decisions of His youth, was a crucial part of His perfect preparation for the sacrificial mission He would one day undertake.

What we see in these years is the human Jesus—the Son of

Man—learning, living, and becoming, without the shortcuts that divine omniscience or omnipotence might have provided. He had to learn like every other human, but His growth was perfectly aligned with God's will. Every challenge He faced, every experience He endured, shaped Him into the Savior the world would need. These "silent years" were not wasted. They were the years of preparation, molding Jesus into the perfect man who could redeem humanity.

The Silent Years

In the quiet years, beneath the sky,
A child grew strong, yet none knew why.
He learned to walk, to talk, to play,
He learned the rules that all must obey.
In Nazareth's streets, in humble grace,
He lived a life, none could replace.
He learned the Law, the prayers, the feasts,
In family's care, He found His peace.
But in His heart, a deeper call—
The Son of God, yet man for all.
He learned to serve, He learned to wait,
Each step He took, ordained by fate.
The wisdom grew, the stature climbed,
The perfect man, by God designed.
In silence lived, yet never still,
God's plan was worked, His heart—His will.
And though the years seemed lost in time,
Each moment built His perfect rhyme.
The world would know, in fullness bright,
The silent years were shaping Light.

Analysis:
The significance of Jesus' "silent years" cannot be overstated. Theologians have long discussed the tension between the divine and hu-

man aspects of Jesus, but the reality of Jesus growing up as a fully human child challenges our perceptions of divinity and incarnation. As the passage we reflected upon indicates, Jesus learned, He grew, and He experienced life in a manner that reflects His humanity.

Hebrews 2:9-10 emphasizes that Jesus was *"made lower than the angels"* for a time, tasting death so that through suffering, He could become *"perfect"* for His mission. This perfection was not about moral flawlessness—Jesus was sinless from birth—but rather, the term is about being fully prepared, fully equipped to serve as the Savior of mankind. The path He walked was not an easy one. He faced the same growing pains, the same frustrations, and the same temptations that every human faces. And yet, He did so without sin, submitting every part of His life to the will of His Father.

The temptation to bypass the human experience in favor of divine intervention is always present, but Jesus, in His self-imposed limitations, did not take that route. He did not jump straight from His birth to His ministry. He lived a full human life, experiencing all the physical, emotional, and spiritual growth that any person would undergo. He learned obedience, not because He was disobedient, but because obedience is a choice—one He made every minute of every day. In the small, mundane moments of life—learning carpentry, dealing with family dynamics, attending synagogue—He was being perfected for the monumental task that lay ahead.

For us, this has profound implications. Jesus didn't just come to die for our sins; He came to live a life that could be held up as the model of humanity at its best. He showed us that being human doesn't mean we are destined to fail or live without hope. His life, from His "silent years" to His public ministry, is the fullest picture of what it means to live according to God's will. His perfection through suffering means that He can identify with us fully, not just as a distant deity but as the man who walked the same path we walk.

The "silent years" are not simply a gap in the historical narrative. They are the quiet foundation upon which the gospel would

135

stand. In those years, Jesus was becoming the perfect sacrifice, the perfect Savior—truly man, yet perfectly aligned with God's will.

The writer of Hebrews addressed this development of Jesus into the person who would become the Christ:

*In the days of his flesh, Jesus offered up prayers and supplications, with loud cries and tears, to him who was able to save him from death, and he was heard because of his reverence. Although he was a son, he learned obedience through what he suffered. And **being made perfect**, he became the source of eternal salvation to all who obey him, being designated by God a high priest after the order of Melchizedek* (Hebrews 5:7-10).

The phrase, *being made perfect*, means "suited or fitted to the task." It is not some abstract concept of perfection. It refers to ***function***. It is perfect for the task it was designed to perform.

I confess a weakness—I love tools. In my collection are tools used as a kid working with my father. I have in my study some of his tools used in his work. They are cherished possessions. When I see them, I remember watching him use them. Some of these tools have unusual design. They might appear odd, but they are designed for a specific application. Their design is dictated by function.

When the writer of Hebrews turns his attention to describing Jesus as our High Priest (4:14-5:1-10), he identifies three essential qualifications of every priest. First, he is appointed on behalf of men in things concerning God. Second, he must be taken from men in order to be sympathetic to their condition. And third, he does not appoint himself, God is the one who appoints him. Jesus met all three of these requirements.

When the writer stated that Jesus was perfectly fitted to the task, he reveals that Jesus was able to sympathize with us because he has been tested as we are—in every way, yet without sin (Heb. 4:15). It was His experiences of being tested and overcoming those temptations that fitted Him to the task. At every juncture of decision between His will and the will of the Father, He chose the Father's

136

will and way. This deepens our understanding of His humanity and underscores the significance of His incarnation.

Jesus' life as a man is integral to our salvation. The phrase from Romans 5, *much more we shall be saved by his life*, is often overlooked, but it's key to understanding the fullness of salvation. It's not merely the death of Jesus that brings us salvation—though His crucifixion is undeniably central—but it is His entire life, the choices He made, His obedience, His perfect alignment with the will of the Father, and His identification with us as a human that becomes the model and foundation of our redemption.

Some want to raise the issue of whether Jesus couldn't sin or chose not to sin. This key theological point is the traditional doctrine of the Impeccability of Christ. The "Impeccability of Christ" is the belief that Jesus could not sin due to His divine nature. It has often been debated. Some hold that because He was God, He was incapable of sinning—suggesting that His humanity was merely a "suit" or vehicle for the divine nature. That reduces His temptation and His life to a farce, a play in which he donned a costume and merely acted a part. Nothing could be further from the truth.

However, the idea that Jesus' sinlessness was due to His deliberate choices, not an inability to sin—is the one that truly honors the mystery of the Incarnation and His full humanity. Look at the evidence of Scripture. He did not sin. But His struggle with temptation led Him to tears. The Amplified Bible caught the essence of this: *And being in agony [deeply distressed and anguished; almost to the point of death], He prayed more intently; and His sweat became like drops of blood, falling down on the ground* (Luke 22:44).

The great Bible scholar, William Barclay noted that the word the writer used in referring to the cry of Jesus in His agony in the Garden of Gethsemane means to wring out. It was an involuntary reaction to the stress and agony of some tremendous tension or searing pain. The struggle was real. The temptations were real. His humanity was full and complete.

137

Jesus' Human Choices in the "Silent Years"

The Luke 2:52 reference is central. *And Jesus increased in wisdom and in stature and in favor with God and man* highlights that Jesus grew. It doesn't just mean He increased in knowledge, but that He developed in wisdom—which speaks to the choices He made in His humanity. The key here is that Jesus had to choose to submit to the will of the Father, to learn obedience, to grow in understanding, and to resist the very temptations and pressures that we face.

If we say that Jesus was incapable of sinning because He was God, we take away the profound significance of His temptations and choices. If He could not have sinned, how could we say He was fully human? How could His experience resonate with our struggles? Jesus had the full capacity to choose—and in His perfect alignment with God's will, He never sinned. This makes His obedience all the more significant, especially when viewed through the lens of His fully-human experience.

The Choice to Obey

Jesus didn't just passively avoid sin because He was divine. Rather, He actively chose obedience to the Father in every moment. Hebrews 4:15 says He was *tempted in every way, just as we are—yet He did not sin*. This isn't merely a statement about His divinity (that He could not sin), but about His full humanity: He faced real temptations, just as we do. But He chose obedience.

When I taught "Introduction to the New Testament" in college as an adjunct, my classes were in the evening. The students came from all backgrounds and jobs. They were working on degrees to help them get ahead. We were at a point in the class where we were dealing with the humanity and the sinlessness of Jesus. One of the students said, "Come on, Professor G, don't you think Jesus did it?" Being as delicate as she could in a class of thirty students, she was also curious about how Jesus could have remained sinless.

She was a 20-something secretary on a Navy base that trained

138

Navy SEALs. She might have been thinking of her own temptations when we were discussing the sinlessness of Jesus. She was struggling with what she knew about temptation and the challenges Jesus must have faced if he lived as a human being. It was one of the more honest moments I can recall. She wasn't a pastor or theologian. She wasn't asking a theoretical, academic question. She was considering real life and wanted to know how Jesus could navigate the temptations that she faced and yet never give in to his appetites and desires.

This is the crux of His sinlessness: His choices. Jesus faced the full range of human temptations and weaknesses, but each time, He chose the Father's will. This wasn't a pre-determined outcome because of His nature; it was the culmination of every small choice, every moment of submitting His will to the Father.

In those "silent years," this obedience was forming Him into the perfect human. It was a training ground for His ministry, His death, and His resurrection. Each choice He made to grow in wisdom, to obey in the small, everyday moments of life was preparing Him for His greater purpose. Every day, He was learning to surrender His will to the Father, and His humanity was tested and refined through those choices. He became perfectly fitted to His function as the sinless sacrifice for the sins of the whole world.

"Much More We Shall Be Saved by His Life"

In that context, Romans 5:10—*much more we shall be saved by His life*—makes sense. It's not just the death of Jesus that saves us (though it's absolutely essential) but His life—the fact that He chose to live in perfect submission to God's will, the fact that He walked the same path we walk and yet remained sinless. That life, lived in the midst of our broken world, is what makes Him our perfect Savior. His life is the model of true humanity. It's the proof that human beings can walk in perfect obedience, and it shows us how we can live through His indwelling Spirit.

This isn't merely about His death on the cross; it's about how

139

He lived—choosing the Father's will in every circumstance, and ultimately, choosing the cross as the ultimate act of obedience. His perfect, sinless life becomes the way of salvation—not just as a doctrinal statement, but as a lived reality that we, through Him, can now follow. We are saved by His life because His life was the perfect example of obedience, submission, and alignment with the will of God.

Connecting to the "Silent Years"

It all comes back to the "silent years," those formative years that the Gospels only briefly touch on. In those years, Jesus was growing, choosing, and learning what it meant to be fully human. His growth wasn't just biological, but spiritual and emotional. As He grew in wisdom and stature, He was learning to submit to the Father's will in the most mundane and ordinary ways. The simple, ordinary choices He made—from learning a craft (carpentry) to engaging with His family—were all part of His preparation for the ultimate choice of obedience—the cross.

In these years, Jesus was not bypassing His humanity—He was fully embracing it. Every choice, from the mundane to the profound, was a step towards salvation for all of humanity. It is in this light that the "silent years" become powerfully significant. They show us that Jesus' life, His choices, and His obedience in every moment—not just His death—are what save us.

17

Laying Aside Rank and Privilege
Reflections on the Humanity of Jesus

In the reflection of Jesus' humanity, we explore the profound reality of the Word becoming flesh. His journey through human life was not one of privilege, but one of self-emptying, where He experienced all the limitations, struggles, and emotions that we as humans do. The *Logos* chose to lay aside his divine prerogatives and take on our human frailties—not as an act of necessity for Himself, but as the most profound expression of love and empathy toward humanity. In doing so, He not only identified with our suffering but also demonstrated the power of obedience and self-sacrifice, becoming the perfect model of what it means to live a life fully surrendered to God's will.

This exercise will lead you through a series of reflections on key passages that reveal the deep humanity of Jesus, allowing you to connect with His experiences of growth, emotion, physical needs, and suffering. These reflections invite you to consider the significance of Jesus' humanity in relation to God's plan of salvation, His identification with our struggles, and the power of His choice to walk among us. Use your Bible to find and read these texts. This exercise contains several passages. Don't feel that you have to rush through them. Meditate your way to a deeper understanding of the humanity of Jesus and what He did on our behalf.

As you reflect on these verses, ask yourself how the humanity of Jesus challenges your understanding of your own humanity, your relationship with God, and the life of faith that He calls you to live.

1. John 1:1, 14
- Why do you think the *"Word became flesh"* was essential for

God's plan of salvation?

- How does this passage challenge the way we view the physical world and our own humanity in relation to God?
- Who do you think needed the incarnation the most: humanity or God? Why?
- What does it mean to you that the eternal Word chose to dwell among us, living as a human being?

2. Romans 8:3

- Why do you think Jesus had to come in *the likeness of sinful flesh*?
- How does this passage shed light on the nature of sin and the way Jesus addressed it?
- How does it impact your understanding of Jesus' empathy toward humanity's struggles with sin?
- What does it mean for you personally that Jesus, in his full humanity, was able to overcome sin in the flesh?

3. Hebrews 2:9-18

- How does the fact that Jesus had to suffer as a human change the way you view suffering in your own life?
- Why do you think Hebrews emphasizes that Jesus came to help "the offspring of Abraham" and not angels?
- What does this passage reveal about the way Jesus identifies with us in our human struggles?
- How does this shift your perspective on the idea of God "coming down" to us?

4. Hebrews 4:14-5:9

- What does it mean that Jesus can sympathize with our weaknesses? How does this deepen your understanding of God's approach to human suffering?

142

- In what ways can you relate to Jesus' temptation and struggles, despite his sinlessness?
- How do you think Jesus' humanity and his ability to empathize with us informs his role as our High Priest?
- What role does prayer and dependence on God play in your life as a response to Jesus' own prayerful dependency on the Father?

5. Philippians 2:6-8

- Why do you think Jesus chose to *"empty himself"* and take on human limitations?
- What would it look like for you to imitate this kind of humility in your daily life?
- How do you understand the concept of humility through the lens of Jesus' human experience?
- In what ways does Jesus' example of self-emptying challenge how you view your own privileges or status in life?
- How does this passage shape your view of what it means to live a life of obedience to God, especially in moments of personal sacrifice?

6. Matthew 4:2

- What significance does Jesus' hunger hold for you, considering that he could have chosen not to experience physical needs?
- Why might it be important for us to recognize that Jesus experienced human limitations, like hunger and fatigue?
- How does this human experience of Jesus help you trust him more in your own moments of physical weakness?
- What does Jesus' hunger teach you about God's understanding of human vulnerabilities?

7. Luke 2:40

- What does Jesus' growth in wisdom and strength suggest about the nature of his human experience?

- How do you think Jesus' childhood and development can inform your understanding of his humanity?
- Why is it important to realize that Jesus did not skip any stage of human development in his journey on earth?
- What aspects of Jesus' growth in this passage speak to your own need for spiritual, emotional, and physical growth?

8. Luke 2:52

- What does it mean for you that Jesus increased in wisdom and stature, and that he experienced human development?
- Why might the Bible emphasize the importance of Jesus' growth in favor with both God and man?
- How does this passage challenge your own understanding of what it means to be fully human?
- How does Jesus' example of growth and learning shape your approach to growth in your own life?

9. Matthew 26:38

- Why do you think Jesus expressed such intense sorrow and distress in the Garden of Gethsemane?
- How does Jesus' openness about his emotional distress influence the way we are called to handle our own emotions?
- What does it mean to you that Jesus, though fully divine, expressed the full range of human emotions?
- How does this passage challenge the way we view emotional vulnerability in the context of faith?

10. John 11:35

- Why do you think Jesus wept at Lazarus' death, even though he knew he was about to raise him from the dead?

- What does Jesus' weeping teach you about the depth of his compassion and empathy for the pain of others?
- How does Jesus' humanity inform the way you respond to sorrow and loss in your own life?
- What does it mean that Jesus, despite being the Son of God, chose to feel and express sorrow like us?

11. Mark 6:3

- Why do you think the people of Nazareth were so offended by Jesus? How does this reflect the challenge of seeing the extraordinary in the midst of the ordinary?
- How does Jesus' experience as the carpenter's son inform the way we view his humanity?
- What role does familiarity play in how we recognize or fail to recognize the divine at work in the world?
- How can Jesus' humanity help you engage more authentically with those who are close to you?

12. John 19:28

- What do you think Jesus' declaration of thirst on the cross teaches us about his identification with human suffering?
- How does the physical nature of Jesus' suffering shape your understanding of his sacrifice?
- What does it mean to you that Jesus fully embraced the physical limitations of humanity, even in his final moments?
- Why is it significant that Jesus didn't avoid or minimize his human experiences, even on the cross?

13. 1 Timothy 2:5

- What does it mean that Jesus is the "man Christ Jesus" as the mediator between God and humanity?

- Why is it important that Jesus is portrayed as a man, and not just a divine figure, in this role?
- How does this passage help you understand the significance of Jesus' humanity in reconciling us with God?
- What are the implications of Jesus' full humanity for your personal relationship with God?

14. Matthew 27:46

- How does Jesus' cry of abandonment on the cross deepen your understanding of his emotional and spiritual struggle in his humanity?
- What does this passage reveal about the intimacy of Jesus' relationship with the Father, even in moments of perceived separation?
- Why is it significant that Jesus felt forsaken by God in this moment of suffering?
- How do you process the tension between Jesus' divine nature and his deep emotional cry of anguish?

15. Acts 2:22

- How does the declaration that Jesus was "*a man attested to you by God*" shape your understanding of his earthly ministry?
- Why do you think the early church emphasized Jesus' humanity alongside the miraculous works that God did through him?
- How does this passage challenge you to see the divine working through the human Jesus?
- What role does Jesus' humanity play in your own faith and understanding of his mission?

16. 1 John 4:2-3

- Why is it essential to affirm that Jesus "*has come in the flesh*" according to this passage?

- How does this passage challenge misconceptions about Jesus or the incarnation?
- What does it mean that Jesus' physical incarnation is a fundamental part of your faith?
- How does this affirmation of Jesus' humanity shape the way you understand salvation?

17. Hebrews 5:7

- What do you think the author means by *"in the days of his flesh"*—how does this emphasize the real, lived humanity of Jesus?
- How does Jesus' earnest prayers and supplications reflect his deep humanity in facing death?
- What can we learn from Jesus' prayerful dependence on God in our own times of distress?
- How does this passage shape your view of the importance of prayer in times of trial?

18. Luke 24:39

- Why is it significant that Jesus, even after resurrection, presents himself with a physical body?
- How does this passage affect your understanding of the resurrection and its implications for the human body?
- What does it mean for you personally that Jesus retains his humanity, even after his victory over death?
- How does this post-resurrection encounter with Jesus affirm the goodness of God's creation, including our own bodies?

These passages help us look at the humanity of Jesus from multiple angles. Through our reflections, we understand how the *Logos* lived as the man, Jesus. The incarnation of the *Logos* was the means God chose to bring about our redemption and forgiveness. Jesus lived the

147

life God wants all of us to live—a life fully surrendered to His will. Jesus gave us a model, but more than a model. He became the man by His choices, who would be the Sinbearer and the Sacrifice for not just our sins, but for the sins of the whole world.

Notes and Observations

Investigative Journal Entry: Date: _____ / _____ / _____

How does the concept of Jesus growing in wisdom, stature, and favor with God and man (Luke 2:52) challenge our understanding of His humanity? What does this reveal about His choices during His early years?

Why is it significant that Jesus chose to live a fully human life with all its limitations and challenges? How does this enhance our understanding of His obedience to the Father?

How does the idea that Jesus *"learned obedience"* (Hebrews 5:8) deepen our understanding of His humanity? What role did His choices, especially during the "silent years," play in preparing Him for His ultimate mission?

In light of Romans 5:10, why is it crucial to recognize that we are saved not only by Jesus' death, but by His life as well? Why was His sinless life through His choices essential?

How does His real human struggle with temptation help us understand the depth of Jesus' humanity and His identification with us in our struggles?

How does Hebrews 4:15, which emphasizes that Jesus was *"tempted in every way, just as we are—yet He did not sin,"* help us relate to Him more deeply?

148

18

Jesus: A Model—but More

Sinful humanity needed much more than a role model. We needed a savior, a redeemer. Consequently, Jesus left heaven. *For the Son of Man has come to seek and to save that which was lost* (Luke 19:10). *For even the Son of Man did not come to be served, but to serve, and to give His life a ransom for many* (Mark 10:45).

Who Jesus was (His character) shaped what He did (His ministry). What He did revealed who He was—and still is. Therefore, Jesus set an example for us (character + ministry) when He saved us, *the* purpose of His earthly life.

Jesus did more than speak. He didn't merely practice what He preached—He preached what He practiced. Jesus showed His followers how to live, modeling three enduring priorities.

1. The Priority of the Kingdom of God
2. The Priority of Persons over Things, even "holy" Things
3. The Priority of Servanthood as a Way of Life

1. The Priority of the Kingdom of God

Twenty-first century citizens of democracies have difficulty grasping the idea of kingdom. Submitting to the rule of a king is foreign to most. A better way to conceive the concept of kingdom is to think of the **kingdom** of God as the **will** of God in our lives.

Jesus Himself pursued the will of God at every juncture: *My food is to do the will of Him who sent Me, and to accomplish His work* (John 4:34). Consequently, He exhibited the lifestyle that pleases God.

149

For Jesus, obeying God's will was a matter of the heart, *the* way to love God (see John 14:15, 21, 23). The scribes and Pharisees, on the other hand, were legalists. They kept the Law in order to exploit God and to impress the masses. God's will was their "credit card," the means to earn points and reap rewards (see Mt. 6:1-6, 16-18).

Obeying the will of God cost Jesus His life. At Gethsemane, the shadow of the cross shrouded Him. Imminent death, however, did not shake His resolve nor weaken His submission to the Father. He prayed, *Not My will, but Thine be done* (Luke 22:42b).

As the mob approached with clubs and swords, Jesus made clear that His arrest was not the result of weakness or surprise. "*Do you think that I cannot appeal to My Father, and He will at once put at My disposal more than twelve legions of angels?*" (Matt. 26:53). A Roman legion numbered around 5,000 soldiers—twelve legions would mean over 60,000 heavenly warriors poised for intervention. At His word, the armies of heaven could have descended in force. But Jesus did not call them. His authority was real—but so was His restraint.

This moment reveals the heart of Jesus' mission: His surrender was not the absence of strength but the highest expression of it. He chose obedience, even unto death, refusing to sidestep the cross with divine privilege. His refusal to call down angelic defense shows the depth of His commitment to the Father's will. It also shows that sinlessness was not an automatic outcome of divine nature—it was the result of perfect, voluntary submission. In this, Jesus models the victory of obedience over self-protection, of sacrificial love over coercive power.

The Kingdom of God was not just a place; it was a matter of God's rule, His will being done on earth as it is in heaven. Jesus' life and ministry were entirely shaped by this rule. In every act of obedience, in every healing, in every word He spoke, He embodied the very will of God. Recall His words to His disciples at the well, *My food is to do the will of Him who sent Me, and to accomplish His*

150

work (John 4:34). Jesus never shied away from submitting His will to the Father's, even when it led Him to the cross.

2. The Priority of People over Things—even "holy" Things Jesus modeled <u>sacrifice</u>.

Greater love has no one than this, that one lay down his life for his friends. You are My friends if you do what I command you (John 15:13-14).

"Let us not forget that any relationship whatever between God and man rests today on the fact that God lived the life of a common man—was born in a stable, sweated in a carpenter shop, preached from a little fishing boat, sat down tired beside a well and conversed with a courtesan, ate and drank and walked with ordinary men, and submitted to an ignoble death—in order that we could recognize Him. Nobody called Him a hero or a martyr. He was simply doing what His Father told Him to do, and doing it with *delight*." (Elisabeth Elliot, *Shadow of the Almighty*)

- In word *and* deed, Jesus loved people. Recall insightful moments from His ministry.
- In Sychar, at Jacob's well, Jesus violated social mores. He conversed with a Samaritan woman. The Twelve *marveled that He had been speaking with a woman* (John 4:27). John apprised us, *Jews have no dealings with Samaritans* (John 4:9b).
- As a healer, Jesus willingly touched the <u>unclean</u>: lepers, a woman who had hemorrhaged for twelve years, even dead bodies.
- Jesus welcomed children. The disciples, on the other hand, tried to deter them. Jesus responded, *Let the children alone, and do not hinder them from coming to Me; for the kingdom of heaven belongs to such as these* (Mt. 19:14).
- On the Sabbath, Jesus exorcised a demon at the synagogue in

Capernaum (Luke 4:31-37); He also healed a man whose right hand had withered (Luke 6:6-11), another man afflicted with dropsy (Luke 14:1-6), and an arthritic woman too stiff to stand upright (Luke 13:10-17). When the synagogue ruler complained, Jesus chided, *You hypocrites, does not each of you on the Sabbath untie his ox or his donkey from the stall, and lead him away to water him? And this woman, a daughter of Abraham as she is, whom Satan has bound for eighteen long years, should she not have been released from this bond on the Sabbath day* (Luke 13:15-16)?

- On the Sabbath, Jesus let the disciples pluck grain and eat. When the Pharisees protested, He stated, *The Sabbath was made for man, and not man for the Sabbath (Mark 2:27).*

- Jesus offers followers an "abundant life." Consequently, the Twelve feasted more, fasted less (Mt. 9:14-17). They ate but skipped ritual hand washings (Mark 7:1-13). Such behavior upset the Pharisees and disciples of John the Baptist. They preserved religious traditions—traditions of the elders (Mark 7:5).

- James and John cornered Jesus, requesting seats of honor. Their ambition angered the other disciples. Jesus, however, remained calm. He quieted everyone, testifying, *For even the Son of Man did not come to be served, but to serve* (Mark 10:45a).

- A lawyer asked Jesus, *Who is my neighbor?* (Luke 10:29b). In a parable, Jesus pictured a neighborhood without boundaries. The "good" neighbor was a Samaritan man (Luke 10:30-37).

- A crowd at Jericho surrounded Jesus. Nevertheless, He noticed Zacchaeus, a tax collector who had climbed a sycamore tree. The locals grumbled when Jesus went home with Zacchaeus. They did not appreciate His sacrifice of precious time for one person. For Jesus, the next stop was Jerusalem.

These actions reflected a deeper reality—a radical reordering of val-

152

ues. These were the guiding priorities of Jesus. Every decision He made, every word He spoke, every action He did reflected these values and the rule of God in every aspect of His life. He gave us a model that we are to do as He has done.

A Matter of Values

Sometimes, critics unintentionally give the best compliments. The Jewish religious leadership charged, *This man receives sinners and eats with them* (Luke 15:2; see also Mt. 9:11; 11:19). Jesus embodied Kingdom values, upending the status quo.

The last shall be first, and the first last (Mt. 20:16).

You know that those who are recognized as rulers of the Gentiles lord it over them; and their great men exercise authority over them, but it is not so among you, but whoever wishes to become great among you shall be your servant; and whoever wishes to be first among you shall be slave of all (Mark 10:42b-44).

For whoever wishes to save his life shall lose it, but whoever loses his life for My sake, he is the one who will save it (Luke 9:24).

Whoever exalts himself shall be humbled; and whoever humbles himself shall be exalted (Mt. 23:12).

Consequently, Jesus threatened the establishment.

Jesus was the antithesis of current culture. Jesus valued persons above things—even "holy" things. He defied mores of proper behavior in order to speak with persons and to change lives. He irritated His enemies by violating religious laws when people were at stake. Often Jesus made the sinners the heroes of his stories while the upright became the villains. When persons or things were in the balance, His scale always tilted toward persons.

Jesus modeled self-sacrifice in His relationships with people. His willingness to violate societal expectations, to touch the "unclean," to engage with sinners, and to serve those considered beneath Him by the religious elite, revealed His deep commitment to valuing people over things—even "holy" things.

His actions transcended ritual and law, pointing to a love for humanity that would culminate in His ultimate sacrifice on the cross. Jesus put the needs of individuals above all else, including tradition or reputation, consistently elevating the value of the person over the legalistic interpretations of the law.

3. The Priority of Servanthood as a Way of Life

Jesus, the servant-leader, foils ambitious plans, frustrating the power -hungry. The world's view of greatness is captured in Mark 10:42: *You know that those who are recognized as rulers of the Gentiles lord it over them; and their great men exercise authority over them.* Greatness, for the world, is reaching the top of the pyramid.

In this view, the pinnacle is the place of success. "Underlings" obey what "higher-ups" decide. The incentive is to climb—leave the bottom, pass as many people as possible, and get to the top at all costs. Those who make it are applauded and rewarded. They are called famous. Successful. Influential.

But is the pinnacle of the pyramid where the great congregate? Jesus turned the world's view of greatness upside down. He invites His followers to join Him at the bottom of an inverted pyramid. True greatness is observable and measurable. Each member of God's Kingdom should ask, "How many people do I serve?" rather than "How many people serve me?"

Years ago, Jesus paved a different path to greatness. As the *Logos*, eternally the form of God, He became flesh and took upon Himself the form (essential, intrinsic attributes) of a servant. If we are His followers, we too should be servants. *Do nothing from self-*

154

ishness or empty conceit, but with humility of mind let each of you regard one another as more important than himself; do not merely look out for your own personal interests, but also for the interests of others (Phil. 2:3-4).

Jesus' ministry was characterized by His selfless servanthood. In contrast to the world's view of greatness, Jesus taught that the greatest among His followers would be the servant of all. *Whoever wishes to become great among you shall be your servant; and whoever wishes to be first among you shall be slave of all* (Mark 10:43-44).

His choice to serve, even to the point of death, exemplifies the humility that would become the hallmark of His followers. The ultimate act of servanthood was His sacrifice on the cross, where He gave His life, not just as a model, but as the perfect sacrifice for the sin of humanity.

Priorities: His and Ours

In these priorities, we not only see Jesus' model for living but also the deliberate choices that defined Him as the **spotless Lamb of God**. His character—His obedience to the will of the Father, His love for people, and His servanthood—was never passive. Each decision He made, each act He performed, led Him closer to the cross. This is where the beauty of the gospel shines through. Jesus was not merely a model for us to follow; He was the sinless Savior who, through His perfect obedience, made it possible for us to be redeemed from the consequences of our rebellion.

By making the choice to fulfill God's will, even when it meant His own suffering and death, Jesus didn't just set an example; He became the ultimate sacrifice. His choices—rooted in His love for humanity and His obedience to the Father—made Him the one who could take away the sin of the world. The Lamb of God, foreordained before the foundation of the world, was revealed at the perfect time to restore what was lost in Eden.

155

In this way, Jesus became more than a model. He was the sacrifice that made our redemption possible, and His choices, made in love and obedience, were the means by which salvation was brought to humanity—proving He was far more than a model.

Notes and Observations

Investigative Journal Entry: Date: _____ / _____ / _____

What does it mean that Jesus "practiced what He preached" and "preached what He practiced"? How does this challenge the idea that sin is inherited by nature, rather than a matter of personal choice?

In chapter 18, Jesus' consistent submission to God's will is emphasized as key to His sinlessness. How does His obedience highlight the role of personal choice in avoiding sin, in contrast to the concept of inherited sin?

Jesus chose to prioritize God's will above His own, even in the face of death. How does this act of willful submission challenge the notion that sin is inherited and instead emphasize personal choice?

How does the idea of Jesus' sinlessness as a result of personal obedience reshape our understanding of human responsibility, in contrast to the belief in inherited sin?

If Jesus was fully human yet without sin, how does this show that sin is not inevitable, but rather a product of individual choices? How does this support the view that sin is not inherited?

19

The Progression of Sin
From Innocence to Spiritual Death

Interpretation is crucial to the correct use of the Bible and establishing a grounded faith. To abuse the Bible by making it say something it doesn't say, is almost as bad as not believing it at all. As Paul instructed Timothy, *we must be diligent to present* [ourselves] *approved to God as a workman who does not need to be ashamed, handling accurately the word of truth* (2 Tim. 2:15).

That verse came to mind vividly during a pastors' retreat I was leading in 2008. I had been writing a doctrinal text on the nature of man, sin, and salvation. I was surprised to find little support for the traditional dogma of inherited sin in the text of Scripture. In the retreat, the pastors were enlisted as a case study. They were assigned in groups of three, to take fifteen minutes and list all the biblical passages that clearly teach the "doctrine of *original* sin."

After a few minutes, frustration began to bubble up. Most groups had only listed three texts: Genesis 3, Psalm 51:5, and Romans 5:12. They had heard this doctrine all their lives, taught it, preached it—but now, confronted with the task of grounding it in Scripture, they found themselves at a loss. And, understandably, some began to focus their frustration on the one who had made them doubt: me.

Months later, I returned to the area for another engagement. A group of those same pastors asked to meet with me again. I walked in with a cheeseburger and a soft drink—only to realize I had stepped into an intervention. They had their Bibles, commentaries, and study tools spread out like a war council. They were there to take me to task and to defend their traditional view of *original* sin. I asked for only one ground rule—that we limit the discussion to only the text

157

of the Bible. What unfolded was a serious inquiry into the biblical foundation of inherited sin. But the longer they looked, the more the foundation crumbled.

One pastor, clearly exasperated, defended the dogma of inherited sin based on Genesis 3: "It's implied!" he said. I replied, "You would think that a doctrine that affects every man, woman, boy, or girl who ever lived—or ever will live—would have been written on a billboard so no one could miss it!"

A good rule of thumb: a foundational doctrine should have a foundation. If it has to be "implied," it probably doesn't exist.

Rethinking *Original* Sin: The Case for Personal Choice

In the quest to understand the nature of *original* sin, few texts are more central to traditional Christian dogma of sin than those found in Genesis 3, Psalm 51:5, and Romans 5:12. In the pastors' retreat, these were the very passages they listed—texts long used to support the dogma of inherited sin. Yet, there is another passage that offers a startlingly different view. It's often overlooked, rarely explored in depth when discussing sin, but James 1:14-15 presents an entirely different way of interpreting human nature, sin, and salvation.

This passage raises questions of whether we are born into sin or whether sin is a choice—a progressive act that begins in the heart, takes root in desire, and culminates in rebellious action. It challenges the idea that we are sinners at conception—suggesting instead that innocence remains intact until a conscious decision to rebel.

Let's explore James 1:14-15 alongside the traditional texts on *original* sin and uncover the progression James outlines.

The Progression of Sin: James 1:14-15

James writes:

> *"But each person is tempted when he is lured and enticed by his own desire. Then desire, when it has conceived, gives birth to sin; and sin, when it is fully grown, brings forth death."*

158

The structure of this passage outlines a process, a progression that's key to understanding how sin operates in human lives:

1. **Temptation:** James begins with the reality of temptation—universal, yet not in itself sin. Everyone experiences it; it's part of being human. But it's how we respond that matters.

2. **Desire:** From temptation comes desire—an internal force that leads us to be drawn toward that which is forbidden or contrary to God's will. Here, desire is personal, a choice that rises from within. It is not an external force compelling us to sin, but rather an internal pull that entices us.

3. **Sin:** Desire, once acted upon, gives birth to sin. The choice to give in to temptation is what leads to sin—an active decision that springs from internal desire.

4. **Death:** The final result of sin, when it is fully grown, is death. This death is not just physical but spiritual, the ultimate separation from God.

James' framework is clear: sin is not an inherited condition from birth, but a choice made when we allow temptation and desire to take root and lead us astray.

Comparing James 1:14-15 to Traditional Texts

Genesis 3: The "Fall" of Humanity

In Genesis 3, we read the story of Adam and Eve's rebellion. Here, the serpent tempts Eve, she desires the forbidden fruit, and then she makes the choice to eat it. This moment has traditionally been seen as the origin of *original* sin—the moment when sin entered the world and became the inheritance of all human beings.

- **Traditional View:** The "Fall"— Adam's choice to disobey God, is seen as the event that corrupted human nature. From that moment on, all humans are born sinful, their nature inherently flawed by Adam's disobedience.

- **James' Challenge:** James, however, doesn't emphasize the

159

inherited nature of sin. Instead, he focuses on the individual process by which sin occurs—through temptation, desire, and choice. While Adam and Eve's choice was momentous, the focus here is on their personal decision to disobey, not on a condition they were born into.

In this light, Genesis 3 might be less about the inheritance of sin and more about individual responsibility. Even Adam and Eve, before they ate the fruit, were innocent until they made the choice. This supports the idea that sin is not an inherited condition but results from personal volition.

Psalm 51:5: A Confession of Sin

In Psalm 51:5, David famously confesses, *"Behold, I was brought forth in iniquity, and in sin did my mother conceive me."* Traditionally, this verse has been interpreted that all humans are born with an inherent sinful nature, tainted from the moment of conception.

- **Traditional View:** This is often cited as evidence that all humans inherit the sinful nature of Adam and Eve. It's seen as an affirmation that *original* sin is something passed down genetically, making every person inherently sinful from birth.

- **James' Challenge:** James gives us an alternative understanding. Rather than asserting that we are born into sin, James 1:14-15 suggests that sin arises through personal desire and choice. David's words in Psalm 51:5 are an expression of personal guilt, but they don't provide a mechanism for how sin is inherited. James' teaching is clear: temptation and desire lead to sin—it's not something embedded in our nature from birth, but rather a progressive act.

While Psalm 51:5 shows David's awareness of his own sin, it does not confirm that all humans are born in sin. It might speak to David's personal experience, but it doesn't suggest that sin is inherited at birth in the way that Romans 5:12 has been interpreted.

Romans 5:12: The Spread of Sin

Romans 5:12 is perhaps the most cited verse for the dogma of *original* sin. Paul writes, *Therefore, just as sin came into the world through one man, and death through sin, and so death spread to all men because all sinned.* This has traditionally been read to mean that all people inherit the guilt of Adam's sin, making them guilty from birth.

- **Traditional View:** Paul's words are often interpreted to mean that all humans are born guilty because of Adam's sin, and that *original* sin is passed down from generation to generation. This lays the foundation for the belief that humans are born with a sinful nature.

- **James' Challenge:** James' view of sin is fundamentally different. He does not describe sin as something inherited but as something personal—the result of internal desire that grows into action. While Paul's focus is on the spread of death, James clarifies that sin and death are not about inherited guilt but about individual choice. Romans may speak to the universal presence of death, but it does not specify that sin is inherently passed down from one generation to the next in the way that traditional dogma suggests. It actually states that death is due to personal sin.

Personal Nature of Sin: A Progressive Act of Rebellion

The progression in James 1:14-15 offers a critical framework for understanding sin. Rather than seeing sin as an inherent condition that is passed down at birth, James emphasizes the volitional nature of sin—a decision that begins with temptation, grows into desire, and ultimately results in rebellious action. This stands in stark contrast to the traditional dogma of *original* sin, which often suggests that we are born with a sinful nature, unable to avoid sin.

- **Sin is a Choice:** According to James, sin is a choice. It arises from internal desire and is not something we inherit. While

161

temptation is universal, we remain innocent until we make the decision to act on that temptation.

- **Temptation is Universal:** Temptation does not make us sinful; how we respond to it does. Temptation is a part of life, but sin arises only when we give in to our desires.

- **Rebellion, Not Inheritance:** Sin is a willful rebellion against God, not an inherited condition. The path to sin is progressive: it begins with temptation, becomes a desire, and culminates in sinful action. This means that we are not born into sin, but are accountable for our choices.

Reframing *Original* Sin

James 1:14-15 presents a compelling challenge to the traditional view of *original* sin. It offers a view of sin that is not about an inherited sinful nature but about personal responsibility and choice. If we adopt James' perspective, we see that sin is not inevitable from birth but arises when individuals are lured by their desires and choose to act in disobedience.

This reframing of *original* sin emphasizes the importance of choice in the human experience—temptation may be universal, but sin itself is a conscious act. This understanding opens the door for a more personal and empowering view of salvation: if sin is a matter of choice, then redemption is also a matter of choice, available to all who choose to turn away from rebellion and embrace God's grace.

By shifting the focus from inherited sin to personal responsibility, we can better understand the full depth of the gospel message—that salvation is about making a choice to follow Christ, not being trapped in a sinful condition over which we have no power. And, as we'll explore further, this understanding of sin and salvation leads us to a richer, more personal relationship with God, grounded in choice, obedience, and grace.

20

The Flesh
The Source of Temptation and Sin

When God formed Adam from the earth—shaping him from the red clay—He breathed into him the breath of life, and man became a living soul. This divine breath animated not just his body, but his soul and spirit—forming a holistic human nature encompassing physical form, self-awareness, and God-consciousness. But it is from this very nature that sin takes root.

At its essence, sin is egocentrism—the desire to assert our self-rule over God's perfect rule. It is the spirit of rebellion, the sin principle, the force that moves us toward self-centeredness. How often do we find ourselves asserting self-rule over God's will in our daily decisions?

The phrase often used by translators of the New Testament to describe the concept of inherited or *original* sin is **sin nature**. In the Greek New Testament, this phrase is simply *sarx*—flesh. Much like Jerome when he mistranslated Romans 5:12, we tend to let our theological biases creep into our translations. These translators seem to be reaching for something more than *flesh*—suggesting that sin is more than physicality, more than mere biomass. And so, the notion of "sin nature" gets carried over into the translations. It is difficult to say if their adherence to Augustine's dogma influenced the outcome. Are they looking through tinted lenses? Let me show you what I mean...

I was discussing the progression from innocence, to temptation, to sin, to spiritual death detailed in James 1:14-15 in a conference a number of years ago. A lady asked if Jesus shared our "sin nature." (She was coming from the base of inherited sin and potentially

163

slanted Bible translations.) My response was immediate—and it was not something I had ever expressed in just the way I did in that moment: *"No. He didn't share our sin nature; He shared our human nature."*

Human nature is the composite of our physical appetites and psychological needs. Jesus was fully human. He shared both. He hungered, thirsted, desired. He longed for connection, belonging, fulfillment. Yet none of these ever crossed into sin.

A Biblical Exercise

Let's do a quick biblical exercise—

Read closely what Paul stated in Romans 8:1-11:

1There is therefore now no condemnation for those who are in Christ Jesus.

2For the law of the Spirit of life has set you free in Christ Jesus from the law of sin and death.

3For God has done what the law, weakened by the flesh, could not do. By sending his own Son in the likeness of sinful flesh and for sin, he condemned sin in the flesh,

4in order that the righteous requirement of the law might be fulfilled in us, who walk not according to the flesh but according to the Spirit.

5For those who live according to the flesh set their minds on the things of the flesh, but those who live according to the Spirit set their minds on the things of the Spirit.

6For to set the mind on the flesh is death, but to set the mind on the Spirit is life and peace.

7For the mind that is set on the flesh is hostile to God, for it does not submit to God's law; indeed, it cannot.

8Those who are in the flesh cannot please God.

9You, however, are not in the flesh but in the Spirit, if in fact the Spirit of God dwells in you. Anyone who does not have the Spirit of Christ does not belong to him.

10But if Christ is in you, although the body is dead because of sin, the Spirit is life because of righteousness.

11If the Spirit of him who raised Jesus from the dead dwells in you, he who raised Christ Jesus from the dead will also give life to your mortal bodies through his Spirit who dwells in you.

- Highlight every time the word, *flesh*, is used in this passage.
- What distinctions can you make in the way these words are used by Paul?
- What does it mean that God sent his own Son in the likeness of sinful flesh?
- How many ways can you identify from the life of Jesus that reveal that He struggled with the same temptations of the flesh that we do?

Allow one more brief exercise to show what I mean when I said that our translators, like Jerome, allow preconceptions or biases to creep into their translations. Compare the following versions—all of 1 Corinthians 3:3. See how the choice of words reflect a particular theological perspective. Our focus is on the word, *worldly*, *fleshly*:

"*worldly*" translation of σαρκικοί (*sarkikoi*); an Adjective - Nominative Masculine Plural meaning: fleshly, carnal, earthly. From *sarx*; pertaining to flesh, i.e. bodily, temporal, or animal, unregenerate.

Berean Standard Bible: "*for you are still worldly. For since there is jealousy and dissension among you, are you not worldly? Are you not walking in the way of man?*"

New Living Translation: "*for you are still controlled by your sinful nature. You are jealous of one another and quarrel with each other. Doesn't that prove you are controlled by your sinful nature? Aren't you living like people of the world?*"

Young's Literal Translation: "*for yet ye are fleshly, for where there is among you envying, and strife, and divisions, are ye not fleshly, and in the manner of men do walk?"* (This is a literal translation from the Greek—explaining why it reads a bit awkwardly to us.)

What is your observation? Is theological bias shown?

Dimensions of Humanity

The term *sarx* in the New Testament refers to more than just the body (*soma*); it encapsulates the entirety of human experience—the physiological, psychological, and emotional dimensions of our existence. Paul addressed this in his letter to the Thessalonians: *Now may the God of peace himself sanctify you completely, and may your whole spirit and soul and body be kept blameless at the coming of our Lord Jesus Christ. He who calls you is faithful; he will surely do it* (1 Thess. 5:23-24).

These three-fold dimensions of our being—physical, psychological, and spiritual—interact in ways that are crucial to understanding our human nature. The physical appetites of hunger, desire, pleasure, and the psychological demands of ego, intellect, emotions, and will are in constant tension. The spiritual dimension is the hinge that determines whether we choose life or death. Our spirit, which comes from God (Ecc. 12:7), remains alive in innocence until the moment we consciously choose rebellion—when we assert our will above His will, choosing self-rule over God's rule.

This desire for self-rule, or egocentrism, is the essence of sin. The sin of Adam and Eve was not simply in the act of eating the fruit. The act of eating the fruit of the tree of the knowledge of good and evil was the outward expression of a rebellion that had already occurred within their spirit. This <u>sin principle of the desire for self-rule</u> was what Paul spoke of in his anguished struggle described in Romans 7, when he cries: *O wretched man that I am! Who will deliver me from this body of death?* (v. 24, English Revised Version).

The desire for self-rule rather than God-rule (theocentrism) is the true nature of sin. Isaiah captured this essence in his prophecy against the king of Babylon: *But you said in your heart, 'I will as-*

166

cend to heaven; I will raise my throne above the stars of God. I will sit on the mount of assembly, in the recesses of the north. I will ascend above the heights of the clouds; I will make myself like the Most High' (Is. 14:13-14).

When Isaiah put the words, *I will*, into the king's mouth, he revealed the essential nature of sin: it is the desire to ascend, to claim power, to dethrone God and establish self-rule. It is this desire, rooted in the flesh, that manifests in the three primary sources of temptation that confront humanity in every generation: the lust of the flesh, the lust of the eyes, and the pride of life.

These are the same temptations that faced Eve in the garden, and later, that faced Jesus in the wilderness—and which have faced every human being throughout history. Sin's origin lies within the human *sarx*—our appetites, desires, and innate self-centeredness.

The Temptations of Eve

The first instance of sin in Scripture occurs in Genesis 3, where Eve is tempted by the serpent. His temptation mirrors the threefold nature of temptation, which is a constant theme in Scripture:

Lust of the Flesh: The desire to satisfy physical appetites, as seen in Eve's attraction to the fruit of the tree of the knowledge of good and evil, which was *good for food* (Genesis 3:6).

Lust of the Eyes: The fruit *was a delight to the eyes* (Genesis 3:6). The enticement of what is visually pleasing or desirable leads to temptation.

Pride of Life: The serpent suggests that eating the fruit will make them *like God, knowing good and evil* (Genesis 3:5). The desire for self-rule and to assert their identity independent of God's will is the essence of pride.

This initial act of rebellion highlights the truth that sin begins within the flesh—the physiological and psychological dimensions of our being. The desires of the body and ego act as catalysts that lead to

167

separation from God. In their desire to become "like God," Adam and Eve succumb to temptation, and thus sin enters the world, bringing death and spiritual separation.

The Temptations of Jesus

The temptation of Jesus in the wilderness (Matthew 4:1-11, Luke 4:1-13) offers a direct parallel to the temptations of Eve. Satan tempted Jesus in the same three areas but with very different results:

Lust of the Flesh: The devil tempted Jesus to turn stones into bread, appealing to His hunger after forty days of fasting. Here, Jesus was tested to trust in His own power to satisfy physical hunger, rather than rely on God's provision (Matthew 4:3-4).

Lust of the Eyes: The devil showed Jesus all the kingdoms of the world and promised to give them to Him if He would worship him. This temptation appealed to the desire for dominion, power, and control over the world, offering the kingdom on the devil's terms, not God's (Matthew 4:8-9).

Pride of Life: Finally, the devil tempted Jesus to throw Himself down from the pinnacle of the temple to prove that God would protect Him. This was a test of ego—challenging Jesus to test God's promise for His own benefit, rather than trusting in God's plan for His life (Matthew 4:5-7).

In each of these temptations, Jesus faced the same basic elements as Eve—temptation through the flesh, through desires, enticements, and ego. He resisted the desires of the flesh, the seductions of the world, and the demands of self-exaltation. Just as Eve's temptation was rooted in the desire to assert her own self-rule, Jesus was tempted with the same desires but chose to submit to God's will. Unlike Eve, Jesus did not give in to the temptation of the flesh. Instead, He relied on God's word and His submission to the Father's will, providing the perfect model of victory over sin.

As we consider the struggle of Eve, and Jesus, we can now turn

168

our attention to the root of these temptations—the flesh itself.

The Flesh and Sin: The Root of Temptation

The flesh, therefore, serves as the root of temptation. Note how Paul echoes James 1:14-15 in his epistle to the Romans: *For while we were living in the flesh, our sinful passions, aroused by the law, were at work in our members to bear fruit for death* (7:5). Paul, in his letters, frequently speaks of the flesh as that which opposes the will of God. For instance, in Romans 7:18, Paul writes: *For I know that nothing good dwells in me, that is, in my flesh.* He was referring to the self-centered nature that resides in the human experience and not merely the body (*soma*) itself.

His warning to the Galatian Christians was: *But I say, walk by the Spirit, and you will not carry out the desire of the flesh. For the flesh sets its desire against the Spirit, and the Spirit against the flesh; for these are in opposition to one another, so that you may not do the things that you please.* (Gal. 5:16-17). His focus was the tendencies that arise from the flesh—the spirit of rebellion.

In Galatians 5:19-21, Paul contrasts the works of the flesh with the fruit of the Spirit. The desires of the flesh—sexual immorality, idolatry, jealousy, and the like—are contrary to the life led by the Spirit. They are, at their core, expressions of rebellion and self-rule, which is why the flesh is seen as the source of sin.

When Paul contrasted the *fruit* of the Spirit to the *works* of the flesh (Gal. 5:19) he used the word, *ergon. Works* signify that which comes from the world of techniques and artisanship. Works are produced by a person's own efforts. The meaning is that we produce the *works* of the flesh. And as Paul states in Roman 6:23, the works of the flesh receive a wage—*For the wages of sin is death, but the free gift of God is eternal life in Christ Jesus our Lord.*

In contrast is the *fruit* of the Spirit. The word for fruit, *karpos*, signifies that which grows as a matter of course, drawing life from another source. The image is of a plant drawing nutrients from the

169

soil and transforming those nutrients into fruit. The fruit is produced through no activity of the plant. It occurs as a matter of course.

The fruit of the Spirit is not merely emotions or feelings. The fruit of the Spirit is the characteristics of Jesus created in the lives of believers simply by their connection with the Spirit. These qualities are not produced by human effort. They are the natural (actually, supernatural) outgrowth in the life of a believer controlled by the Spirit. These characterize *"Christians."* As we bear these, we are *like Christ.* This term was applied to the followers of Jesus first in Antioch (Acts 11:26). Those believers were marked by Christ's life.

This connection between the flesh and sin is further highlighted by Jesus in His teachings about the human heart. It is interesting that He was addressing the people in response to the inquiry (accusation) by the Pharisees about His disciples eating with defiled hands (Mark 7:1-13). He states that it is not the things from without that defile you but the things from within. In Mark 7:21-23, He says: ***For from within, out of the heart of man,*** *come evil thoughts, sexual immorality, theft, murder, adultery, greed, wickedness, deceit, sensuality, envy, slander, pride, foolishness. All these evil things come from within, and they defile a person.* The heart, a biblical symbol of the center of our being, is shaped by the flesh, sin's base of operation.

And it is this same connection that James was making: *But each person is tempted when he is lured and **enticed by his own desire.** Then desire when it has conceived gives birth to sin, and sin when it is fully grown brings forth death* (James 1:14-15). We are enticed by our desires that are rooted in the flesh, the seat of sin.

Know this, temptation is not sin—it is the yielding that is sin. The hymn writer, H.R. Palmer, got it right—"Yield not to temptation, For yielding is sin." Dr. Frank Stagg noted about temptation that it is the invitation to sin. Temptation does not mean that we will sin. The sin is in yielding. When we yield to temptation, we cross a line that can never be uncrossed. We are in rebellion against God. Innocence lost cannot be regained. We go from tempted to sin.

And ultimately, the end of sin is death. Jesus alluded to this when He told the Pharisees that they were like whited sepulchers—pretty on the outside but filled with death and decay. James stated it plainly—the end of sin is death (James 1:15). Paul called it the wages of sin—*For the wages of sin is death* (Rms. 6:23). And all of this echoes what God told Adam—*in the day you eat, you will die*.

The Remedy: The Cross and the Flesh

The remedy for the flesh is found in the cross of Jesus Christ. Paul writes in Galatians 2:20, *I have been crucified with Christ. It is no longer I who live, but Christ who lives in me*. The flesh, with its sinful desires, must be put to death in order for the believer to walk in the Spirit. The death of Jesus on the cross provided the ultimate answer to the problem of the flesh. Through His death, the power of sin was broken. The believer is invited to victory over the desires of the flesh by identifying with Christ's death and resurrection.

In Romans 6:6, Paul declares: *We know that our old self was crucified with him in order that the body of sin might be brought to nothing, so that we would no longer be enslaved to sin*. The victory over the flesh is not achieved through mere self-discipline, but through the work of Christ on the cross, where He took the penalty of sin and the power of sin upon Himself.

On the cross, Jesus died for our sins and broke sin's power so that through our faith we can appropriate His death as our own. As Paul declared to the Galatian Christians: *I have been crucified with Christ. It is no longer I who live, but Christ who lives in me. And the life I now live in the flesh I live by faith in the Son of God, who loved me and gave himself for me* (Galatians 2:20). In Jesus is freedom… *If the Son sets you free, you will be free indeed!* (John 8:36).

In the victory of Christ over the flesh, we find not just freedom from sin but the invitation to live in the fullness of His grace. As we seek His strength, let us surrender our own self-rule and submit to His perfect will.

171

Paul stated to the Roman Christians:

Neither yield your members to sin as instruments of unrighteousness, but yield yourselves to God, as living out from the dead, and your members to God as instruments of righteousness (Romans 6:13, Berean Literal Bible).

The verb Paul uses here for "yield" carries the idea of continually presenting ourselves, not as instruments of unrighteousness, but as instruments of righteousness to God.

Paul stresses that we have been raised from the dead and are functioning not under law but under grace:

Therefore do not let sin reign in your mortal body so that you obey its desires. Do not present the parts of your body to sin as instruments of wickedness, but present yourselves to God as those who have been brought from death to life; and present the parts of your body to Him as instruments of righteousness. For sin shall not be your master, because you are not under law, but under grace (Romans 6:12-14, BSB).

Through Christ, the chains that once bound us to sin are broken. We are no longer slaves to the flesh. No longer should we yield ourselves to the desires of our mortal bodies, but rather, yield in total surrender to God. Under the reign of grace, we find freedom—not only from the dominion of sin, but to be made instruments of righteousness for His glory. Yieldedness is the key to true freedom.

Notes and Observations

Investigative Journal Entry: Date: _____ / _____ / _____

How does recognizing the flesh as the seat of temptation—not an inherited sin nature—reshape our understanding of human responsibility and Christ's example of overcoming sin?

172

Section 3
A Time of Turbulence

The period from AD 100 to 420 was a time of profound change for the Christian Church. After the apostles, the faith entered an era of significant doctrinal and structural transformation, marked by internal divisions and external pressures from the Roman Empire. That turbulence was like the swirling fog a CSI team enters before the yellow tape goes up. This period set the stage for the later shaping of Christian doctrine and the development of the powerful institutional structures that emerged during the medieval period.

As we continue our investigation, think of this era as the crime scene—one where pieces are scattered, and it's up to us, as forensic theological detectives, to unravel the truth. The teachings of the apostles set a strong foundation for Christian doctrine. Recall that Jude described it as the faith that was *once for all delivered to the saints* (v. 3). Over time, church leaders and thinkers began to build upon—and sometimes diverge from—those teachings. Theological shifts began to take shape, and we must examine these developments to piece together how and why certain doctrines took hold.

Key figures like Ignatius of Antioch, Irenaeus, Tertullian, and Cyprian laid foundations for early Christian thought, each introducing pivotal ideas. Ignatius, for example, developed the concept of a distinct clergy, creating a separation between clergy and laity. These men grappled with questions about God, Christ, and salvation—issues crucial to the formation of Christian orthodoxy. In investigations, every clue contributes to a larger narrative. Our investigation demands that we carefully consider each clue.

By the 4th and 5th centuries, the church found itself at a crossroads—a pivotal moment in our investigation. The period between AD 380 and 420 was marked by intense theological conflict. Powerful bishops, like Damasus of Rome, and the growing involvement of emperors such as Theodosius in church matters, helped shift the church toward a more centralized, politically influential, and doctrinally rigid institution. This was a time when ideas were colliding, much like competing theories at a crime scene.

It was in this charged environment that the debate over *original* sin and free will came to a head. Augustine of Hippo championed the doctrine of inherited sin, while Pelagius, denying *original* sin, offered a radically different view. Their conflict became the central "crime scene"—defining how sin, salvation, and grace have been understood ever since. As detectives, our task is to examine the evidence, explore the motivations of these key figures, and determine how their theories shaped Christian doctrine.

This period of turbulence not only forged Christian doctrine but also laid the foundation for the church's growing influence in both spiritual and political realms—especially the church of Rome. As we move through this history, we'll encounter names and ideas that might be unfamiliar, but they were key players in shaping the dogmas that still influence Christian practice today. Just as a detective unravels the mystery step by step, we will follow the thread of this investigation to understand how this pivotal dogma was born.

Our focus here is on how a scripturally-unsupported dogma took hold and shaped the Western Christian understanding of sin and salvation. Like detectives assembling the final pieces of a long-unsolved mystery, we will trace how these debates emerged and how they impacted the church and the world. If a particular name or event piques your interest, further research is just a click away.

For now, let's explore how the concept of *original* sin emerged and became the defining lens through which salvation has been interpreted for generations.

21

Empire and Church

"Facts, Hastings, facts, those are the cobbles that make up the road along which we travel." —Hercule Poirot

The first three centuries marked a time of immense change for both the Roman Empire and the emerging Christian church. The empire was struggling under increasing internal and external pressures—economic decline, barbarian invasions, and political instability. Yet in the midst of these crises, the church was beginning to grow and strengthen its influence, slowly but surely. Christianity had suffered regional and sometimes empire-wide persecution. But this persecuted minority was steadily gaining influence. Relief came from an unexpected source.

Constantine was battling for control and position in the western Empire. In 312, he had a dream in which he was directed to mark his army's shields and banners with the symbol of the letters *chi* and *rho*—the first two letters of the Greek word for *Christos*. Under this banner, he won a victory that made him emperor of the Western Roman Empire. With his victory, he became a supporter of Christianity. He was the first "Christian" emperor. But it was not until the point of his death that he was baptized.

Chi-Rho

However, the rise of Constantine marked a significant change in the status of the fledgling faith. His Edict of Milan in 313 officially recognized Christianity as a legal religion. This began the faith's march toward imperial dominance. When Constantine became sole emperor in 324, one-fifth of the population identified as Christian.

As Constantine embraced Christianity and learned more about this faith, he found it embroiled in internal doctrinal battles. For un-

175

believers, salvation lies just beyond the unavoidable question: "Who is Jesus?" Answering it is a struggle. To believe or to reject Jesus has eternal consequences.

Interestingly, church history reveals that believers have struggled with the question more than unbelievers. Christians were debating the nature of Jesus for hundreds of years after His earthly life had ended. The one question—"Who is Jesus?"—spawned more questions: Was He human? Was He divine? Was He both? If both, how did the two natures interact?

Just as Constantine embraced Christianity and began promoting it across the Empire, he found the faith embroiled in a struggle between competing factions. The division was over the nature of Jesus. One of the first things Constantine did as the sole emperor of the entire Roman Empire was to convene the Council of Nicaea (AD 325)—a churchwide council to determine the nature of Jesus. At question—was Jesus God or not? The Council asserted that Jesus was truly God. The Nicene Creed would guide the faith to dominance in the Roman world—and wherever else the faith would be spread. By the end of Constantine's reign in 337, 40% of the population claimed to be Christian.

As the church had developed in the first three centuries prior to Constantine, much of the biblical and theological development was influenced not from Jerusalem or Rome, but from North Africa. Scholars known as the Early Church Fathers came from Alexandria, Carthage, and Hippo. Origen of Alexandria, Tertullian and Cyprian of Carthage, and Augustine of Hippo would guide the development of Christian faith.

Of these, Tertullian and Cyprian laid the foundation for what would become the most powerful institution on earth—the Catholic Church. They could never have known they were writing or guiding key components of a power structure that would rule the world. Nor could they have imagined that Augustine would use their teachings to establish a dogma that would encompass the whole of humanity.

Tertullian's Legacy

Born in Carthage, Tertullian was one of the church's earliest theologians to engage with the intellectual currents of the time, including Roman legalism and philosophy. Quintus Septimius Florens Tertullianus (AD 155-225) was the son of a Roman military official. He received an excellent education in grammar, rhetoric, literature, philosophy, and law. He studied in Carthage, second only to Rome in the Western Roman Empire. He went on to study in Rome but returned to Carthage. While in Rome, he became interested in Christianity. Toward the end of the second century, Tertullian embraced Christian faith around 40 years of age.

Training and disposition pushed him to explore his new faith. He avidly read books of the Bible that had been collected and that he had available. Although not having a set canon of Scripture, he quoted liberally from the Old Testament and from several New Testament writings—the four Gospels, the letters of Paul, Hebrews, 1 Peter, 1 John, Jude, and Revelation. For Tertullian, Scripture was authoritative, forming the basis for almost every chapter of his work.

From about AD 200 until his death (maybe 225), Tertullian wrote extensively about the doctrines and practices of the Christian faith. His home city of Carthage would become a powerhouse of Christian thought over the next 200 years due, in large part to the influence of Tertullian.

In Tertullian, Christianity found one of its more ardent thinkers, teachers, and writers. Never a priest. Just a follower of Jesus. He served the church as a prolific lay theologian dedicated to literary pursuits in the dissemination of Christian teaching and thought. His explanation of baptism as an initiation rite would eventually shape much of Christianity and, in particular, the Catholic Church.

His book *De Baptismo* is the first Christian book on baptism. It is here that the first mention is made of "sacrament" in relation to any Christian rite or practice. Tertullian introduced the concept of the sacrament into Christian theological vocabulary.

177

In his work, he compared the Christian act of baptism to the Roman soldier's oath of loyalty to the emperor, which he called the *sacramentum*. Though this was merely an analogy, it set the stage for a deeper development of sacramental theology. In his mind, baptism was a ritual of commitment—much like the soldier's oath, it marked an irrevocable bond between the Christian and their Lord.

However, Tertullian's theology was still individualistic. His primary concern was with the personal relationship between the believer and God. In his view, the role of the church was more about providing order and structure rather than controlling access to salvation itself. The practices of baptism and the Lord's Supper were seen in a more personal and volitional context.

Tertullian's search for an analogy to help explain what baptism was in the life of an individual and the church would be used later as the instrument of the church's power and control. Such analogies can take on a theological life of their own. While Tertullian sowed the seed of the "sacrament"—Cyprian institutionalized it.

Cyprian's Influence

Enter Cyprian, a bishop of Carthage who would take Tertullian's work and build upon it in a way that would forever alter the ecclesiological landscape. Cyprian was an avid student of the writings of Tertullian. He simply called Tertullian, The Teacher. However, Cyprian was not interested in theology merely for its own sake. His work as the spiritual leader of Carthage was driven by the practical needs of a community that had been rocked by persecution.

Here's the situation: Emperor Decius (reigned AD 249-251) pressed a revival of civic religion in an effort to unite the Empire. The persecution of Christians began indirectly from an edict issued by Decius. He required all people (except Jews) to perform a sacrifice to the Roman gods and deified emperors. This might have been to strengthen the eclectic religion of the Empire and bring some sense of unity to an empire in disarray.

Religion was a civic duty in the Roman Empire. And since the sacrifice was made in front of the image of the emperor, it would have also been a declaration of loyalty to Decius.

The edict required all citizens to do the sacrifice in the presence of a Roman magistrate and obtain a certificate (*libellus*) that the sacrifice had been performed. While some of the Christians submitted, most did not. Persecution was unleashed. Though lasting only 18 months, several thousand Christians were killed. Especially hard hit was Carthage where Cyprian was bishop. Interestingly, he had been selected as bishop of Carthage in AD 249, the same year that Decius rose to emperorship. Talk about a baptism with fire.

The persecution under Decius ended when he died in 251. In the aftermath of the persecution, the Christian community was divided. The wedge issue was what to do about those who had abandoned their faith, sacrificing to the Roman gods and the emperor. Many of the *lapsi* (those who had recanted, denying their faith) wanted readmission to the Christian community. Questions arose: Should they be readmitted? If so, how should they be admitted? What should be required of them? Out of these questions would come the second "sacrament" of the church—Tertullian having established the first.

Often we assume that a practice has been in the church from the beginning of the church in the book of Acts. It is a failure of not knowing our origins and history. The system of "Saints" in the Catholic Church is a concoction. But the concept grew out of the persecution of Decius. And specifically out of the position taken by Bishop Cyprian of Carthage over the readmittance of the *lapsi* into the fellowship of believers.

The Decian persecution left the Christian community divided into three classifications:

- Martyrs–those who had died for their faith.

- The *Lapsi*–those who had recanted, denying their faith in Christ.

- Confessors–those who remained faithful during the persecution, suffering for their faith.

The persecution was particularly focused on Carthage. Chris-

179

tians in the church there believed that the Confessors had, through their faithfulness and courage, obtained a special power from God. They held that the Confessors had been ordained to absolve the *Lapsi* from their sins. The merit of the Confessors could cover the demerits of the *Lapsi*. Cyprian, bishop of Carthage, was urged to use the merits of the Confessors to allow the *Lapsi* to return to the fellowship of the church. Out of this pastoral challenge, Cyprian made decisions that would carry implications far beyond Carthage—and would reverberate for centuries.

Church historian Bruce Shelley captures succinctly the situation that confronted the Christian community following the persecution of Decius. He notes the development of a system that involves a ranking of sin, appropriate levels of penance, and the mediation or absolution of the bishop. Does any of these terms sound familiar? Here's where they began. Additional elements of ecclesiastical constructs would be added later—

"Many urged Cyprian to announce such a blanket pardon.

"Cyprian declined, however, in favor of a system of readmission based on the degrees of seriousness of the sins. Leniency, he said, should be extended to those who had sacrificed only after excruciating torture and who well might plead that their bodies, not their spirits, had given way. Those, however, who had gone willingly to make sacrifices must receive the severest punishment.

"His argument won general approval, so to deal with these degrees of guilt, the church created a graded system of penance. Only after varied periods of sorrow for sin (penance) were the sinners allowed to return to the Lord's Supper.

"The bishop extended forgiveness to the fallen, provided they proved their sorrow by coming before the congregation in sackcloth and with ashes on their heads. After this confession and act of humility, the bishop laid his hands upon the penitent as a symbol of restoration to the church.

"The proposal from the North African confessors, however, was only temporarily defeated; it did not die. It reappeared years later in the Roman Catholic doctrine of the Treasury of Merit and the practice of indulgences. In these, too, the church transferred the merits of the unusually spiritual (the saints) to needy sinners." (Bruce L. Shelley, Church History in Plain Language, 5th edition, 88-89)

Penance and absolution trace to Cyprian and the readmission of the *Lapsi* during and after the persecution of Decius (250-251). The use of indulgences as a means of dealing with sin began after this persecution. They were first exercised on behalf of the *lapsi*.

Unless you were paying close attention to the actions that came in the aftermath of the persecutions of Decius, you would hardly notice this development. And you probably would not think that a whole system would grow out of the issue of those who had lapsed from the faith under the persecutions. But what happened there would affect practices in churches around the world every day right now. Whole systems would grow out of the writings and practices of the Christian leaders primarily based in Carthage from AD 200–418.

Tertullian had used the word *sacramentum* to describe or explain the nature of Christian baptism, drawing a parallel to the oath taken to the Emperor by soldiers of the Roman military. This was the only rite to which Tertullian applied the metaphor. Cyprian took the application of the term further, applying it to other rites and practices. He linked these to salvation and the authority of the church. His position was that the only valid sacraments were in the church. Therefore, salvation was only in the church.

Darius Jankiewicz wrote, "Cyprian also applied the OT passages regarding priesthood to the ministry of Christian bishops, thereby contributing to the development of *sacerdotalism*. (*Sacerdotalism* is 'religious belief emphasizing the powers of priests as essential mediators between God and humankind'—Merriam-Webster.com Dictionary.) This new terminology—of sacrament and bishop as priest—was applied especially to the Eucharist and to baptism, of which, according to Cyprian, the bishop was the only celebrant.

181

"This innovation elevated the authority of the episcopate and contributed to the rise of clericalism, a doctrine that promotes separation between the clergy and laity, as it caused the spiritual life of the faithful to be entirely dependent upon the bishop." ("Sacramental Theology and Ecclesiastical Authority." Andrews University Seminary Studies, Vol. 42, No. 2, 361-382. Copyright © 2004 Andrews University Press.)

Cyprian's chief contribution to sacramental theology was the notion that salvation was tied to the church itself. In Cyprian's world, no salvation could occur outside the church, and the church could only be accessed through the sacraments, which were administered by the bishop, analogous to the Old Testament priest.

His views would have a profound effect on the development of sacerdotalism—the belief that priests and bishops had the exclusive ability to mediate God's grace through the sacraments. In his theological framework, only the church's sacraments could guarantee salvation, and as such, the bishop became a powerful figure, one who could bind or loose the faithful from sin.

Augustine Changes the Church

Augustine (AD 354-430), another North African bishop from Hippo near Carthage, defined sacrament as: "symbolical actions…pertaining to divine things; the visible sacred sign of an invisible sacrifice; the sign of a sacred thing; an outward and visible sign of an inward and invisible grace." Augustine opened the way for almost any rite, ritual, or practice to be a sacrament. It took nearly 200 years for *sacrament* to go from Tertullian's analogy to core dogma.

In the following centuries after Augustine, the list of sacraments included, in addition to baptism and the Lord's Supper, such practices as ordination, recitation of the Lord's Prayer, the veneration of relics, pilgrimages, the use of holy water, the sign of the cross, and the recitation of the Christian creeds. Augustine's understanding prevailed for 700 years until the Middle Ages.

Augustine made contributions to the beliefs, practices, and structures of the church that would stretch over centuries. But it was

182

a conflict with another theologian—a British monk named Pelagius—that would leave the most lasting mark on the church.

Note on Terminology:

In this work, the word *church* refers broadly to the community of Christian believers. The term *Church of Rome* is used to describe the early organized leadership centered in Rome, especially as it began to assert doctrinal and institutional authority. The *Catholic Church* refers to the formal, hierarchical institution that developed over time—especially after the fifth century—claiming universal jurisdiction and doctrinal authority rooted in apostolic succession.

Notes and Observations

Investigative Journal Entry: Date: _____ / _____ / _____

1. Constantine's Influence on the Church

- How did Constantine's conversion and the Edict of Milan (AD 313) shape the relationship between the Roman Empire and Christianity, particularly in terms of its political and spiritual development?

- Given that Constantine was baptized on his deathbed, how does his conversion affect the narrative of Christianity becoming the official religion of the Roman Empire, and what does this reveal about the intersection of political power and religious influence?

2. Theological Struggles – Who is Jesus?

- Why did early Christians struggle for centuries to define the nature of Jesus, and how did this influence the church's understanding of His divinity and humanity?

- How did the Council of Nicaea's declaration of Jesus' divinity

183

shape the orthodox view of the Trinity, and what were the significant dissenting opinions?

3. Tertullian's Legacy

- How did Tertullian's use of the term "sacrament" and his analogy between baptism and Roman military oaths influence early Christian sacramental theology?

- Tertullian emphasized personal commitment in faith, but how did later theologians like Cyprian shift the focus toward the institutional church?

4. Cyprian and the Aftermath of Persecution

- In response to the *lapsi* (those who renounced their faith under persecution), Cyprian's decision to establish a system of penance and readmission had long-term effects on church authority. How did this influence the church's handling of sin, forgiveness, and hierarchy—especially the Church of Rome?

5. Sacramental Theology and the Power of the Church

- How did Cyprian's concept of salvation through the church's sacraments contribute to sacerdotalism, and what role did the bishop play in this system?

- Augustine expanded the definition of sacraments. How did this broadened view shape Christian rituals and the church's growing influence in both spiritual and political realms?

6. The Development of Doctrine

- How did Tertullian and Cyprian's writings help shape the Church of Rome's (what would emerge as the Catholic Church) institutional power and its balance of faith with practical needs?

- How did Augustine's teachings on sin, grace, and salvation, particularly in his conflict with Pelagius, influence later Christian doctrine, including the concept of *original* sin?

Timeline: The Road to Carthage
A Chronology of Events Surrounding
Jerome, Pelagius, and Augustine

To understand what happened at the Council of Carthage in 418, we must revisit the key events that led up to it—and what followed. Within this timeline lies the thread of the assassination—the deliberate, systematic destruction of Pelagius's character and credibility. Every turning point is a clue. The dates, writings, and theological developments listed here aren't just background—they are evidence. As you read, trace the patterns. Watch how ideas emerge, how alliances form, and how an entire doctrinal shift takes shape. The connections will not merely inform you—they will leap from the page.

Note: All dates listed in this timeline are given in AD (*Anno Domini*) unless otherwise specified.

Jerome's Personal Journey and Theological Development

- **347**: Birth of Jerome in Stridon (modern-day Croatia).

- **c. 360**: Jerome is baptized at age 13.

- **c. 373**: Jerome experiences a call to ministry and embraces the ascetic life.

- **374–378**: Lives as a monk in the East, studying theology and living in the Syrian desert.

- **376–377**: Writes *Letter to Damasus*, appealing to the "chair of Peter" as a foundation of ecclesiastical authority.

- **382**: Writes Letter 15 to Damasus from Bethlehem, seeking favor and outlining his translation goals.

- **382–384**: Begins translating the Old and New Testaments into Latin under Pope Damasus' commission.

- **384–385**: Following Damasus' death and a cloud of scandal,

185

Jerome permanently relocates to Bethlehem.

- **386–392**: Writes his *Commentary on Ephesians* and other works on sin and grace.

- **405**: Completes the full Latin translation of the Bible—known as the *Vulgate*.

- **410**: Writes *Letter 133*, a public condemnation of Pelagius' teachings.

- **412–417**: Resides in Palestine, where he actively opposes Pelagius during the growing controversy.

- **415**: Participates in opposition to Pelagius during the Council of Diospolis.

Pelagius' Arrival and Development in Rome
- **c. 354**: Birth of Pelagius, likely in Britain.

- **c. 380**: Arrives in Rome, quickly gaining respect as a theologian and moral teacher.

- **c. 390s**: Begins teaching against the doctrine of original sin, promoting moral responsibility and free will.

- **c. 395–400**: Composes *De Natura* (On Nature), laying out his views that humanity is born morally neutral.

- **410**: Flees Rome during/after the sack by the Visigoths; relocates to Carthage.

- **412–417**: Resides in Palestine. Defends his teachings against opposition from Jerome and Orosius.

- **415**: Stands trial at the Council of Diospolis; no verdict is rendered and the case is referred to Rome.

- **417**: Pope Zosimus initially acquits Pelagius after receiving his letter and statement of belief.

- **418**: Excommunicated by Zosimus under pressure from African bishops; formally condemned at Council of Carthage.

- **c. 420–430**: Lives in exile, likely in Palestine or Egypt, until his death. His final years are unrecorded.

Augustine's Early Years and Theological Development
- **354**: Birth of Augustine in Tagaste (modern-day Algeria).

- **370s**: Studies rhetoric in Carthage; later influenced by Manichaeism and Neoplatonism.

- **386**: Converts to Christianity under the influence of Ambrose of Milan.

- **391**: Ordained a priest in Hippo.

- **395**: Consecrated as bishop of Hippo.

- **397–400**: Writes *Confessions*, detailing his conversion and view of sin.

- **397–400**: Begins formulating doctrine of original sin and divine grace.

- **411**: Leads the synod of Carthage in debating Pelagius' teachings—no formal condemnation issued.

- **412–417**: Mobilizes allies to formally oppose Pelagianism.

- **413–426**: Writes *De Civitate Dei* (*The City of God*), reinforcing his theological positions on sin and grace.

- **418**: His influence secures the official condemnation of Pelagius at the Council of Carthage.

Councils and Key Events in the Conflict
- **380**: *Edict of Thessalonica* by Theodosius I makes Nicene Christianity the state religion of the Empire.

187

- **411**: First Synod of Carthage—Pelagius is debated but not condemned.

- **415**: Council of Diospolis—no verdict against Pelagius.

- **415**: Synod of Carthage (second)—led by Augustine's allies, condemns Pelagianism.

- **417**: Pope Zosimus initially acquits Pelagius after receiving his statement of faith.

- **418**: Council of Carthage (Third)—formally condemns Pelagius; Zosimus reverses his decision and excommunicates him.

- **431**: Council of Ephesus confirms Pelagianism as heresy, closing the chapter on his influence in official Church doctrine.

Writings and Doctrinal Developments

- **Letter 15 (382)** by Jerome to Damasus—appeal for ecclesiastical authority and Roman primacy.

- **Jerome's *Vulgate* Bible (completed 405)**—contains key Latin translations such as *in quo* for Romans 5:12.

- **Pelagius' *De Natura* (c. 395–400)**—teaches human moral neutrality and free will.

- **Jerome's *Letter 133* (410)**—public rebuke of Pelagius' theology.

- **Augustine's *On Nature and Grace* (411)**—formally refutes Pelagius' denial of *original* sin.

- **Augustine's *The City of God* (413–426)**—lays theological foundation for Christian worldview rooted in grace and inherited guilt.

Influential Theological Developments and Context

Edict of Thessalonica (380): Emperor Theodosius I makes Nicene Christianity the official religion of the Roman Empire, setting the stage for increased ecclesiastical authority, particularly for Rome and Alexandria, and influencing the theological debates of the time.

The *Vulgate* Bible (completed 405): Jerome's Latin translation becomes the standard Bible of the Western Church, influencing theological discussions of sin, grace, and salvation. This translation of the New Testament helped shape the Christian view of *original* sin, especially in his interpretation of passages like Romans 5:12.

Concluding Points:
By connecting these key dates and events, you can see how the personal motivations of Jerome and Augustine, their theological development, and their responses to Pelagius's teachings all intersected to form the basis of the Pelagian controversy. The tension between these three figures—and especially Jerome's behind-the-scenes influence—could be framed as the key to understanding how the "crime" of Pelagianism was eventually "solved" through the condemnation of the Council of Carthage. The meticulous unraveling of their interactions and the shifting allegiances among the church's power players during this period will ultimately bring to light the strategic, theological, and personal motivations behind the battle for control over Christian orthodoxy.

Notes and Observations

Investigative Journal Entry: Date: _____ / _____ / _____

What patterns emerge? Reviewing the events, dates, and writings in the timeline, what patterns do you notice? Do you see connections between key writings and political or ecclesiastical developments?

Jerome's influence: How did Jerome's personal journey—including his departure from Rome and the completion of the *Vulgate*—position him to shape the church's theological trajectory? How did his experiences influence his opposition to Pelagius?

Augustine's rise to power: Trace Augustine's theological development from *Confessions* to *The City of God*. How did his growing authority influence the outcomes of the councils, particularly Carthage in 418?

Pelagius in motion: How did Pelagius' movements—from Rome to Carthage to Palestine—reflect both his vulnerability and his determination to defend his teachings? What effect did his absence from key moments have on the narrative formed about him?

The role of the *Vulgate*: Consider the significance of Jerome's Latin translation, especially the phrase *in quo* in Romans 5:12. How might this small but pivotal translation choice have influenced the doctrine of original sin?

Turning points: Identify at least two moments in the timeline that you consider decisive in sealing Pelagius' fate. What made these moments so critical?

Power and narrative control: How did the church's increasing alliance with imperial authority (*e.g.*, the Edict of Thessalonica) influence the outcomes of theological disputes? Who controlled the narrative—and how?

Foreshadowing the crime scene: In light of the timeline, how would you characterize the direction things are heading by 418? What clues already point toward an orchestrated outcome rather than an open debate?

190

22

A Storm Arising

In 380, the year that Theodosius made Christianity the state religion of the Roman Empire, a young theologian arrived in Rome. His name was Pelagius, and though few knew it then, his ideas would soon stir a theological storm that would echo through the halls of the church for centuries to come.

Pelagius was born somewhere in the British Isles—though the exact location is debated—sometime around AD 354. By the time he came to Rome, he was already deeply versed in Christian thought, having spent years honing his intellectual pursuits. He arrived in the heart of the empire at a time of immense religious and political upheaval. Christianity, now the official religion of the Roman Empire, was growing rapidly, but it was also embroiled in fierce theological debates about the nature of salvation, grace, and free will.

Rome, once the imperial capital and the seat of Roman paganism, had been gradually transformed. When Constantine established his new imperial capital in Constantinople in 330, Rome's luster was dimmed. Even before Constantine, Diocletian's Tetrarchy in the late third century had seats of power scattered over the divisions of the Eastern and Western Roman Empire as Diocletian sought to improve governance of the sprawling empire. Seats of the four governing men were placed in four different regions and cities. Rome was not one of the cities. Though diminished, Rome remained the leading city in the Western Empire and was home to a powerful church.

In the wake of Emperor Theodosius's decree, the bishop of Rome along with the four other Sees of Constantinople, Antioch, Jerusalem, and Alexandria became primary heads of the newly adopted state religion--Christianity. Now, Christian bishops were

191

beginning to wield political power, and theological disputes were no longer confined to the halls and walls of churches or monasteries but had moved into the very courts of emperors. It was during this period that Pelagius would make his mark.

As a theologian, Pelagius brought a fresh perspective to these debates. He rejected the growing doctrines of original sin and divine grace as articulated by Augustine of Hippo. For Pelagius, human beings had the capacity to choose between good and evil without needing divine intervention. Salvation, he argued, was not a matter of divine grace alone but also the free will of individuals to live righteous lives. In his eyes, every Christian was capable of following Christ's teachings without the need for God's overwhelming grace.

Pelagius' teachings were clear and systematic. Six key statements outlined the framework of his beliefs regarding sin and the means of salvation:

1. Even if Adam had not sinned, he would have died.
2. Adam's sin harmed only himself, not the human race.
3. Children just born are in the same state as Adam before his fall.
4. The whole human race neither dies through Adam's sin or death, nor rises again through the resurrection of Christ.
5. The Mosaic Law is as good a guide to heaven as the gospel.
6. Even before the advent of Christ, there were men who were without sin.

Most Christians agree that Pelagius went too far in some aspects of his theology. It was clearly not fully informed by the text of Scripture. For instance, he believed that a person could be righteous before God through one's personal efforts. Isaiah instructs us that our righteousness is like filthy, disease-ridden wraps and rags from a leprous body. The best moment we have lived is insufficient in the light of God's holiness.

Pelagius held that while the grace of God might assist a person in righteousness, it was not necessary—just helpful—in achieving a right standing before God. And yet, we know that it is only by grace

192

that we are saved. Paul, throughout his writings in Romans, Ephesians, Galatians, makes this abundantly clear.

Although Pelagius was wrong on some points of his theology, this does not discount every position he held. His opposition to a deterministic view of salvation, for instance, raised important questions about the nature of human responsibility, and in some ways, his insistence on free will could be seen as an expression of human dignity. This optimistic view of human nature, however, would bring him into conflict with some of the most powerful theologians of his time.

In the early 400s, Pelagius found himself at odds with Jerome of Bethlehem. Jerome was born in AD 347, baptized at age thirteen, and experienced a call into ministry at age 26. He was trained in rhetoric and philosophy but had a real aptitude for languages. Jerome became a protégé of Damasus, the bishop of Rome.

Because of some accusation (if not an actual indiscretion), Jerome left Rome and went to live for a number of years in the Syrian desert. We know this from his famous Letter 15 to Damasus. Jerome writes: "But since by reason of my sins I have betaken myself to this desert which lies between Syria and the uncivilized waste, I cannot, owing to the great distance between us, always ask of your sanctity the holy thing of the Lord."

While there, he became dismayed at the disunity of the Christian community in the East. Around 376, Jerome wrote to Damasus, the bishop of Rome. In this letter, Jerome would give the basis for the bishop of Rome to claim primacy in the churches and this argument would become full-blown when Theodosius made Christianity the state religion of Rome. Here are pertinent segments of that letter:

- Since the East, shattered as it is by the long-standing feuds, subsisting between its peoples, is bit by bit tearing into shreds...I think it my duty to consult *the chair of Peter*...

- My words are spoken to the successor of the fisherman, to the disciple of the cross.

193

- As I follow no leader save Christ, so I communicate with none but your blessedness, that is with the chair of Peter.
- For this, I <u>know</u>, is the rock on which the church is built! <u>Matthew 16:18</u>
- This is the house where alone the paschal lamb can be rightly eaten. <u>Exodus 12:22</u>
- This is the <u>Ark of Noah</u>, and he who is not found in it shall perish when the flood prevails. <u>Genesis 7:23</u>

These points and the reference, especially to Matthew 16:18, would be the basis for the assertion that the bishop of Rome was the true successor of the Apostle Peter. This would have immense implications for the future of the western world. (And this is beyond the scope of this work, I am sorry to say.)

However, for us, the takeaway is how Jerome used the Scripture to make his point. It reveals that he has a tendency to use the text to make a point. He is not <u>exegeting</u> the text, he is <u>eisegeting</u> the text. He is viewing Scripture through his own lens. It reveals something about how he approaches a text and a situation. This will be important as the conflict over inherited sin intensifies.

Jerome was commissioned by Pope Damasus in 382 to revise the Old Latin text of the four Gospels from the best Greek texts. By the time of Damasus' death in 384 he had thoroughly completed this task and had also produced a new translation of the Psalms into Latin. What began with this commission in 382 lasted until 405 and resulted in the Latin translation known as the *Vulgate*, a modern translation of the time. Jerome was prolific in writing. From his study in Bethlehem, over 34 years, he would become the second most prolific writer of the early church—next only to Augustine of Hippo.

As a man who had spent much of his life translating the Bible into Latin and was deeply concerned with the precise doctrines of salvation. Jerome, whose views on grace were heavily shaped by his admiration for Augustine, quickly grew critical of Pelagius' teachings. And the storm continued to build.

In **AD 410**, Jerome penned a scathing letter (**Letter 133**) attacking Pelagius for what he saw as a dangerous misunderstanding of Scripture. For Jerome, Pelagius was a threat to the foundational Christian belief in the necessity of divine grace. To deny the role of grace was to deny the very basis of salvation, and Jerome wasted no time warning the church of the implications of Pelagius' ideas.

Pelagius, ever confident in his position, responded vigorously, defending his doctrine as a return to the original teachings of the apostles. Yet, despite his eloquence, the tension between him and Jerome would only escalate. Their war of words and letters would dominate the theological landscape of the early 5th century.

But it was Augustine of Hippo, the towering intellectual figure of North Africa, who would prove to be Pelagius' most formidable adversary. Augustine had long held that human beings, due to *original* sin, were incapable of saving themselves. Only by the grace of God, dispensed through the church, could salvation be attained. His views were revolutionary and had already begun to shape the theological identity of the Western Church. When Pelagius arrived in Rome, Augustine's influence was growing rapidly, and the stage was set for a dramatic clash between the two men.

As the debate raged on, Pelagius' ideas gained a following in Rome, especially among those disillusioned by the growing power of the church's bishops and the increasing bureaucracy of Christian life. But as Pelagius' influence grew, so too did the opposition from Jerome and Augustine.

In **AD 411**, Pelagius found himself in direct conflict with Augustine. The debate reached its zenith when Pelagius' views on free will and grace came under formal scrutiny. Augustine, ever the theological giant, wrote against Pelagius in *"On Nature and Grace"*, refuting the idea that human beings could live sinless lives apart from divine grace. To Augustine, Pelagius' denial of *original* sin was a direct threat to the foundation of Christianity. He argued that salva-

195

tion was not from human effort alone but of God's mercy.

The controversy intensified as Pelagius' ideas gained traction in Rome. Yet, his opponents were growing more vocal.

Pelagius spent a period in Palestine beginning around 412 having fled Rome after the sacking by the Visigoths in 410. Jerome, who also lived there, became involved in the debate. Jerome and Orosius, a pupil of Augustine in Palestine at the same time, publicly condemned Pelagius. Their resistance to Pelagius and their public condemnation moved Bishop John of Jerusalem, a personal friend of Pelagius, to call a synod in July 415 to hear charges of heresy against the monk. This was the Council of Diospolis (Lydda)—often referred to as the Synod or Council of "Jerusalem." Pelagius' defense centered around his belief that the church had misunderstood the true nature of Christian free will, but his critics were relentless.

The council rendered no verdict and passed the controversy to the Church in Rome.

In the same year (415), the Synod of Carthage, led by Augustine's allies, condemned Pelagius' teachings, officially labeling them as heretical. Despite this condemnation, Pelagius refused to recant. Pelagius continued to be harassed over the next two or three years by various segments and leaders of the church. However, he was not uniformly condemned. His guilt in the eyes of the church was undecided during this period.

Following the Council of Diospolis, Pelagius wrote a letter and statement of belief showing himself to be guiltless of heresy. By the time the letter reached Rome in 417, Zosimus had become Pope. He was impressed with the statements and declared Pelagius innocent.

Augustine was shocked that Pelagius was not declared heretic.

Pelagius' positions attracted quite a number of devotees, but his views were rapidly met with resistance, particularly from Augustine, the bishop of Hippo and one of the great intellects of the church. The clash between these two minds would shape the course of Christian theology for centuries to come.

As this theological storm brewed, the fate of Pelagius—and the church's understanding of free will and grace—hung in the balance. This chapter, however, serves as the backdrop for one of the most significant theological disputes in early Christianity—one that would define the trajectory of Western Christianity for centuries. In the next chapter, we will turn to the Council of Carthage, where Augustine, with the support of key figures in the church, would seek to have Pelagius officially condemned as a heretic. The stage was set for a final showdown. But it would be a one-sided fight.

Notes and Observations

Investigative Journal Entry: Date: _____ / _____ / _____

Jerome: The Overlooked Architect
Jerome's influence on the condemnation of Pelagius and the entrenchment of inherited sin might be greater than commonly recognized. Like Poirot, we must examine the clues carefully, assembling the evidence piece by piece.

The Primacy of Rome and Jerome's Hand
Jerome played a critical role in elevating the authority of the Bishop of Rome. His letters to Damasus (376–377) framed Matthew 16:18 as proof of papal supremacy, helping consolidate Rome's power. This had long-term doctrinal consequences, including who had the authority to define orthodoxy.

The same "binding and loosing" language appears in Matthew 18:18, applied to the whole church, yet Jerome's interpretation favored centralization in Rome. If he was willing to construct an argument to bolster Roman primacy, could he have done the same to support Augustine's theological agenda?

The Mistranslation of Romans 5:12—A Smoking Gun?
Jerome's Latin rendering of Romans 5:12 was a pivotal moment.

197

The Greek phrase *eph' ho* ("because" or "on the basis of which") is not ambiguous, yet Jerome translated it as *in quo* ("in whom"), fundamentally altering its meaning. In Greek, Paul states that death spread to all *because all sinned*. Jerome's Latin made it appear as though all sinned in Adam, a shift that became the cornerstone of Augustine's dogma of inherited guilt. (More on this to come.)

Was this an innocent mistake? Jerome was fluent in Greek and had access to Origen's writings, which did not support an Augustinian reading of Romans 5:12. The shift appears less like a linguistic necessity and more like a deliberate theological maneuver.

The 415 Inquiry Against Pelagius—Jerome's Political Play
Jerome's role in the 415 Council of Diospolis was anything but neutral. His opposition to Pelagius was not just theological—it was personal. Pelagius undercut the asceticism Jerome championed. If human nature was not tainted by Adam's sin, then Jerome's extreme views on celibacy and self-denial lost their theological foundation.

Pelagius' acquittal in 415 frustrated Jerome and Augustine. Only councils at Carthage (418) and Ephesus (431) condemned him.

Jerome as Iago to Augustine's Othello? A Bit of Shakespeare!
Like Iago feeding Othello half-truths to steer him toward a predetermined conclusion, Jerome might have played a similar role.

- Augustine's ideas on inherited sin were forming, but Jerome's *in quo* gave them scriptural weight.
- Augustine was deeply invested in his conclusions—Jerome, the political thinker, might have simply provided the final nudge.
- Jerome's ambitions show his involvement beyond scholarship.

Though overshadowed by Augustine, Jerome's fingerprints are unmistakable. His strategic use of Scripture, influence on translation, and political savvy may have done as much to establish the dogma of *original* sin as Augustine's theological arguments themselves. Jerome might not have invented Augustine's theology, but he amplified and weaponized it—just as Iago didn't create Othello's jealousy but masterfully exploited it.

198

23

The Crime Scene
Council of Carthage (418)

By the year 418, the church stood at a theological crossroads, its identity at the center of fierce scrutiny and debate. The controversy surrounding Pelagianism—a belief system that rejected the dogma of *original* sin and the necessity of divine grace for salvation—had erupted into one of the most significant theological crises of early Christianity. This conflict threatened to unravel the very core of Christian teaching, challenging the church's authority to define the nature of salvation and the role of divine grace.

The battle waged by Jerome and Augustine against Pelagius had reached a crescendo. Augustine was aghast that Pelagius had not been declared a heretic at the earlier Council of Diospolis—often referred to as the synod or Council of Jerusalem—in 415. He was determined not to let that verdict stand.

A Church in Crisis

By 418, Pelagianism had spread across the Western Church, especially in North Africa, though its most notable champion at the time was Julian of Eclanum, an Italian bishop and disciple of Pelagius. The controversy came to a head when Bishop Aurelius of Carthage called for a council to address the issue. With the support of Augustine of Hippo, the church leaders of the region sought to put an end to the theological turmoil by confronting Pelagianism head-on.

As the influential bishop of Hippo and the most prolific writer in Christendom at the time, Augustine wielded great sway with his fellow bishops. The council at Carthage in 418 was to take up two primary matters: 1) the teachings of Pelagius and 2) the response to the Donatists. For Augustine, the Donatist matter was secondary. His major concern was dispatching his theological opponent.

It was against this backdrop of division and unrest that the Council of Carthage convened. Over 200 bishops from across North Africa gathered in Carthage, and the decisions made at this council would forever shape the future of Christian beliefs about sin. Pelagius himself was not present—a notable absence that would shape the Council's tone and outcome.

The questions before the bishops were not just about one man's teachings. At the center, these questions were about the very nature of humanity, sin, and grace. The Council was poised to make a decision that would forever shape Christian belief and practice. The teachings of Pelagius, the monk whose views on free will and grace challenge the dominant understanding of *original* sin, were to be formally condemned. At the heart of this moment is a battle not merely for theological supremacy, but for the soul of Christianity.

The Great Gulf

The theological chasm between the followers of Augustine and Pelagius had become a deep rift. On one side, Augustine, the Bishop of Hippo, argued that humanity, due to Adam's fall, was incapable of choosing good without the grace of God. He taught that all are born with *original* sin, and only God's grace, through Christ's death and the sacrament of baptism, can save them.

On the other side stands Pelagius, a monk from Britain, whose teachings challenge Augustine's understanding of sin and grace. He asserted that humans are born innocent, with the inherent capacity to choose between good and evil. In his view, Adam's sin was his alone, and it did not have any lasting effects on the human race. Humans, therefore, were capable of achieving salvation through their own free will, without the need for divine grace.

The debate is not merely academic; it is intensely practical. It touches on the very nature of salvation—whether humanity requires God's grace for salvation, or whether each person, through their own will and effort, can earn it.

The Role of Augustine: Guiding the Council

Central to the debate was the figure of Augustine of Hippo, whose theological writings had made him a formidable voice against Pelagianism. Augustine's influence cannot be overstated; his works, particularly *The Confessions* and *The City of God*, had already established him as the Church's most significant theologian of the time. Augustine's personal journey from a life of sin to a profound conversion had deeply shaped his understanding of grace and salvation. His *Confessions*, a raw and introspective recounting of his conversion, revealed how deeply he believed in the necessity of God's grace in overcoming human weakness.

Augustine's teachings emphasized the absolute need for divine grace to overcome the effects of *original* sin. In contrast to Pelagius, who argued that human beings could, through their free will, live righteous lives unaided by grace, Augustine insisted that all humans were inherently flawed due to *original* sin and could only be saved through God's unmerited grace.

It was precisely this theological conviction that made Augustine's voice so critical at the Council of Carthage. As Pelagius' followers continued to gain support, Augustine's writings on grace—particularly his reflections on the power of God's grace to transform the human will—became central to the church's response.

Augustine, having already fought theological battles with Pelagius, played a central role at the Council of Carthage. His letters, his theological writings, and his personal influence shaped the direction of the council. By 418, Augustine's teachings on *original* sin, grace, and predestination had become the dominant framework within the Western Church. His dogma stood in stark contrast to Pelagius' opti-

201

mistic view of human free will. With Pelagius refusing to back down, the time had come for the church to decide once and for all whether Pelagius' teachings are heretical.

Jerome's Latin translation of the Bible, the *Vulgate*, played a pivotal role in this theological battle. The *Vulgate*, a product of years of painstaking scholarship, had become the standard for the Western Church. Damasus, the bishop of Rome, had commissioned the "modern" translation for the Latin-speaking western church. Although Damasus died in 384, Jerome continued the work he had been commissioned to do, laboring from 382 until 405. This translation would be THE Bible for the Western Church for a thousand years. And when new versions developed, the *Vulgate* remained the most used text in the western church until the twentieth century.

Jerome's translation of Romans 5:12, particularly his rendering of the phrase "in whom all have sinned," becomes a central piece of evidence in the defense of Augustine's position on *original* sin. The *Vulgate's* support of Augustine's theology of inherited sin is critical in the church's condemnation of Pelagianism.

The Battle Over Romans 5:12 and the Doctrine of Original Sin—The Crucial Passage

The theological battle over the dogma of *original* sin was decisively shaped by one biblical passage—Romans 5:12. This verse would become the foundation for a monumental dispute within early Christianity, determining the understanding of humanity's sinful nature and, consequently, the need for salvation.

In Jerome's *Vulgate* translation, the verse reads: *Therefore, just as sin entered the world through one man, and death through sin, and in this way death came to all people, because all sinned.*

At first glance, the passage seems straightforward—sin entered the world through Adam, leading to death, which affected all of humanity. However, its implications were far from clear, sparking a fierce debate about the nature of sin: Was sin inherited, passed down

202

through human generations, or was it simply a matter of individual choice? This theological conflict profoundly impacted Christian doctrine, giving rise to two competing interpretations: one that emphasized human free will and moral responsibility, and the other that underscored the inherited corruption of human nature.

Theological Battle: Pelagius vs. Augustine

Pelagius' interpretation of Romans 5:12 was rooted in his rejection of the concept of inherited sin. He argued that this passage did not support the idea of *original* sin or inherited guilt passed down from Adam. Instead, Pelagius emphasized that while sin entered the world through Adam's actions, it did not introduce a metaphysical corruption that would affect all subsequent generations. Rather, Pelagius viewed sin as a matter of individual choice, a decision that each person makes freely.

For Pelagius, Romans 5:12 highlighted the possibility of moral choice in human action. He understood that death and sin spread to all men not because of a fallen human nature passed from Adam but because each individual chose to sin. Pelagius maintained that humanity was born morally neutral, with the ability to choose between good and evil, and he rejected the notion that divine grace was necessary for humans to make the right choice. He believed that every person had the free will to choose righteousness, just as every person had the free will to sin.

Thus, in Pelagius' view, Romans 5:12 did not proclaim a universal inheritance of sin, nor did it declare humanity's nature to be hopelessly corrupt. Instead, it was a declaration of universal human responsibility. The passage, for Pelagius, was a call to moral responsibility and accountability, reminding every individual that they were capable of choosing their path and bearing the consequences of those choices. It was not a statement of mankind's inability to live righteously but an affirmation that the power of choice—both for good and for evil—resided in every human being.

Jerome's Translation: The Seed for Augustine's Doctrine

Jerome's *Vulgate* translation subtly shifted the understanding of Romans 5:12. His use of "all people" reinforced the idea that sin and death were passed down to every human being—not merely as an example to follow, but as an inherited condition. This shift in understanding helped lay the groundwork for Augustine's dogma of *original* sin.

Jerome's Mistranslation and Its Impact

Jerome's translation (actually, mistranslation) of Romans 5:12 played the key role in the development of the dogma of *original* sin. Following is an exploration of that text. Approach these sections where the languages are written as visual illustrations.

Take a look at the highlighted text. It is crucial to your understanding. (This will be a bit technical, but there is no way to clarify this but to show you the Jerome's Latin translation and the corresponding Greek text. You might read neither Latin or Greek, but you can see differences in the texts. Use this as a visual illustration.)

propterea sicut per unum hominem in hunc mundum peccatum intravit et per peccatum mors et ita in omnes homines mors pertransiit **in quo omnes** *peccaverunt* (Rms. 5:12, *Vulgate*)

Here's an English translation of the Latin...we'll find it a bit easier: *Wherefore as by one man sin entered into this world and by sin death: and so death passed upon all men,* **in whom** *all have sinned* (English translation of Rms. 5:12 from the *Vulgate*).

Here's the key phrase to focus on: *"in whom all have sinned."* This addition did not appear in the original Greek text. It was a mistranslation of the Greek phrase $\dot{\epsilon}\varphi' \ddot{\omega}$ (eph'hō), which actually means *since, because, for that,* or *inasmuch,* and refers to humanity's shared responsibility in sin, not their collective participation in Adam's personal act.

204

In contrast, the Greek text of Romans 5:12 reads:

"Διὰ τοῦτο ὥσπερ δι' ἑνὸς ἀνθρώπου ἡ ἁμαρτία εἰς τὸν κόσμον εἰσῆλθεν καὶ διὰ τῆς ἁμαρτίας ὁ θάνατος, καὶ οὕτως εἰς πάντας ἀνθρώπους ὁ θάνατος διῆλθεν, ἐφ' ᾧ πάντες ἥμαρτον."

Notice the phrase *ἐφ' ᾧ* (*eph'hō*), which Jerome misinterpreted as *"in whom all have sinned."* This mistranslation was not simply a minor error but one with profound theological implications. The Greek phrase should have been translated in a way that emphasizes human responsibility for sin due to individual actions (*since all have sinned*), rather than suggesting universal participation in Adam's sin.

This misstep created confusion around the passage's meaning, and in the centuries that followed, it became a cornerstone of the doctrine of original sin. The phrase *"in whom all have sinned"* helped fuel the idea that sin was inherited from Adam, setting the stage for Augustine's interpretation.

Augustine Rejects Pelagius: Sin as an Inherited Condition
Augustine, influenced by Jerome's *Vulgate* and his own theological insights, interpreted Romans 5:12 as evidence of *original* sin—a condition passed down from Adam to all humanity. For Augustine, this passage was central to understanding the state of human nature after the Fall. He argued that Adam's sin corrupted human nature, making all subsequent humans guilty of sin from birth.

Augustine's interpretation of Romans 5:12 emphasized that death spread to all people not because they personally sinned, but because of their shared participation in Adam's sin. The phrase *"death spread to all people because all sinned"* represented the universality of sin. Humanity's corrupted nature could not be remedied by human effort alone; divine grace was necessary for redemption.

In contrast to Pelagius, who believed humans had the capacity to choose righteousness through free will, Augustine believed that humanity was spiritually dead and in need of divine grace to restore

205

them to life. For Augustine, grace was the only means of salvation, as humanity was incapable of choosing good on its own.

Augustine's Personal Struggles and Philosophical Influences
To fully appreciate why Augustine's views won out at Carthage and beyond, we need to consider the personal and philosophical factors at play in his development of the dogma of *original* sin.

1. Augustine's Past and Its Influence:
Augustine's personal history played a significant role in shaping his theological conclusions. His early life of indulgence, marked by struggles with lust and desire, made the concept of *original* sin particularly compelling for him. It wasn't merely a philosophical or theological idea for Augustine; it was a deeply personal issue, one that reflected his own internal conflicts. His famous line from *Confessions*, "Give me chastity, but not yet," captures the essence of his spiritual battle. This experience made him more attuned to the idea that human beings are inherently predisposed to sin.

Augustine's own transformation—his experience of God's grace as a means of overcoming sin—deeply influenced his belief that grace was necessary to break free from humanity's sinful nature. This personal struggle between desire and grace led to his firm conviction that only divine intervention could overcome the power of sin in the human heart.

2. Manichean Influence:
Augustine's early association with Manicheanism also influenced his worldview. Manichean dualism, with its strict separation of good and evil, likely shaped Augustine's understanding of sin as a corrupting force originating from a source separate from God's goodness. His eventual departure from Manicheanism heightened his skepticism about human autonomy and reinforced his belief that humans could not overcome sin without God's help. This shift might have led Augustine to adopt a more expansive view of grace, which

emphasized divine assistance over human effort.

3. Pelagius and the Battle for Status:
The dispute between Pelagius and Augustine wasn't just a theological matter; it was also about intellectual and ecclesiastical authority. Pelagius's optimistic view of human nature posed a direct challenge to the authority of Augustine and Jerome, who both supported the necessity of divine grace. Pelagius's teachings suggested that humans could achieve holiness through their own efforts, casting doubt on the validity of Augustine's ideas about *original* sin and grace.

This challenge to Augustine's theological system was also, in part, a challenge to his status as a leading authority in the church. The tension between the two figures, and their followers, was as much a power struggle as it was a theological debate.

4. The Role of Rhetoric and Power Dynamics:
The rhetorical skills of Augustine and Jerome were also critical in this theological conflict. In the ancient world, rhetoric wasn't just about persuasion—it was a tool for shaping public opinion and cultural discourse. Augustine and Jerome used their rhetorical training to present their views as not just theologically sound, but as authoritative. The power dynamics at play—status, influence, and persuasion—were just as important in this debate as the ideas themselves.

The Philosophical Roots of Augustine's Doctrine
Augustine's view of Romans 5:12 was not just an exegetical one—it was deeply influenced by his broader philosophical beliefs. His interpretation reflected his understanding of human freedom, the nature of sin, and the necessity of grace.

Philosophy vs. Exegesis: The Roots of Augustine's Doctrine of *Original* Sin
One of the central issues in Augustine's theology was the tension between philosophy and exegesis—how Scripture should be interpreted in light of human nature, sin, and salvation. Augustine's

background in Neoplatonism and Stoicism greatly influenced his understanding of sin. These philosophies emphasized human will, moral responsibility, and the relationship between the soul and the divine, all of which played a key role in his formulation of the doctrine of *original* sin.

While Augustine's philosophical assumptions shaped his reading of Romans 5:12, Pelagius took a more literal, expository approach to Scripture. Pelagius emphasized free will and human responsibility over the inherited nature of sin. Augustine, on the other hand, used philosophical frameworks to guide his interpretation of Scripture, ultimately developing a system that viewed human nature as inherently corrupted by sin.

Implications: Theological Development and Church Practice

The interpretive choices made by both Pelagius and Augustine had profound consequences for the early church. Augustine's dogma of *original* sin reshaped Christian practice, leading to the widespread adoption of infant baptism as a means of cleansing the inherited stain of sin. By contrast, Pelagius's emphasis on human effort and free will would be condemned as heretical.

The adoption of Augustine's view of *original* sin also led to a shift in the church's understanding of grace. Salvation was no longer seen as something humans could work toward through their own efforts, but rather as an unmerited gift from God. This view would shape church practices and doctrine for centuries, influencing ideas of baptism, salvation, and the necessity of grace.

The Legacy of Romans 5:12 and *Original* Sin

The interpretation of Romans 5:12 has had a lasting impact on Christian dogma. Jerome's mistranslation, combined with Augustine's philosophical and theological commitments, solidified the dogma of *original* sin as central to Christian understanding of human nature. This dogma emphasized that all humans inherit a sinful nature from Adam and need divine grace for redemption.

Augustine's emphasis on *original* sin has shaped Christian thought for centuries. It led to practices such as infant baptism and reinforced the belief in the necessity of divine grace. While Pelagius's interpretation was rejected, his views on free will and moral responsibility continue to be relevant in modern discussions of sin and salvation.

The Council's Action: The Canons and Their Impact

The bishops at the Council of Carthage, under the leadership of Bishop Aurelius of Carthage, made a definitive move. They issued eight canons—binding declarations that formalize the church's position on Pelagianism and *original* sin. The first eight canons of the Council specifically address Pelagius and his teachings. They condemn Pelagius and affirm the dogma of *original* sin, explicitly rejecting his claims that humans can achieve salvation without grace.

These canons are more than theological statements—they are the instruments of church authority. The *anathemas* (curses) declared against Pelagius and his followers serve as a clear message: the church is not merely offering a theological opinion, but exercising its power to define orthodoxy. The canons are a declaration that Pelagianism is not just wrong—it is heretical.

The First 8 Canons: The Condemnation of Pelagius

The first eight canons of the Council of Carthage are a direct response to Pelagius and his theology. Let's look at them closely, for they represent the turning point in church history:

Canon 1: Denounces the idea that Adam's sin was confined to himself and did not affect his descendants. This canon affirms the dogma that Adam's fall introduced sin to all of humanity.

Canon 2: Rejects the idea that infants, who have not sinned personally, do not require baptism to remit the sin of Adam. This canon firmly establishes the necessity of baptism for all, emphasizing the dogma of *original* sin.

209

Canon 3: Reaffirms the essential role of baptism in remitting *original* sin. The church declares that baptism is the means by which *original* sin, inherited from Adam, is forgiven.

Canons 4-7: These canons emphasize the indispensability of grace in human salvation. They reject any suggestion that human beings can attain salvation or perform good works without divine assistance. Grace is not optional; it is necessary.

Canon 8: Denies Pelagius' view that Christ's death and grace are not necessary for all humanity. It reinforces the idea that Christ's sacrifice is universal and essential for salvation.

Each of these canons drives home a single point: Pelagianism is incompatible with the teachings of the church. Grace is not optional— it is essential for salvation. *Original* sin is not a metaphor or a historical relic; it is a living reality that affects every human being.

Canon 1 formally condemned Pelagius' teaching about Adam, declaring it (and thereby, him) heretical. This was a decisive moment in the battle against Pelagianism, as the church unequivocally rejected Pelagius' denial of *original* sin and the necessity of grace.

Here's the full text of Canon 1:
That Adam was not created by God subject to death. (Canon 1 of 418 Synod)
That whosoever says that Adam, the first man, was created mortal, so that whether he had sinned or not, he would have died in body— that is, he would have gone forth of the body, not because his sin merited this, but by natural necessity, let him be *anathema*.

Canon 2 addressed the issue of baptism, which was at the heart of the Pelagian controversy. Pelagius had argued that baptism was unnecessary for the remission of sin in infants, a view that contradicted the church's long-standing tradition of infant baptism. This canon emphasized the necessity of baptism for all, explicitly stating that it was through baptism that *original* sin was cleansed. The significance of this canon extended beyond theology, as it reinforced the church's practice of infant baptism, which became and remains a cornerstone of the Catholic Church's dogma.

Here's the full text of Canon 2:

That infants are baptized for the remission of sins. *(Canon 2 of 418 Synod)*
Likewise it seemed good that whosoever denies that infants newly from their mother's wombs should be baptized, or says that baptism is for remission of sins, but that they derive from Adam no *original* sin, which needs to be removed by the laver of regeneration, from whence the conclusion follows, that in them the form of baptism for the remission of sins, is to be understood as false and not true, let him be *anathema*. For no otherwise can be understood what the Apostle says, *"By one man sin is come into the world, and death through sin, and so death passed upon all men in that all have sinned,"* than the Catholic Church everywhere diffused has always understood it. For on account of this rule of faith even infants, who could have committed as yet no sin themselves, therefore are truly baptized for the remission of sins, in order that what in them is the result of generation may be cleansed by regeneration.

Other canons sought to clarify the relationship between free will and grace, affirming that human beings, while endowed with free will, could not attain salvation apart from divine grace. These canons were not only theological declarations but practical directives that shaped the church's worship practices, including its rites of baptism and penance.

The canons not only defined the theological boundaries of the church but also laid down the ecclesiastical foundation for combating heretical teachings.

211

The Knock-Out Punch: Augustine's Victory

The church's decision at Carthage is not just a theological victory; it is a triumph of Augustine's vision for the human condition. The inclusion of Jerome's *Vulgate* translation of Romans 5:12 in Canon 2—the phrase "in whom all have sinned"—is the theological knock-out punch that secures Augustine's position. Augustine used Jerome's mistranslation as the final weapon to silence his opponent.

Pelagius' doctrine, with its emphasis on human free will and the possibility of salvation without grace, is now officially condemned. The idea that *original* sin is inherited from Adam is solidified and the necessity of divine grace for salvation is affirmed as a central doctrine of the church.

The Council condemned Pelagius and his teachings as heretical. However, it is crucial to note the controversial nature of this decision. Pelagius was condemned without being given an opportunity to defend himself at the Council, a practice that raises questions about fairness and transparency in the process. He was declared a heretic *in absentia*, a tactic that many saw as cowardly and unfair.

It is widely believed that Augustine, using his considerable influence, was primarily responsible for pushing through the condemnation of Pelagius without giving him a proper opportunity for defense. Both Jerome and Augustine, skilled rhetoricians, employed their intellectual and theological resources to frame Pelagius as a heretic for years, effectively silencing him through the power of dogma and influence, rather than through direct confrontation.

This approach, while rhetorically effective, highlights the manipulative nature of theological battles in the late 4th and early 5th centuries. Augustine and Jerome, both using their considerable intellectual influence, orchestrated a victory in the battle for theological supremacy, shaping the future of Christian thought in the West.

The Council's Legacy

The Council of Carthage represented the culmination of a theological battle that had raged for years. The church, under the leadership of Augustine, formally condemned Pelagianism, affirming the necessity of divine grace and the reality of *original* sin. The first eight canons issued by the Council are a powerful declaration of the church's official stance on these matters, shaping Christian theology and practices for generations.

This council is not just a moment in church history—it is a turning point. The decision at Carthage set the stage for the church's growing authority in defining orthodoxy, and it marked the triumph of Augustine's theology over Pelagius' humanistic vision of free will and salvation. For better or worse, the doctrine of *original* sin became a cornerstone of Christian thought, deeply influencing the development of Western Christian identity.

Pelagius' Defeat and the Rise of Augustine's Theology

Following the Council of Carthage, Pelagius is marginalized, and his ideas are officially declared heretical. While Pelagius himself is never fully excommunicated, his followers are increasingly ostracized, and his teachings lose credibility within the church. The Council's decision cements Augustine's theology as the dominant framework for understanding sin, grace, and salvation in the Western Church.

Pelagius' influence wanes, but his ideas never disappear completely. They will resurface in various forms throughout Christian history, but the Council of Carthage marks a decisive moment in the struggle for doctrinal purity. The dogma of *original* sin, now officially affirmed, will remain a defining feature of Western Christianity for centuries to come.

The culmination of the Council's work was the formal condemnation of Pelagianism. While this decision was theological in nature, its implications were far-reaching. Augustine's theological writings, combined with the authority of the Council, left little room for Pelagius and his followers to maneuver. The canons of Carthage firmly established the necessity of grace for salvation and rejected Pelagi-

213

us' teachings on free will and sin.

However, the decision was not without consequences. Pelagius' followers, especially those in Britain and Gaul, did not accept the Council's ruling without resistance. Some continued to propagate Pelagian ideas, leading to further theological disputes in the years that followed. Moreover, the condemnation of Pelagianism sparked tensions between the Western Church and other parts of the Christian world, particularly in the East, where some theologians questioned the Western interpretation of grace.

Despite the ongoing resistance, the actions of the Council of Carthage marked a decisive moment in the history of Christian doctrine. The rejection of Pelagianism laid the groundwork for the church's understanding of *original* sin, grace, and salvation.

In the aftermath of the Council, the Pelagian heresy was largely contained within the Western Church. However, its lingering influence can still be seen in later theological debates, particularly those surrounding the nature of free will and grace. The long-term effects of the Council of Carthage would continue to reverberate throughout the church's history, shaping its doctrines and practices well into the medieval period and beyond.

Both Were Right—Both Were Wrong

Pelagius was right to affirm the innocence of birth and the power of human free will. But he was wrong to dismiss the need for divine grace and to stress humanity's ability to attain righteousness on its own. Augustine was right to emphasize the necessity of grace for salvation. But he was wrong to portray sin as inherited guilt, bypassing personal choice and requiring infant baptism. His personal animosity, rhetorical dominance, and reliance on Jerome's mistranslation of Romans 5:12 clouded the fairness of the Carthage verdict— especially in the absence of Pelagius. Each saw in part, but their extremes pulled the church toward dogma rather than balanced truth.

214

24

The Detective
The Real Meaning of Romans 5:12

Blunt observed: "You're an odd man, Monsieur Poirot."

Hercule Poirot replied: "Oh, yes, I am. Very odd. That is to say, I am methodical, orderly, and logical, and *I do not like to distort facts to support a theory*." (from ITV Production of "One, Two Buckle My Shoe" based on Agatha Christie's 1940 novel by same name)

Jerome's mistranslation of Romans 5:12 is a fascinating example of how a single translation error can have lasting theological consequences. It's like becoming a detective, piecing together a complex case. And just as a detective identifies a crucial piece of evidence that shifts the direction of an investigation, uncovering this mistranslation becomes a turning point. The entire dogma of *original* sin hinges on one key two-word phrase from the Greek New Testament.

As I was explaining this to Sue, my barber, her eyes widened with disbelief. "Wait," she said, pausing with scissors in the air, as if trying to grasp the enormity of what I had just said. "You mean the whole thing—this doctrine that shaped so much of Christian thought—comes down to a two-word phrase?"

Sue's surprise was palpable. "So, all that history, all those debates and teachings, could have been built on a misunderstanding of a single line in a translation?" She shook her head, her fingers frozen mid-air. "It's like finding out that a detective's whole case is based on a misinterpreted clue. That's incredible!"

As Sue rightly pointed out—uncovering a single overlooked clue in a cold-case file can change everything. In the dogma of *original* sin, the entire case hinges on a key piece of evidence, a misinterpretation that shaped Christian theology for centuries. This distorted "proof" changes everything we thought we knew for sure.

215

The Antidote to the Council of Carthage

The issue with Augustine's approach—particularly his argument at the Council of Carthage and his interpretation of Romans 5:12—lies in the eisegetical lens through which he viewed the text, rather than allowing the text to speak for itself. This is a powerful critique that directly addresses the hermeneutical error underpinning much of Western Christian theology regarding *original* sin.

Eisegesis vs. Exegesis: Augustine was deeply entrenched in his own views, and his theological conflict with Pelagius was intensely personal—likely clouding his reading of Scripture. Eisegesis, opposed to exegesis, involves reading one's own ideas *into* the text to support a pre-existing theological stance, rather than allowing the text to reveal its meaning. Augustine's approach was shaped not only by his desire to defeat Pelagius but also by his broader philosophical commitments. These external influences led him to impose meanings on the text that were not inherent within the scriptural passage itself.

Exegesis, on the other hand, demands that the text be allowed to speak on its own terms, in context, and with its original meaning intact. When Romans 5:12 is read in isolation, as Augustine did, it is easy to distort its message to support inherited sin—especially when viewed through the lens of Augustinian anthropology, which emphasizes sin as a condition passed down through generations. However, when we examine the passage in its broader context, it becomes clear that the verse does not necessarily support this conclusion.

The Innocence of Humanity at Birth: All persons are born in a state of innocence, much like Adam and Eve before the Fall. This innocence is critical, as it aligns with the biblical understanding of humanity's original condition: Adam and Eve were created "*very good*" (Genesis 1:31) and in a state of moral innocence until they made the choice to sin. Their spiritual death—separation from God—was the consequence of their choice to rebel, not some inherited flaw.

216

While physical death did enter the world through Adam's sin, it is important to distinguish between spiritual death (separation from God) and physical death. The Bible consistently portrays sin as a result of personal choice and desire, rather than something inherited from a distant ancestor. This theme is echoed throughout Scripture, notably in Ephesians 2:1-10 and James 1:14-15, where sin is described as arising from human desire and decision, not from *original* guilt passed down by birth.

By contrast, the dogma of *original* sin (as formulated by Augustine) teaches that all humans are born spiritually dead and guilty because of Adam's sin. This view is not supported by the broader sweep of Scripture. In fact, when you examine the full evidence carefully, it becomes clear that Romans 5 itself does not argue for the hereditary corruption of human nature. Instead, it presents two universal realities: the universal condemnation in Adam and the universal justification in Christ. The central theological question is: ***How are we to understand this universality in Paul's argument?***

Augustine's Eisegesis: A crucial hermeneutical issue arises in Augustine's interpretation of Romans 5:12. His reading was deeply influenced by his ongoing theological battle with Pelagius. Rather than allowing the text to unfold its natural meaning, Augustine read Romans 5:12 through the lens of his pre-existing doctrine. This is an example of eisegesis—where a theological stance dictates how a passage is understood, rather than deriving meaning from the text.

In fairness to Augustine, Jerome's translation of Romans 5:12 might have further exacerbated this issue. Much like a piece of evidence that's misinterpreted and misused, Jerome's translation of Romans 5:12 might have turned what could have been a straightforward case into a theological mystery. Like a detective who must question the motivations of those involved, we must consider Jerome's own theological sympathies. His translation of the passage might have been shaped by that bias.

Jerome's translation provided Augustine with a theological weapon to support his stance. While Augustine's Greek skills might have been limited, his rhetorical expertise made him highly capable of leveraging Jerome's translation in his theological debates.

Context and the "Pretext" for Prooftexting: The adage "a text out of context is just a pretext for a prooftext" perfectly captures Augustine's approach. He used Romans 5:12 as a prooftext for *original* sin without considering the larger biblical narrative and the full argument of Romans 5. It's as though a new piece of evidence changes the entire trajectory of the case. When we bring the full context of Romans 5—especially verses 18–19—into the investigation, a completely different picture emerges, one that dismantles the inherited guilt hypothesis. These verses strongly suggest the universal scope of Christ's redemptive work, which parallels the universality of the effects of Adam's disobedience.

The parallelism between Adam and Christ in Romans 5:18–19 implies that just as condemnation came to all through one man's disobedience, justification also comes to all through one man's obedience. If one accepts a universal consequence in Adam without personal choice, one must also accept the universal availability of justification in Christ—apart from personal merit or choice. The logic of Paul's argument compels consistency: either both are inherited, or both are a matter of personal choice. Romans 5:15–19 highlights not only the damage done by Adam's sin but the far greater effect of Christ's super-abounding grace.

Theological and Hermeneutical Implications: Had Augustine approached Romans 5:12 with more rigorous exegesis, he might have recognized the theological symmetry in Paul's argument—universal consequence in Adam balanced by universal provision in Christ. Rather than forcing the text to support a dogma in need of validation, Augustine could have acknowledged that Romans 5 presents Christ's redemptive act as universally sufficient, even if not univer-

218

sally applied or appropriated through personal faith. Unfortunately, his eisegesis led to a system of thought that imposed theological conclusions—dogmatic presuppositions—onto the text, rather than allowing the text itself to shape the theology.

The Foundation Is Faulty

Romans 5:12 cannot support the dogma of *original* sin, especially when the surrounding context (Rms. 5:18-19) presents a contrasting universal scope of salvation in Christ.

This approach is akin to an investigator twisting evidence to fit a predetermined narrative. Augustine's *eisegesis* of Romans 5:12 forced the text to support a conclusion rather than allow it to lead to a natural understanding of sin. His preconceived theory of the case based on his personal experience with a dissipateed life or maybe his exposure to Manichaeism allowed the dogma of *original* sin to become a central tenet of Christian theology—despite its insufficient biblical foundation.

By returning to *exegesis*, we see that sin is a result of personal choice, as it was with Adam and Eve, and not inherited from them. God's grace, however, remains abundantly available to all, offering the opportunity for restoration and reconciliation, just as it was offered to Adam and Eve after their fall.

In his battle with Pelagius, Augustine was trying to prove that human beings were incapable of choosing righteousness apart from divine grace. He used Romans 5:12 as evidence that all humanity shares in Adam's guilt and thus, spiritually dead, unable to choose good without the intervention of God's grace. Augustine quoted Jerome's Latin translation, the *Vulgate*, for the only reference to Romans 5:12. Following is the exact text. You do not need to know either Latin or Greek (thank goodness). Now, just as every clue must be examined with precision, look closely for the differences—put on your detective hat and see how one small mistranslation shifts the entire case.

Latin (*Vulgate*):

*Propterea sicut per unum hominem in hunc mundum peccatum intravit et per peccatum mors, et ita in omnes homines mors pertransiit, **in quo** omnes peccaverunt.*

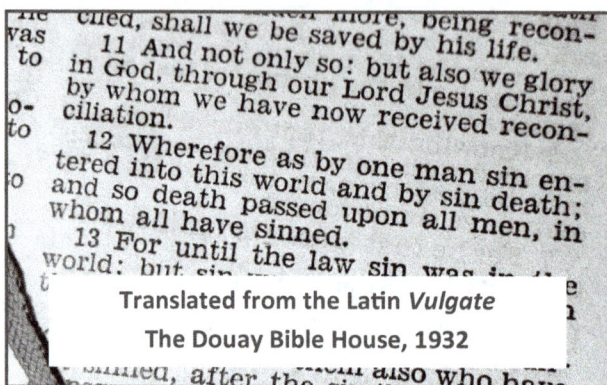

Translated from the Latin *Vulgate*
The Douay Bible House, 1932

"Wherefore, as by one man sin entered into this world, and death by sin; and so death passed upon all men, in whom all have sinned."

At first glance, the Latin translation seems reasonable. But the smallest detail can be the key to breaking a case wide open. When we dig deeper into the Greek text—the very source Jerome worked from—we start to see the pivotal problem hiding in plain sight.

Greek (Romans 5:12):

Διὰ τοῦτο ὥσπερ δι' ἑνὸς ἀνθρώπου ἡ ἁμαρτία εἰς τὸν κόσμον εἰσῆλθεν καὶ διὰ τῆς ἁμαρτίας ὁ θάνατος, καὶ οὕτως εἰς πάντας ἀνθρώπους ὁ θάνατος διῆλθεν, ἐφ' ᾧ πάντες ἥμαρτον.

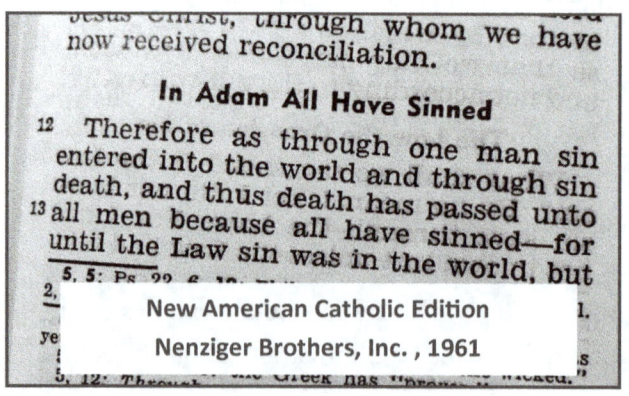

New American Catholic Edition
Nenziger Brothers, Inc., 1961

"Therefore, just as sin entered the world through one man, and death through sin, and in this way death came to all men, because all sinned."

220

The key difference lies in a single phrase. Jerome translated the Greek word $\dot{\epsilon}\varphi'\,\tilde{\omega}$ (eph'hō) as **in quo**, meaning *"in whom."* This insertion of *"in whom"* implies a corporate, inherited sin—that all humanity sinned in Adam and thus inherited his guilt.

However, the Greek word $\dot{\epsilon}\varphi'\,\tilde{\omega}$ does not mean *"in whom"*. It is better translated as *"because"*, *"since"*, or *"inasmuch as"*. The phrase $\dot{\epsilon}\varphi'\,\tilde{\omega}$ suggests that all sinned because of their own individual actions, not because they were inherently tainted by Adam's transgression.

This reading, however, overlooks the broader context of Romans 5, where Paul presents a much more nuanced understanding of sin and salvation.

The Larger Context of Romans 5: The Parallel Between Adam and Christ

When considering the larger context of Romans 5, we gain a fuller understanding of Paul's message. Many interpreters of Romans 5:12 -21, such as Dr. MacGorman, have pointed out that a careful reading of this passage—set within the context of Paul's broader argument in Romans—reveals that the real focus is not on inherited guilt but on the contrast between Adam and Christ.

Dr. MacGorman writes:

"Many interpreters of Romans 5:12-21 have tended to ignore both its general and immediate context in the letter. In Romans 1:18 to 3:20, Paul set forth his doctrine of sin. Here he showed how all men, Gentiles and Jews, alike, have become guilty, because all men have sinned (3:9, 19, 23). Human guilt derives from human sin; it is not inherited. No interpretation of Romans 5:12-21 that obscures or refutes the plain teaching of Romans 1:18 to 3:20 can be correct. Is it not interesting that Paul managed to demonstrate the guiltiness of all men in this earlier passage without any reference to Adam?

"Romans 5:12-21 is set in the immediate context of Romans

3:21 to 5:21. Here Paul set forth the gospel of the grace of God revealed through Jesus Christ his Son (3:21-31). Through faith in Christ, sinful men may be justified before God or made right with him (3:24-25). Abraham himself was justified by faith and has become the father of all who believe (4:1-25). In Romans 5:1-11, Paul rejoiced in the benefits that have come to men through God's justifying grace.

"And in Romans 5:12-21, he continued to magnify God's grace by showing the universal scope of Christ's accomplishment on the cross. As Adam headed an old humanity characterized by sin and death, even so Christ heads a new humanity characterized by righteousness and life. Indeed, the theme of this passage is superabounding grace. Paul insisted that what mankind lost in Adam was more than regained in Christ." (*Romans: Everyman's Gospel*, pp.79-80)

This emphasis on grace—the idea that Christ's redemption surpasses what was lost in Adam—serves as the framework for understanding the true purpose of Romans 5:12-21.

The **Principle of Context** instructs us to seek the broader setting of any passage to properly understand its meaning. Regarding Adam, we find that neither the Old nor New Testament writers give much more than a passing acknowledgment of his role as the head of humanity. Often, the word *'adam* is used simply to mean *humanity* or *mankind*. It is only in Paul's writings that we find an extensive use of Adam, and he is presented as an analogy—either in comparison or contrast to Christ.

When we place the single verse—*and a mistranslated one at that*—used as the foundation for inherited sin into its proper context, it takes on a much different hue than the one cast over it for generations.

Adam and Christ: A Contrast, Not a Continuity
To fully grasp Paul's argument in Romans 5:12-21, it is crucial to recognize that his focus is on comparing Adam and Christ. Paul re-

222

peatedly contrasts the results of Adam's actions with those of Christ. Adam's transgression led to death and condemnation, while Christ's obedience leads to life and justification. This comparison is not about a shared nature or inherited guilt, but rather about the choices each made and their respective consequences.

As Dr. Walter T. Conner, professor of theology at Southwestern Baptist Theological Seminary, put it: "I am no more individually responsible, and hence guilty, for what Adam did than I am for what Julius Caesar did. But I am affected in my life by what both did."

It is also noteworthy that some Roman Catholic scholars today are challenging their church's traditional views regarding *original* sin. Herbert Haag, for example, writes: "The idea that Adam's descendants are automatically sinners because of the sin of their ancestor, and that they are already sinners when they enter the world, is foreign to Holy Scripture."

MacGorman also asserts: "There is no evidence for either of these theories of original sin in this passage."

This statement directly challenges the theological tradition that has sought to read inherited guilt into Romans 5. Paul's focus is not on explaining how Adam's sin is transmitted to his descendants but on contrasting the consequences of Adam's sin with the consequences of Christ's redemptive work. The central theme is not the inherited nature of sin but the contrast between death and life, condemnation and justification.

The Law's Role: Revealing, Not Condemning
Another key aspect of the passage is Paul's discussion of the law. In Romans 5:13-14, he writes: *For sin indeed was in the world before the law was given, but sin is not counted where there is no law. Yet death reigned from Adam to Moses, even over those whose sinning was not like the transgression of Adam.*

Paul's point here is that sin existed before the law, but it was not accounted as sin in the same way because there was no law to

223

transgress. The law, when it arrived, revealed sin but did not create guilt in the way traditional doctrines of inherited guilt suggest.

As Hobbs points out, "The burden of responsibility upon each individual person" is crucial to understanding the role of the law. Sin becomes transgression when individuals knowingly violate God's commands, not because they inherit guilt from Adam. The law simply reveals that sin exists in the world, highlighting personal responsibility before God. Hobbs further clarifies: "He is personally guilty and condemned when spiritually he follows his tendency toward sin even as did Adam."

Sin is a personal choice, not an inherited condition.

The Absence of Inherited Guilt in Scripture

MacGorman's assertion that "The idea that Adam's descendants are automatically sinners because of the sin of their ancestor, and that they are already sinners when they enter the world, is foreign to Holy Scripture" emphasizes a critical point. This idea of inherited guilt, central to the dogma of *original* sin, is not biblically grounded in Romans 5 or anywhere else in Scripture.

While it is clear that Adam's sin brought death into the world, Paul's language does not suggest that humanity is born guilty because of that sin. Rather, Paul's focus is on the fact that all have sinned—each person makes a choice to sin, and that's why death and condemnation spread to all.

Dr. Dale Moody, in his commentary on Romans, notes that "Augustine's doctrine of original sin, or inherited guilt, resulted from his small knowledge of Greek." Hobbs also underscores that Augustine's misunderstanding of the Greek language led to a doctrinal error that has had profound theological consequences. The dogma of inherited guilt, popularized by Augustine, rests on a linguistic mistake rather than sound biblical exegesis. This invites a reassessment of the foundations upon which traditional interpretations of Romans 5 have been built.

Superabounding Grace: The Focus of Romans 5

One of the most powerful points made by MacGorman is his assertion that "Paul insisted that what mankind lost in Adam was more than regained in Christ." This shifts the entire discussion of Romans 5:12-21 from focusing on the negative consequences of Adam's sin to the far greater triumph of Christ's grace. What Adam lost, Christ restored—and more. Paul's emphasis is on the superabounding grace of Christ, which not only overcomes the death and condemnation that came through Adam but exceeds it abundantly.

MacGorman captures this central theme well when he notes: "Paul's overall thrust is obvious enough... the theme of this passage is superabounding grace."

Grace is the dominant theme in this passage, and it is grace that leads to life—not inherited guilt.

Personal Responsibility and Faith

Finally, it is essential to recognize that salvation is not inherited any more than sin is. Hobbs emphasizes: "God deals with people as individuals, not *en masse*."

Each person is responsible for their own sin, and each must choose to accept Christ's salvation through faith. As MacGorman notes: "We do not inherit salvation through Christ's obedience apart from our personal involvement in faith."

Salvation is not automatic but requires a personal decision to accept God's grace and respond in faith. This personal responsibility stands in stark contrast to the idea that we inherit sin from Adam.

The Hobbs' Conclusion

A careful reading of Romans 5 reveals that the passage does not support the dogma of inherited guilt in the way traditional theology has often understood it. Rather, Paul's focus is on the contrast between Adam and Christ, death and life, condemnation and justification. The law's role is to reveal sin, not to impose guilt. Grace is the ultimate answer to sin, and Christ's work on the cross is far greater than Adam's transgression. Each individual is responsible for their own actions, and salvation comes through personal faith in Christ—not through inherited righteousness or guilt.

As Hobbs rightly affirms, "The burden of responsibility is upon each individual person." We are not guilty because of Adam's sin, but we are all responsible for our own choices and must each respond to God's grace individually.

The grace of Christ is the true answer to the problem of sin, and it is through Christ that humanity finds redemption—not through inherited guilt.

The Whole Counsel of God

In Acts 20:27, Paul's farewell address to the elders of the church in Ephesus contains a crucial and sobering charge: "*I have not shunned* [hupesteilamēn] *to declare unto you all the counsel of God.*" This word *hupesteilamēn* (hoo-peh-stay-LAH-men) though somewhat technical in its meaning, carries profound implications when applied to our understanding of the faithful delivery of God's message. (Please pardon the technical aspects of this—but sometimes if a detective is to solve a case, technical exploration is essential.)

Paul's message to the elders was clear: *he had not withheld, concealed, or minimized any part of the gospel truth*. He had proclaimed the full counsel of God without fear of how it might be received. He had boldly declared what God had revealed in its entirety—without trimming, adjusting, or selectively quoting Scripture to support a specific agenda.

Much like a detective committed to solving a case, Paul did not leave any clue unexamined or any lead unexplored. He did not fear the consequences of uncovering uncomfortable truths but instead pursued the case of God's full revelation with relentless integrity, ensuring no vital piece of the puzzle was hidden or manipulated.

Contrast this with the tactic employed by Augustine centuries later, when he, seeking to prove the dogma of inherited sin, relied on a mistranslation from Jerome's *Vulgate*. Through his selective reading of a small portion of a text, Augustine introduced a dogma that became deeply embedded in Christian theology. This move was not unlike *hupesteilamēn*—the deliberate withholding, disguising, or concealment of a fuller truth in favor of a more convenient or persuasive interpretation. It was as if Augustine, instead of faithfully considering all the available evidence, selectively picked a single piece of evidence to support his theory, ignoring or downplaying other relevant details that could have led to a different conclusion. He wasn't after truth; he was after victory over Pelagius.

The Problem with Withholding Truth

Paul's words carry the weight of both a warning and an invitation: Do not withhold, disguise, or obscure any part of God's revelation. However, Augustine, in his confrontation with Pelagius, did exactly that. His argument was built upon a passage of Scripture that, when read in context, did not fully support his claims. But by focusing on a single, isolated piece of the text, Augustine could make a more compelling case for the dogma of inherited sin. He selectively emphasized a part of Scripture, disregarding other passages that might counteract or clarify the message. The result was the crafting of a theology that was, at best, incomplete and, at worst, misleading.

In this case, Augustine's actions resemble the approach of an investigator who, instead of considering all the evidence from every angle, focuses solely on one piece of the puzzle that aligns with his initial hypothesis, while dismissing contradictory or complex evidence. It's as if he created a case file based on a single misleading clue, ignoring other important pieces that would have revealed a fuller truth.

Augustine's choice to use a fragment of a text rather than the whole counsel of God highlights an important danger—one that still affects theology today. Many who subscribe to the dogma of inherit-

227

ed sin do so without recognizing that it rests on a passage of Scripture that has been, in essence, *hupesteilamēn*—hidden from view.

The argument is often convincing and is supported by centuries of tradition, but it is based on a selective interpretation of the Bible, not a comprehensive one.

Just as a detective would be foolish to base a case on one piece of evidence without considering the entire investigation, so too are we, as believers, called to look at the whole counsel of God, not just a few isolated verses. To do otherwise would be to risk building a theology that is only partially true, much like a detective building a case on a false assumption.

This is where the challenge lies: To accept Augustine's view is to unknowingly accept a theological construct that has been built on a skewed interpretation of Scripture. It's not that people have maliciously sought to hide the truth, but the historical and institutional weight of tradition can be blinding. Often, devout believers do not realize that their beliefs rest on the selective reading of a few verses rather than on the full counsel of God's word. It's as if they're following a trail of misleading evidence, convinced that the case is solved, without realizing they've missed crucial pieces of the puzzle.

If we are to take Paul's charge seriously, we must ask ourselves: Have we, in our own theology, *hupesteilamēn*—withheld or disguised the full counsel of God? In the case of inherited sin, it is clear that many, knowingly or unknowingly, have accepted a theology that draws on only a fraction of God's word. To uncover the whole counsel of God is to let the entirety of Scripture speak—unhindered by tradition, uncolored by human agenda, and unfiltered through the lens of institutional control. Only then can we come to a truly biblical understanding of sin, salvation, and grace. Like a detective who digs deeper, looking beyond the surface, we must be committed to uncovering all the clues and not settling for an incomplete picture of the truth.

228

The Tension Between Tradition and Truth

For many, the appeal of tradition is strong. Augustine's argument was compelling in its time, and his position was embraced as the foundation of much of Christian thought. But the burden of proof lies with those who claim to know the truth. Are we willing to investigate Scripture with fresh eyes? Are we willing to challenge the traditions that have been handed down to us, asking whether they are truly rooted in the full counsel of God, or if they are merely the result of selective reading and theological convenience?

In the same way a detective might challenge old assumptions in an investigation, we too must be willing to test the long-held traditions against the evidence found in the full counsel of God's word. Augustine's stance, while influential, was not an objective proclamation of God's will. Instead, it was an argument strategically constructed to support a particular theological system. When we look back at this moment in history, we see that the foundation of the dogma of *original* sin is built on a narrow interpretation, a *hupesteilamēn* approach, in which a portion of Scripture was elevated above the whole counsel of God.

To proclaim the gospel, we must commit to declaring all of God's counsel—the full scope of His plan for salvation, as revealed through Scripture. This means embracing theology grounded in the whole of Scripture, not one that selectively picks and chooses which parts of God's word to emphasize. It means confronting the temptation to suppress the parts of Scripture that challenge our comfort or understanding, and instead, letting every part of God's word shape our theology. Just as a thorough investigation requires examining all the facts, our theology must engage the entirety of Scripture.

Reclaiming the Whole Counsel

The choice to reject *hupesteilamēn*—the concealing of truth—is an invitation to rediscover the fullness of the gospel. As we move forward in our journey of faith, we must be willing to embrace the uncomfortable, the difficult, and the challenging aspects of Scripture, even if they conflict with our preconceived notions or long-held beliefs. The goal is not simply to build a theological system that makes us feel comfortable or secure, but to proclaim and live by the truth as God has revealed it in His word, in all its fullness. It's like being a detective who, instead of avoiding the hard truths, follows the investigation wherever it leads, no matter how challenging it might be.

In this light, Augustine's interpretation of Scripture is a stark reminder that tradition, while valuable, must never supersede Scripture. The call for a reformation of the heart, mind, and soul is, at its core, a call to recover the whole counsel of God, not a truncated or distorted version of it. To follow Paul's example by refusing to *hupesteilamēn* is to embrace the full spectrum of truth—the hard, the beautiful, and the liberating truth that sets us free.

Just as a detective uncovers the truth no matter how inconvenient, we too must seek the fullness of God's revelation, letting the entirety of Scripture guide us to the complete and unblemished truth.

Notes and Observations

Investigative Journal Entry: Date: _____ / _____ / _____

Choice or Inheritance? According to Pelagius, sin is a matter of individual choice and not inherited from Adam. How does Pelagius' view of sin challenge Augustine's dogma of *original* sin?

Tiny error—Seismic Shift: Jerome's translation of Romans 5:12 in the *Vulgate* is crucial in shaping the dogma of *original* sin. How does Jerome's mistranslation of the Greek phrase $\dot{\epsilon}\varphi'\ \tilde{\dot{\omega}}$ ("because all sinned") to *in quo* ("in whom all have sinned") influence Augustine's interpretation of this passage? Why did this mistranslation have such a significant impact on the spread of Augustine's view on inherited or *original* sin in the Western Church?

25

Romans 1-5 and the Four "Therefores"

Following is a sketch of Paul's message to the Roman Christians in the first five chapters. For this exegetical exploration, you will need your Bible so you can refer to it throughout this brief exercise. While the outline provides a guide for your study, the Spirit of illumination and the Scripture He inspired will be your true guides.

Romans 1-5: Foundation of the Gospel

Romans 1:1-17 introduces Paul's thesis: the gospel is the power of God for salvation to all who believe, both Jew and Gentile. Paul sets the stage by emphasizing that salvation is through faith. From the opening 6 verses, Paul gets right to the essence of the letter: the gospel of God. He culminates this section with his great declaration in verses 16 and 17.

Romans 1:18-3:18 highlights the universal guilt of humanity. Whether Gentile or Jew, all have turned away from God. The wrath of God is revealed against all unrighteousness, both through the rebellion against the natural order and the Law, which all have failed to follow.

Romans 3:19-31 underscores the fact that righteousness is not obtainable through human works but only through faith in Jesus Christ, who was sacrificed for our sins. Here, the doctrine of justification by faith is solidified.

Romans 4:1-25: Abraham as the Example of Justification by Faith—Paul turns to **Abraham** to illustrate justification by faith. Abraham, who trusted in God's promise, was credited with right-

231

eousness (Gen. 15:6), proving that justification has always been based on faith, not works.

Romans 4:22 introduces the *first* "Therefore"—meaning "on the basis of." What Paul states now is based on what he has said previously. It is a summary of what has been said and a springboard for what is to come. Paul states that Abraham's faith was counted as righteousness, showing that the principle of justification applies not only to Abraham but also to all believers.

Romans 5:1-11: Justification and Peace with God

Romans 5:1 introduces the *second* "Therefore,"—based on the argument for justification by faith: *Therefore, since we have been justified by faith, we have peace with God.*

Paul goes on to explain the benefits of justification, including peace with God, hope in the glory of God, and perseverance through suffering, which produces character and hope.

The passage climaxes with God's love being poured out through the Holy Spirit (Romans 5:5), affirming that Christ died for the ungodly while we were still sinners (Romans 5:6-11). While we were at enmity against God, Christ died for us and that through faith in Him we will be "much more" saved from the wrath of God (v. 9; see also Romans 1:18), not just through His death but through His life—for without the sinless life, the death would have been just another death. But because of His sinless life, His death, and His resurrection—we have been justified through faith.

Romans 5:12-21: Adam, Christ, and the Role of Death

Romans 5:12: With the *third* "Therefore," Paul begins the discussion of sin and death entering the world through one man—Adam. It introduces the universal problem of death resulting from sin (*because all have sinned*), but Paul leaves his thought unfinished;

the mention of death causes him to "chase a rabbit" by explaining how death reigned over humanity because of their sin.

Romans 5:13-14 clarifies that sin was in the world from Adam to Moses, but it was not counted as transgression without the law. Death reigned because of sin, but not all sin is the result of direct disobedience to a command, as Adam's was.

Romans 5:15-17 begins a series of contrasts between Adam and Christ, emphasizing that Christ's act of righteousness overflows to many, in stark contrast to Adam's trespass.

Romans 5:18-19 introduces the *fourth* "Therefore," completing Paul's argument: *Therefore, as one trespass led to condemnation for all men, so one act of righteousness leads to justification and life for all men.* What Paul began to state in verse 12, he returns to and completes here in verses 18 and 19. This passage refutes the idea of inherited guilt, showing that just as one man's disobedience led to death, one man's obedience leads to life.

The verses in 18 and 19 are direct parallels. Note the use of "as" and "so" in both verses. Most believers recoil at the thought of universalism—yet here it is: if you believe in universal guilt and sin through Adam, you must also allow for universal redemption through Christ—and not only just the same but "much more" shall grace reign (Romans 5:10, 17, 20). Without the element of choice, universalism is the only logical conclusion. But if we must choose Christ, we also must allow choice for sin and disobedience.

Romans 6-8: New Life in Christ
Although these chapters go beyond our immediate focus, they reinforce the principle of new life in Christ. Through Jesus' sacrifice, believers are freed from the dominion of sin and can live in the righteousness of God and nothing shall separate us from the love of God that is in Christ Jesus (Romans 8:31-39).

Theological Implications:
  Correcting the Error of Inherited Guilt

1. Romans 5:12-21: Adam's Sin and Christ's Obedience

- The key to understanding Romans 5:12-21 is recognizing that Paul's argument is not about inherited guilt but about the contrast between the consequences of Adam's sin and the redemptive work of Christ. The death that came through Adam's sin is contrasted with the life that comes through Christ's obedience.

- Jerome's mistranslation led to a misunderstanding of this passage, suggesting that all humans inherit Adam's guilt. However, Paul's argument emphasizes that while all men are affected by Adam's sin (death reigning over all), all can be justified through Christ's righteous act.

- The four "therefores" in Romans 4:22, 5:1, 5:12, and 5:18 (and the "*for*" in verse 19—if you are counting!) provide a logical flow: justification by faith leads to peace with God, which is made possible by the work of Christ, who overcomes the consequences of Adam's disobedience.

2. Role of Tradition and Need for Correcting the Narrative

- Augustine, while not at fault for the misuse of the text, followed Jerome's mistranslation. As a result, the dogma of *original* sin became enshrined in Christian tradition, despite its questionable theological foundation.

- The challenge now is not only to correct this error but to challenge the long-held tradition that has shaped views on *original* sin and the necessity of infant baptism. The antidote lies in returning to the source text, understanding Paul's true message, and embracing a theology of grace that centers on Christ's redemptive work, not Adam's disobedience.

Reflections

Here is an opportunity for you to dive deeper into this foundational section of Paul's letter to the Roman Christians. You can expand your understanding by using the reflection questions and observations to guide you in your faith journey. These questions draw from the rich theological truths in the Bible Exploration Exercise and encourage practical application, while also helping you wrestle with difficult concepts and cultivate personal reflection.

1. The Power of the Gospel: Romans 1:16-17

Question: Paul says that the gospel is the power of God for salvation to everyone who believes. What does it mean for you personally that the gospel is *the* power of God? How do you experience that power in your life today?

Observation: The message of salvation through the gospel is not just a theoretical concept—it's a transformative power that can change lives. Reflect on moments when you have experienced God's power through faith in Christ. How can this understanding empower you to share the gospel more boldly with others?

2. The Wrath of God: Romans 1:18-3:18

Question: How does the idea of God's wrath in response to unrighteousness challenge or comfort you? In what ways do you see the wrath of God manifesting in today's world, both in personal and societal contexts?

Observation: Paul paints a stark picture of the universal need for salvation due to the rebellion of all humanity. It's easy to overlook the seriousness of sin, but reflecting on God's wrath helps us understand the weight of the gospel message. How does understanding the gravity of our sin help us appreciate God's grace more deeply?

3. Justification by Faith: Romans 3:19-31

Question: Paul says that righteousness comes not through human works but through faith in Christ. How does this challenge our cultural understanding of earning worth or striving for perfection? What are some ways you have tried to "earn" God's approval, and how does this passage shift that mindset?

Observation: The doctrine of justification by faith is radical—it goes against human nature to believe that we are made right with God simply by trusting in Jesus' work, not our own. This freedom is both liberating and humbling. Reflect on how your faith in Christ changes your approach to life's challenges and your relationship with God.

4. Abraham as the Example of Faith: Romans 4:1-25

Question: Paul uses Abraham as the model of faith. How does Abraham's story challenge you in your own walk with God? What does it mean for you to have "faith in God's promises" in your current season of life?

Observation: Abraham's life shows us that faith is not passive—it's active trust in God's promises, even when circumstances seem to contradict them. Reflect on an area of your life where you might be struggling to trust God's plan. How can you follow Abraham's example of faith, knowing that God credits faith as righteousness?

5. Peace with God: Romans 5:1-11

Question: Paul says that through justification by faith, we have peace with God. How does this peace differ from the temporary or worldly peace we often seek? In what areas of your life do you need to embrace the peace that comes from being reconciled to God?

Observation: Peace with God is foundational to living out the

236

Christian faith. It isn't about the absence of problems, but the assurance of God's presence and favor. Reflect on moments when you've experienced peace from God, even in difficult circumstances. How can that peace serve as a witness to others who need reconciliation with God?

6. The Role of Suffering: Romans 5:3-5

Question: In Romans 5, Paul connects suffering to perseverance, character, and hope. How does this perspective on suffering challenge the way you view trials in your own life? What role does hope in God's love play in enduring hardship?

Observation: This passage reminds us that suffering isn't meaningless—it has purpose. God uses it to develop Christlike character in us. Reflect on past sufferings you've endured, and how God has used them to shape your character or deepen your hope. How can you shift your mindset to view challenges as opportunities for growth?

7. Adam and Christ: Romans 5:12-21

Question: Paul contrasts Adam's disobedience with Christ's obedience. How does this contrast shape your understanding of the gospel? What does it mean for you personally that Christ's one act of righteousness brings life to all who believe?

Observation: The comparison between Adam and Christ is profound. Adam's sin brought death, but Christ's sacrifice brought life. Reflect on the magnitude of Christ's obedience. How does recognizing the depth of His sacrifice transform the way you approach sin and salvation in your own life?

8. The Fourth "Therefore" – Romans 5:18-19

Question: Paul writes that just as one trespass led to condemnation for all, so one act of righteousness leads to justification and life.

How does this "much more" in Christ challenge the way you view your own redemption? In what areas do you need to embrace the "much more" of God's grace?

Observation: The idea of "much more" in Christ is a powerful reminder of the abundance of God's grace. It's not just about being saved from sin; it's about the overflowing, superabundant life that comes through Christ's righteousness. Reflect on how your understanding of Christ's gift of salvation impacts the way you live today. How does His "much more" offer hope and strength in your daily walk?

9. Theological Implication: Correcting the Error of Inherited Guilt

Question: How does the concept of universal redemption through Christ challenge traditional dogmas about inherited guilt? What would it mean for you to shift from a theology of inherited guilt to one rooted in Christ's redemptive work?

Observation: The tradition of inherited guilt has shaped much of Christian theology, but Paul's letter to the Romans presents a different understanding: that Christ's redemptive work offers salvation to all who followed Adam's example of rebellion. Reflect on how this changes your view of salvation. How does it deepen your appreciation for the sufficiency of Christ's work on the cross?

10. The Role of Tradition and Correcting the Narrative

Question: As you reflect on the history of Christian doctrine, what role does tradition play in your faith today? How can we challenge theological misunderstandings, like the dogma of *original* sin, while still honoring the wisdom of church history?

Observation: Tradition is a gift that shapes our faith, but it is not infallible. Reflect on areas of church tradition that have shaped your beliefs and practices. Are there aspects of doctrine you've inherited that need to be revisited in light of Scripture? How can you approach tradition with a heart that is open to correction by the Word of God?

11. Living Out the Theology of Justification

Question: How does the doctrine of justification by faith impact your daily life? How do you live out the truth that you have been justified by faith in Christ, not by works?

Observation: Understanding justification by faith frees us from the pressure to perform for God's approval. It also empowers us to live in confidence and humility, knowing that our standing before God is secure in Christ. Reflect on how this understanding of grace affects your relationships, choices, and daily actions. How can you cultivate a deeper awareness of your justification as you walk through life?

12. Final Reflection: Embracing Grace

Question: As you reflect on Paul's message in Romans 1-5, how does the gospel—the power of God for salvation—transform the way you view yourself, God, and others? How can you better embrace grace in your walk with Christ?

Observation: The message of the gospel is not just about what God has done for us in the past; it's about how we live out the implications of grace in every aspect of our lives. Reflect on how embracing grace challenges your self-perception, your relationship with God, and your relationships with others. How can you live more fully in the reality of God's grace today?

Closing Thoughts

By reflecting on these questions, you can deepen your understanding of Paul's message to the Romans and apply these theological truths to your everyday life. As you wrestle with the meaning of justification by faith, the contrast between Adam and Christ, the implications of peace with God, and the transformative power of grace, you increase your ability to give a reason for the hope in you.

Summary

In Chapters 21-25, we traced the historical, doctrinal, and biblical threads that form the basis for the dogma of inherited or *original* sin. The turbulent early centuries laid the foundation for the theological conflict between Pelagius, Jerome, and Augustine, culminating in the Council of Carthage's formal endorsement of Augustine's views on inherited sin. This non-biblical dogma has shaped Christian thought ever since it was adopted in AD 418.

However, by turning to the Bible, specifically Romans 5:12-21, we discovered a profound contrast between the effects of Adam's sin and Christ's redemptive act. Paul's argument against inherited guilt is clear: while death entered the world through Adam's disobedience, life and justification come through Christ's obedience. The four "therefores" in Romans provide a logical framework, proclaiming justification by faith—not inherited sin.

Biblical exegesis challenges the traditional view of *original* sin, reminding us that we do not have inherited guilt because of Adam's sin. Scripture teaches that we become sinners by our own choice. The practical implications are significant: rethinking inherited sin reshapes our understanding of salvation, grace, and the human condition. Instead of inherited depravity, the biblical text reveals that personal choice, responsibility, faith, and the transformative power of Christ's redemptive work constitute the bad news and the good news from God.

26

The Reveal

The stage is set. The players are in position. Yet, what was meant to be a theological debate, a search for truth, became a carefully orchestrated campaign—one that would alter the course of Christian doctrine and reshape the way humanity would understand sin, salvation, and divine grace. And at the center of it all, like a solitary figure on the wrong side of history, stood Pelagius.

The story of Pelagius has long been told as one of heresy and defeat, a narrative crafted and maintained by those who, for reasons both personal and theological, ensured that his voice would never be fully heard. But what if this story—this tale of a lone theologian who was crushed under the weight of ecclesiastical authority—was not the whole truth? What if the true story was far more intricate, far more deliberate, and far more tragic than history has allowed?

In the years leading up to the Council of Carthage in 418, Pelagius found himself at the mercy of not one, but two powerful adversaries. Augustine of Hippo, the undisputed theological heavyweight, and Jerome of Stridon, a man whose own internal conflicts shaped much of his career, would become the architects of his downfall. Together, they engaged in a campaign that was not simply about defending their views but about isolating, discrediting, and ultimately condemning a man whose ideas posed a challenge to their own.

The timeline of events is crucial, for it reveals not just the logic of this theological battle but the deliberate strategy behind it. When we look at the pattern of the attacks against Pelagius, we begin to see the calculated nature of the campaign.

241

The Timeline of Defeat

It begins with Jerome's departure from Rome in 385—a departure that was less of a voluntary retreat and more of a retreat born from scandal and the erosion of his influence. Jerome, having failed in his attempt to establish himself as the definitive voice on Christian teaching, found solace in the desert. But this exile did not erase his bruised ego. It festered.

Meanwhile, in the West, Augustine was rising. His influence began to spread, his theological convictions gaining traction, especially on the dogma of *original* sin. Augustine's personal experiences with the question of human will and divine grace made him the perfect candidate to champion a dogma that would give him, and the church, a clear authority over the moral fate of mankind. But there was a problem. Pelagius, with his belief in human free will and moral responsibility, posed a direct challenge to Augustine's assertions of divine predestination.

The clash was inevitable.

As early as the year 400, Pelagius was already feeling the first sting of opposition. But it was not until around 410, when Jerome began to publicly condemn Pelagius, that the attacks took on a systematic and coordinated form. Jerome, perhaps feeling the sting of his own perceived failure, found in Pelagius the perfect scapegoat. His sharp critiques—laden with accusations of heresy—found a receptive audience among those who were already uneasy with the moral optimism Pelagius espoused. Pelagius' teachings were painted as dangerous, a threat to the moral fabric of Christianity, despite the fact that, in many ways, they were in harmony with the gospel message of personal responsibility.

But Jerome's attacks alone were not enough. He needed a partner, a theologian with the ecclesiastical weight to tip the balance. Augustine, who had spent years refining his dogma of *original* sin, was the perfect man for the job. Augustine's views on grace and predestination had already won him wide acclaim, and his theological

242

authority was nearly unrivaled. What Jerome lacked in personal influence, Augustine made up for in theological might. Together, they formed a strategic—and ruthless—alliance of rhetoric and power, each man playing a calculated role in the demolition of Pelagius.

The Tag-Team
Pelagius became the lone figure in the ring, left to fend off two opponents who would swap in and out with ruthless efficiency. The dynamics of this rhetorical tag-team match were clear. Jerome, with his sharp and often polemical writings, would strike first, accusing Pelagius of heresy. Augustine, more measured but no less forceful, would follow up with sweeping theological arguments that painted Pelagius' views as not just erroneous, but damnable. Each man took his turn, wearing Pelagius down with a combination of personal insult and theological critique. And Pelagius had no one to tag; no one to relieve him from the unrelenting assault.

Jerome's critiques, which began as sharp barbs against Pelagius' personal character, gradually evolved into an all-out assault on Pelagius' doctrine. In one letter after another, Jerome mocked Pelagius, distorting his views and portraying him as a dangerous innovator who sought to undo the very foundations of Christian belief. Jerome's words, though filled with venom, were not simply personal attacks—they were strategic. He was painting Pelagius as a heretic in the eyes of the church, preparing the ground for a formal condemnation.

Augustine, meanwhile, moved more carefully, using his theological writings to solidify the position that *original* sin was a foundational dogma of the Christian faith. The battle over Pelagius was not just a theological debate; it was a struggle for control over the direction of Christian doctrine. Augustine's influence, combined with his rigorous intellectual arguments, served to entrench the idea that salvation could not be achieved by human effort alone, as Pelagius had suggested, but required divine grace.

243

In their respective arenas, both Jerome and Augustine were skillful rhetoricians. They understood the power of words and ideas, and they knew that their combined efforts would be more effective than any isolated attack on Pelagius. With each stroke, each argument, they wore him down, isolating him from the church and undermining his credibility.

Pelagius, meanwhile, was absent. His absence, though often due to exile or avoidance of direct confrontation, proved to be a crucial factor in his defeat. Without his voice in the ring, Jerome and Augustine could continue their attacks unchallenged. The absence of Pelagius allowed the narrative of heresy to solidify without the possibility of defense.

The Personal Motives Behind the Attack

But the question remains: Why? Why did Jerome and Augustine, two men of considerable theological stature, join forces to take down a scholar like Pelagius? What drove them to such lengths? The answer lies not just in their theological differences but in their personal motivations.

For Jerome, the attack on Pelagius was a chance to reclaim some of the influence he had lost in Rome. Having been driven out of the city amid scandal and controversy, Jerome sought to establish himself as a dominant theological voice. In Pelagius, Jerome saw a threat—a man whose ideas about free will and human responsibility seemed to challenge Jerome's own convictions. More than that, Pelagius represented a growing influence in the Christian world, one that Jerome felt he needed to neutralize if he was ever to restore his place in the ecclesiastical hierarchy.

For Augustine, the reasons were more doctrinal but no less personal. Augustine's dogma of *original* sin was not simply an intellectual framework—it was a cornerstone of his understanding of salvation. To accept Pelagius' teachings was to undermine Augustine's entire theological structure. But beyond that, Augustine's personal experiences with the question of grace, his struggle with his own sinful nature, made the dogma of *original* sin profoundly personal. Pelagius, by rejecting this dogma, represented a challenge not only to Augustine's authority but to the very foundation of his theological identity and status.

The Tragic End of Pelagius
In the end, Pelagius was left in the ring alone. The absence of a strong defense, coupled with the relentless attacks from two of the church's most powerful figures, ensured that his fate was sealed. The Council of Carthage in 418, where Pelagius' ideas were condemned as heretical, marked the culmination of the campaign against him. But this was not the conclusion of a fair debate—it was the final blow in a rhetorical battle that had been rigged from the start.

Pelagius' ideas did not disappear, of course. They lived on in the hearts and minds of those who believed in human responsibility and moral choice. But the political, personal, and theological machinery of the church ensured that these ideas would be relegated to the margins, their proponents cast aside as heretics.

Pelagius was not merely defeated; he was discredited. His name became synonymous with heresy, his teachings buried beneath the weight of Augustine's theology and Jerome's relentless rhetoric.

Conclusion: The Real Story
As we step back and examine the events surrounding the condemnation of Pelagius, it becomes clear: this was not simply a theological dispute—it was a political campaign, a calculated effort to destroy a rival and reshape the Christian worldview in a way that suited Jerome and Augustine's ambitions. Pelagius, for all his flaws, was not the heretic he was made out to be. He was a man who stood for something different, something that challenged the dominant narrative, and for that, he was silenced.

In the end, Pelagius is not just a cautionary tale about the dangers of theological rigidity and political ambition. He is a reminder of how easily a man's name and ideas can be destroyed when those in power work together to rewrite the story.

In the final years of his life, Pelagius must have looked back on his work, his vision—a vision where humanity's potential for moral choice was paramount, where the soul's journey was defined not by inherited guilt but by the individual's will to strive for righteousness. He had taught that salvation lay in the heart of the individual, that God's grace was not a force that enslaved, but a call to freedom.

This message of hope, rooted in the belief that human beings could stand upright before God, did not just shape the theology of his time—it was, in its essence, a call to the very dignity of mankind. But in the cold winds of history, this vision would not be the one that endured. The theological establishment, threatened by the possibility that human agency could stand in the balance with divine grace, would ultimately consign Pelagius to the shadows. His name became synonymous with heresy, and his teachings were buried beneath the weight of dogmas that stripped humanity of its moral responsibility.

The irony is staggering: in a world where Augustine's words were embraced as the final authority on human salvation, Pelagius' message—that each person could choose their moral fate, that faith was a living, breathing choice—was cast aside. Yet, the very thing that Pelagius had fought for, the autonomy of human will, was paradoxically used as a weapon against him. The church, in its zeal to protect the dogma of *original* sin, embraced the very notion of human impotence that Pelagius had worked so hard to reject.

But what does it say about a society—about a faith—that must silence a voice calling for the full dignity of the human being? What does it say about a system that believes humanity is too weak, too bound by the sin of Adam to stand before God on its own merits? That this was the answer, the final resolution—Pelagius, in exile, his

246

name sullied, his ideas obscured—was not only a tragedy for him. It was a tragedy for the church, for all of Christianity, and for the centuries of believers who would never hear the message of human agency and hope that Pelagius had so fiercely championed.

The crime against Pelagius was not only the destruction of one man—it was the destruction of an idea. An idea that might have reshaped the very foundation of Christian thought, urging humanity to recognize that salvation is a journey not just shaped by divine grace, but by the choice to walk in that grace. And in the end, as the years wore on and the shadows of history closed in, it became clear that Pelagius' greatest crime was not that he had misinterpreted Scripture—but that he had dared to believe in the power of human choice.

The church moved forward, but Pelagius, condemned and forgotten, would not see the fruits of his labor. His message, drowned out by the tides of power and dogma, faded into obscurity, a footnote in the history of a church that would never fully embrace the hope he had placed in the hearts of men. His voice, though silenced, still lingers in the echoes of history—an unheeded cry for the redemption of human agency.

Epilogue

Imagine Agatha Christie's Hercule Poirot, who liked his soliloquies, having gathered the key players and concluded the investigation, now reflecting on the case with his friend Captain Hastings...

"*Mon ami* Hastings, you have been with me from the very beginning of this investigation, and I believe you now understand the situation in which we find ourselves. This is a tale of intrigue, of a crime committed not in the shadows but in the very halls of power, where dogma and reputation held sway over truth.

"We begin with Pelagius, a man of principle, whose views on human responsibility and the potential for moral choice were founded on reason and faith, untainted by the rigid theological framework of *original* sin that was rapidly gaining traction in the late Roman

247

Empire. He was not a man consumed by ambition but driven by the conviction that humanity could indeed live righteously through free will and God's grace. And yet, this man, this 'heretic,' became the target of a campaign stretching across decades, a slow-burning, relentless series of attacks, designed not to confront him openly but to discredit him, to isolate him, and finally to obliterate his teachings.

"Two men, Jerome and Augustine, emerged as the principal figures in this theological war. Despite their differences, they saw the opportunity to work in tandem, using their positions of influence, their mastery of rhetoric, and their access to the levers of power to advance their shared objective: the destruction of Pelagius' credibility and the establishment of *original* sin as the unquestioned dogma of the church.

"They employed a strategy not of open debate, for they knew Pelagius was a formidable adversary in that arena. No, the true weapon was one of absence. Their weapon was not just the absence of Pelagius from councils and debates, but the careful manipulation of power—their ability to control the narrative and the institutions that shaped theological thought. It was not enough to defeat him in debate; they needed to eliminate his influence from the halls of power, ensuring his ideas could never challenge the orthodoxy they were building. The institutions that Jerome and Augustine wielded gave them not only authority, but the means to bury a philosophy that threatened the very foundations of their growing influence.

"By pushing Pelagius to the margins, by ensuring his physical absence from key councils like that of Carthage, they set the stage for the final blow. They knew that, in his absence, they could wield their rhetoric unopposed, framing Pelagius as a heretic without allowing him the chance to defend himself. For they knew that every time Pelagius was allowed to defend himself and his teachings, he was not pronounced as heretic.

"With every word they wrote, with every accusation they levied, the character of Pelagius was tarnished. And when the final decision came, the condemnation was swift, the verdict passed down as if it were a matter of course, despite the glaring absence of the accused.

"The victors, Jerome and Augustine, were hailed as saints. Their teachings, enshrined in the very foundations of Christian theology, became the foundation upon which much of Christian doctrine would rest for centuries. The power of the church, with its political and doctrinal influence, ensured that their teachings became the bedrock of Christian theology. It was a victory not just for the soul of the church, but for the consolidation of power within the ecclesiastical elite. And Pelagius? He was left in the dust, his name dragged through the mud, his works forgotten, his fate sealed by a theological and rhetorical assassination that remains unmatched in its cruelty.

"And what of Pelagius in the end? We know nothing of his last days. The sources are silent. The history books, written by the victors, tell us only of the heretic. No record of his death, no record of his final thoughts or moments. He is lost to history, forgotten as a footnote, his character and his teachings erased from the annals of church history, all for the preservation of a dogma that had no true basis in Scripture.

"The 'crime,' if we can call it that, was complete. The victors drank to their success, their dogma prevailing, their foe vanquished. But, *mon ami*, is it not strange? History has a way of forgetting the truth when those in power shape the narrative. Pelagius, whose ideas were rooted in the very possibility of human agency and responsibility before God, has been consigned to the ash heap of history. His name tarnished, his teachings discarded, not because they were false, but because they stood in opposition to a dogma that could not be substantiated by the word of God.

"Pelagius' teachings were not discarded because they were proven false, but because they posed a direct challenge to the power structures that had been carefully cultivated by Jerome and Augus-

249

tine. His ideas represented an alternative vision of human responsibility and free will—one that would have undone the theological framework that secured their control over the church's direction.

"And so, Hastings, what are we left with? A theological war fought and won, not on the basis of Scripture, but on the power of persuasion, the manipulation of absence, and the weight of institutional authority. A man who stood for human free will was erased from history, while those who fashioned a dogma from thin air were celebrated as saints. This is the story of Pelagius, a man forgotten by time, but not by truth."

Notes and Observations

Investigative Journal Entry: Date: _____ / _____ / _____

Who were the real power players? How do you interpret the roles of Jerome and Augustine in the condemnation of Pelagius? What were their motivations—personal, theological, or political?

Absent from the trial, silenced in history: How did Pelagius' absence from the Council of Carthage impact the outcome of the debate? How does this absence shape your view of the fairness or legitimacy of his condemnation?

The cost of challenging orthodoxy: What does Pelagius' fate reveal about the dangers of challenging established doctrines or institutional authority in the church?

Human will and divine grace: How does Pelagius' emphasis on moral choice and personal responsibility challenge the dogma of *original* sin? Do you think his view offers a more hopeful or faithful picture of humanity?

The voice that lingers: How would you summarize the core message of Pelagius? Do you believe that message still matters today?

27

The Legacy of Carthage
Evolution of the Doctrine of *Original* Sin

The Council of Carthage in 418 marked not only a theological victory for Augustine, but also the formal establishment of *original* sin as a cornerstone of Western Christianity. In the wake of Pelagius' condemnation, Augustine's vision of humanity—marked by the stain of original sin and in desperate need of divine grace—would begin to shape the course of Christian thought. Yet, the battle was far from over. The legacy of Carthage would echo through the centuries, influencing theological debates, shaping the structure of the church, and becoming a battleground in later struggles over salvation, grace, and free will.

Aftermath: The Struggle for Theological Hegemony
Though Pelagius' ideas were officially condemned at Carthage, eradicating Pelagianism proved far more elusive. Pelagius, ever persistent, remained a figure of theological controversy for decades, especially in the East. His teachings were particularly appealing to some in the Eastern provinces, where the notion of human free will and moral responsibility was given greater emphasis. In regions like Carthage and Africa, remnants of Pelagius' ideas continued to find sympathy, complicating the West's embrace of Augustine's dogma.

Even after Carthage, Pelagius' followers attempted to defend his teachings, challenging Augustine's increasingly dominant influence. It wasn't until the early 5th century, after repeated failed attempts to gain official recognition for Pelagianism, that the church definitively excluded Pelagius from its theological fold. This prolonged battle, one fought with letters, debates, and synods, laid the groundwork for the theological division that would later culminate in the Great Schism of 1054. The ecclesiastical rift that divided the Eastern and Western Churches had its roots in these early struggles over *original* sin.

Pelagius himself would eventually face exile, though his ideas would not entirely disappear. Augustine's doctrines, particularly those on *original* sin and divine grace, had firmly established themselves within the Western Church, though debates over free will and grace would continue to spark theological fires for centuries. Despite Pelagius' efforts, it was Augustine's vision of the human condition that would come to dominate Western Christian thought.

Institutionalization of *Original* Sin in Western Christianity
With the official condemnation of Pelagius at Carthage, the dogma of *original* sin became institutionalized within the Western Church. The church, now in possession of a theological victory, turned to solidify Augustine's views as official dogma.

The *Vulgate* Bible, Jerome's translation of the Scriptures, became the central text in the Latin-speaking world, serving as a powerful ally in the Church's theological campaigns. Jerome's rendering of Romans 5:12, especially the phrase *"in whom all have sinned,"* provided the scriptural backing for Augustine's ideas about *original* sin, further reinforcing the dominance of his theology.

Augustine's view of *original* sin began to shape more than just doctrinal teachings; it influenced the very structures of the church. With the dogma of *original* sin came an understanding of baptism as the means by which humanity is cleansed of Adam's stain. This not only reaffirmed the church's authority in matters of salvation but also solidified its role as the necessary intermediary between God and humanity. The church, as the exclusive channel for grace, grew in power and influence.

Augustine's ideas on grace and salvation were no longer merely theological positions; they became the foundations of ecclesiastical power. The dogma of *original* sin became a tool for the church's authority, as it positioned itself as the guardian and dispenser of divine grace. It was not simply a matter of salvation; it was about the church's role in mediating God's grace to humanity. In this way, the church became both the arbiter and the enforcer of orthodoxy.

The Influence of Augustine's Legacy in the Middle Ages

As Western Christianity entered the Middle Ages, the influence of Augustine's thought on *original* sin only deepened. The intellectual framework Augustine established became the foundation of medieval scholasticism, the dominant theological system of the time. Figures like Anselm of Canterbury, Thomas Aquinas, and Bernard of Clairvaux all built upon Augustine's teachings, making *original* sin a central component of their theological systems.

Anselm, for instance, took Augustine's dogma of *original* sin and integrated it into his understanding of the atonement. Anselm's satisfaction theory of atonement—arguing that Christ's death was necessary to satisfy God's justice—was predicated on the assumption that all humanity shared in Adam's *original* sin and needed redemption from it. For Anselm, Christ's sacrifice became the means of restoring humanity to a state of grace, healing the rupture caused by *original* sin.

By the time of Thomas Aquinas, Augustine's theology was considered the foundation of Catholic dogma. Aquinas, drawing upon Augustine's writings, expanded upon the concepts of grace, salvation, and divine justice. The dogma of *original* sin was fully integrated into Catholic teaching and would remain a key element in the Church's understanding of salvation, grace, and the role of the Church in mediating God's intervention in human affairs.

The Eastern Response and Divergence

While the West fully embraced Augustine's vision of *original* sin,

253

the Eastern Church developed a somewhat different understanding of human nature and sin. The Eastern Fathers, including John Chrysostom, Theodore of Mopsuestia, and Gregory of Nyssa, were more inclined to emphasize human potential and the transformative power of free will. While they did not deny the reality of sin, their theology placed less emphasis on *original* sin as formulated by Augustine.

For the Eastern Church, humanity's potential to choose good and respond to divine grace was more central. The concept of *theosis*—the process by which humans are divinized and made partakers in the divine nature—played a key role in the Eastern understanding of salvation. This idea of salvation was less about the inheritance of *original* sin and more about the potential for transformation and union with God.

Despite these differences, the debate over original sin remained a significant point of tension between the East and the West. This doctrinal divide, especially regarding the nature of grace and human free will, contributed to the eventual schism between the Eastern Orthodox and Roman Catholic Churches in 1054. The theological dispute over *original* sin was not the only issue, but it was one of the key factors that separated the two branches of Christianity.

The Doctrinal Struggles of the Reformation

The next major challenge to the dogma of *original* sin came during the Protestant Reformation in the 16th century. Reformers like Martin Luther and John Calvin both accepted the idea of *original* sin, while challenging the Catholic Church's understanding of salvation, particularly in relation to grace, baptism, and the role of the Church.

Luther's doctrine of justification by faith alone rejected the Augustinian notion that baptism remitted *original* sin. Instead, Luther argued that faith in Christ alone, apart from any human works or sacraments, was the means of salvation. For Luther, salvation was a gift from God, received by faith, not through the mediating work of the church.

254

John Calvin's theology took the dogma of *original* sin even further, developing a radical view of predestination. Calvin argued that the fall of Adam had so deeply corrupted human nature that only God's sovereign grace could save anyone. The consequence of *original* sin, for Calvin, was that only a chosen few would be saved, and this divine selection was entirely beyond human control.

The Reformation debates over *original* sin, salvation, and grace further polarized Christian thought. As the Protestant movement spread, it contributed to the fragmentation of Christianity, as each new denomination grappled with its own understanding of sin, grace, and the role of the church.

The Enduring Legacy of the Dogma of *Original* Sin

The dogma of *original* sin, as formulated by Augustine and solidified at the Council of Carthage, would have a profound and lasting impact on Christian thought for over a millennium. It became a key element in the development of Catholic soteriology (the doctrine of salvation) and helped define the Catholic Church's role as the mediator of grace. Through the Middle Ages, the Reformation, and beyond, the dogma of *original* sin continued to shape the course of theological debates.

From the early theological battles of Rome and Carthage to the doctrinal struggles of the Reformation, the legacy of Augustine's understanding of *original* sin was ever-present. It became a central issue in debates between Catholics and Protestants, and in the East-West divide, influencing the development of Christian traditions for centuries. The theological battle that began in the halls of the Council of Carthage would not end with Augustine's death—it would evolve, challenge, and shape the church in the centuries to come, leaving an indelible mark on the history of Christian thought.

Notes and Observations

Investigative Journal Entry: Date: _____ / _____ / _____

The Influence of Pelagius in the East: Why did Pelagius' ideas resonate more deeply in the Eastern provinces of the Roman Empire? How might the cultural and theological climate of the East have allowed Pelagian thought to persist, even after its condemnation at Carthage?

Augustine vs. Pelagius: How did the condemnation of Pelagius at Carthage shape the development of Western Christianity? What role did the concept of free will play in the ongoing theological debate between Augustine's and Pelagius' views, and how did this debate impact the church's authority?

***Original* Sin and the Church's Authority:** How did the dogma of *original* sin, as formalized at the Council of Carthage, reinforce the church's role as intermediary between God and humanity? In what ways did this reshape the church's relationship with its followers, particularly in regard to its spiritual and temporal authority?

Theological Divisions and the Great Schism: The theological battles over *original* sin contributed to the East-West division that culminated in the Great Schism of 1054. What were some of the lasting effects of this doctrinal divide on the broader development of Christianity, particularly in relation to the authority of the Papacy in the Catholic Church?

28

The Power of the Sacrament
How Baptism and *Original* Sin Empowered the Church

The union of the dogma of *original* sin with the practice of infant baptism gave the Catholic Church a power like no other in the history of Christianity. It not only cemented the Church's authority over the spiritual fate of individuals but also elevated it into a dominant political and economic force. By claiming control over the means of salvation—chiefly through baptism—the Church became the sole mediator between humanity and God. In this chapter, we will explore how the Church's marriage of these two dogmas not only expanded its spiritual reach but also enabled it to consolidate unprecedented levels of material power, wealth, and influence.

How Baptism Became the Gateway to Salvation

As the dogma of *original* sin became deeply entrenched in Christian teaching, the necessity of baptism was no longer a matter of choice but of eternal consequence. In this view, *original* sin, inherited from Adam, left all humans spiritually dead, incapable of salvation without divine intervention. Baptism, then, was not just a symbolic rite of initiation into the Christian community—it was the means by which the soul was cleansed of *original* sin, restoring the individual to a state of grace.

With the widespread practice of infant baptism in the early centuries of the church, this sacrament was universally understood to be essential for everyone, from the moment of birth. Infants, who were incapable of making a personal profession of faith, were still baptized in order to cleanse them of the inherited sin that separated

257

them from God. This meant that every human being—no matter their age—was now indelibly tied to the church from birth. The church became, in essence, the arbiter of salvation, and baptism was the key that unlocked it.

In this framework, the church's authority over baptism translated directly into control over an individual's eternal destiny. No longer merely a provider of spiritual guidance, the church had become the sole authority with the power to grant salvation—its rituals, especially baptism, the gateway to eternal life.

Infant Baptism: Cornerstone of Church Authority

As the Catholic Church solidified in the West, its insistence on infant baptism marked the earliest possible entry into the body of Christ. (Scholars debate when the Roman church became the Catholic Church in the institutional sense. Some point to Leo the Great as the key figure in its emergence; others look to Gregory the Great as the one who cast the vision for a dominant Western Church. Gregory effectively promoted Augustine's dogma. What is clear is that during this era, the church became the Church—capital "C.")

The Church of Rome's insistence on infant baptism to remit inherited sin ensured that its control over salvation began at the very beginning of life. This was not a mere option for believers—it was an imperative. Infants, though innocent and unable to profess faith, were nonetheless included in the Christian covenant by the sacrament of baptism. This policy elevated the Catholic Church to the status of unquestioned authority in all matters of salvation.

Infant baptism became a cornerstone of the Church's authority over the lives of individuals, as it was no longer about the individual's choice to follow Christ; it was about the Church's duty to ensure that every soul was baptized to avoid eternal damnation. The very idea of unbaptized children facing eternity in hell became a source of societal anxiety, one that placed immense pressure on parents to ensure their infants received the sacrament as soon as possible.

258

The Catholic Church's self-promoted monopoly on baptism reinforced its control over the souls of the faithful. Since only priests could administer this sacrament, the Church was not merely a place of worship; it had become the gatekeeper of eternal life. The power to offer—or withhold—baptism was immense. To reject the necessity of baptism, as Pelagius had done, was to challenge the very foundation of the Church's spiritual authority. Such a challenge was not just a theological dispute—it was a direct attack on the Church's claim to control the eternal destinies of humankind.

Making the Church the Mediator of Grace

The increasing prominence of the dogma of *original* sin and the practice of baptism had a profound impact on the way salvation was understood. No longer could salvation be seen as something directly between the individual and God. The Catholic Church's assumed role as the sole institution with the power to mediate grace became an even more dominant force in the spiritual lives of all Christians.

The sacraments—especially baptism—came to be seen as matters of life and death, further solidifying the Church's power. The very act of salvation was no longer something that could be accessed simply by personal faith or good works. It had to be mediated, administered, and controlled by the Church. This transformation marked a pivotal moment in Christian history: salvation was no longer a direct encounter between the believer and God but a communal and institutional matter, with the Church acting as the indispensable channel for divine grace.

The practical consequences of this shift were far-reaching. The Church's control over baptism gave it unparalleled spiritual power, but it also translated into material wealth and political influence. As the most important institution for the salvation of souls, the Church accumulated vast wealth, property, and influence. The faithful, in seeking the grace of baptism for themselves and their children, made generous offerings to the Church, further reinforcing its strength.

The Threat of Heresy and the Power of the Church

The Church's consolidation of power through the sacraments came with a strict policy of orthodoxy, enforced with vigor and ruthlessness. One of the most striking aspects of this period was the Church's uncompromising stance against any heretical challenge to the dogmas of *original* sin or the necessity of baptism. Heresy, once a theological deviation, became a direct threat to the institution's control over salvation—and thus its power.

Pelagius, who rejected the idea of inherited sin, became the most prominent example of someone whose views were seen as a dangerous challenge to the Church's authority. Pelagius and his followers, who advocated for human free will and moral responsibility without the need for baptism to cleanse *original* sin, were condemned as heretics. The Church's response to Pelagianism was not simply theological; it was political. If Pelagius' ideas were allowed to spread, the very structure of the Church's power, built upon the dogma of *original* sin and the necessity of baptism, would collapse.

For the Church, this wasn't just about defending a theological idea; it was about defending its monopoly on salvation. The label of "heretic" became a powerful weapon, suppressing theological dissent and maintaining the Church's control over the spiritual lives of the people. To question baptism, or to deny *original* sin, undermined the very foundation of the Church's authority. The Church could not, and would not, allow such challenges to go unanswered.

Who is the Heretic?

Pelagius and his rejection of *original* sin provides a striking parallel to later events in church history, particularly the previously mentioned condemnation of Copernicus during the Renaissance. In both cases, the Church of Rome wasn't just defending dogma—it was defending its very authority. The Catholic Church's condemnation of Copernicus' heliocentric theory was not just about science—it was about preserving the belief that the Church of Rome itself was the center of human knowledge, and therefore of all creation.

260

Similarly, in the case of Pelagius, the church's condemnation was not just a matter of theological disagreement—it was an effort to preserve its authority as the sole institution capable of mediating salvation. Augustine and Jerome knew that if Pelagius' challenge succeeded, it would set a dangerous precedent that threatened the entire ecclesiastical structure. To reject the dogma of *original* sin and infant baptism was to deny the church's exclusive claim to the keys of salvation—and that was something the church could not allow. Augustine made the church's position unmistakably clear: "Infants, too, are baptized for the remission of sins—not for sins of their own, but because of *original* sin." (*De Peccatorum Meritis et Remissione* [On the Merits and Forgiveness of Sins], Book 1)

Conclusion: The Church's Unassailable Power

As the dogma of *original* sin and the practice of infant baptism became fully entrenched in Christian thought, the Catholic Church solidified its status as the unassailable spiritual and temporal power of the Western world. The Church's monopoly on salvation, mediated through the sacraments, gave it dominion not only over souls but also over wealth, land, and political authority. The sacraments became the instruments by which the Church exercised control over the lives of the faithful.

For those rejecting the dogma of *original* sin, the punishment was excommunication—separation from the grace of salvation, the very lifeblood of the Church's influence. By this, the Church maintained dominance over the both spiritual and material realms.

The dogma of *original* sin, coupled with the practice of infant baptism, gave the Catholic Church staggering power. The union of these two elements created an institution of unparalleled authority, one that would shape the course of Christian history for centuries. Augustine, Jerome, and the Church used these dogmas to forge a legacy that would establish the Church not just as a spiritual authority, but as a pillar of social, political, and economic power.

Notes and Observations

Investigative Journal Entry: Date: _____ / _____ / _____

1. The Social and Political Implications of Baptism

How did the practice of infant baptism transform the Church of Rome—soon to emerge as the Roman Catholic Church—into a powerful political and social institution? What were the broader societal consequences of making baptism a universal necessity?

2. The Concept of Heresy

In what ways did the Church's response to Pelagius reflect its increasing use of theological orthodoxy to secure its authority? How did the concept of heresy evolve from a theological deviation into a direct challenge to the Church's political and social power?

3. Baptism and Control Over Salvation

This chapter presents baptism as the "gateway to salvation." How did the Church's monopoly over this sacrament consolidate both spiritual authority and material wealth? What are the implications of that monopoly for individual believers—and for society as a whole?

4. The Church's Dual Role: Spiritual and Temporal Power

How did the Church's involvement in both spiritual and material realms reshape Christians' understanding of their relationship to the Church? In what ways did this shift empower the Church to control not only individual salvation but also wealth, land, and political influence?

262

29

Rise of the Church of Rome
Ecclesiastical Power and Wealth

To understand the full impact of the Council of Carthage and its decisions, consider a parallel drawn from one of Agatha Christie's most famous mysteries, *Murder on the Orient Express*, featuring Hercule Poirot. In this story, a seemingly straightforward crime—the kidnapping of a little girl, Daisy Armstrong—sets off a chain of events with far-reaching and unintended consequences. The kidnapping leads to the death of a man, but the ripple effects are vast: there are suicides, mental breakdowns, falsely accused victims, financial ruin, and ultimately, widespread grief. The initial crime, though tragic in itself, triggers a cascade of events that affect many lives, each person playing a part in a greater story that builds to a stunning revelation.

Theology, often seen as abstract or academic, can carry profound political and cultural weight—much like the crime in *Murder on the Orient Express*, which reverberated through an entire web of characters. As Poirot uncovers layer upon layer of motive and impact, we are reminded that ideas—like theology—may seem abstract, but their consequences are anything but. In much the same way, the establishment of the dogma of *original* sin at the Council of Carthage (418) triggered a cascade of consequences, all centered around the necessity of infant baptism to "wash away *original* sin."

What began as a theological decree quickly became the catalyst for a series of events that would shift the balance of power in Europe, drawing monarchs, empires, and millions of souls into the fold of the Church of Rome. A seemingly abstract dogma would evolve into the cornerstone of an institution that would shape the fate of kingdoms. It wasn't just a **doctrinal shift**—it was a **power shift**, one that would alter the entire landscape of Europe and the wider world—especially North and South America.

Much like the interconnected lives of Christie's characters, the events set in motion by Carthage would unfold across generations, impacting every facet of European civilization. The Church of Rome, which had once been a persecuted minority, transformed into the wealthiest and most powerful institution in the Western world, with vast lands, immeasurable wealth, and immense political sway—emerging as the Roman Catholic Church.

Augustine's dogma of inherited sin and the necessity of infant baptism would ultimately affect not just Rome or Europe, but the entire world. By tracing these ripple effects, we begin to uncover how this transformation unfolded.

In a way, the Council of Carthage—a theological gathering held in 418 to condemn the teachings of Pelagius and pronounce him as a heretic, to solidify the dogma of *original* sin, and to establish the necessity of infant baptism—was an event of seemingly humble proportions. The decisions made at this council, rooted in the thoughts of Augustine of Hippo and debated among other ecclesiastical authorities, set in motion a series of ripple effects that reached far beyond the confines of the early Christian world. What initially appeared to be an abstract religious debate would ultimately reverberate through the centuries, shaping not only the theological landscape, but the very foundation of the political, social, and cultural systems of Western civilization.

In a manner similar to Agatha Christie's famous detective, Hercule Poirot, we will now begin to trace the clues—examining

264

key moments in history that reveal how a theological decision made in a small African city would change the world.

The Council of Carthage: The Seeds of Power
To understand the scope of the ripple effect, we must first return to the Council of Carthage in 418. The Church of Rome, led by figures such as Augustine, had already begun to formulate a powerful theological foundation that emphasized human depravity due to *original* sin. This dogma painted all of humanity as inherently sinful from birth, requiring divine intervention through baptism to cleanse the soul and ensure salvation.

As Augustine's ideas gained traction, they were enshrined in the decisions made at Carthage, which laid the groundwork for the Church of Rome to become the arbiter of who was saved and who was not. It was not just a spiritual decision; it was a political and social one, allowing the Catholic Church to establish unprecedented control over the lives of millions, embedding itself deeply into the social fabric of the Roman Empire and beyond.

Constantine to Theodosius: A Shift Toward Rome
By 380, Emperor Theodosius I made Christianity the state religion of the Roman Empire, officially recognizing the faith and positioning it as the core of Roman identity. The Council of Nicaea (325) had already settled critical theological issues, such as the nature of Christ, but after 380, doctrinal and textual authority needed to be firmly established. The Church of Rome quickly became the central hub for religious matters in the western empire, and its bishops, particularly the Bishop of Rome, began to assume immense political power.

Leo I, bishop of Rome from 440–461, elevated Rome's status as the primary see in the Western Church. He justified this elevation by appealing to Peter's primacy—a claim rooted in yet

265

another interpretive error (an example of eisegesis) from the pen of Jerome. This position, promoted by Jerome to Bishop Damasus of Rome, set the mold for the eventual elevation of the Church of Rome. Though the imperial capital was in decline, it remained the most powerful city in the Western Empire. The Church of Rome, large and wealthy, exerted growing influence over Western Christianity. Leo I wielded great influence in Rome and beyond.

Irenaeus, a 2nd-century Church Father, recognized the significant influence of the Church of Rome in his writings. In his work *Against Heresies*, he pointed out the importance of the Church of Rome due to its proposed founding by the apostles Peter and Paul and its central location in the capital of the Roman Empire. He wrote, "For it is a matter of necessity that every Church should agree with this Church [of Rome], on account of its preeminent authority." (*Against Heresies*, 3.3.2)

He did not, however, suggest the supremacy of the bishop of Rome over other bishops, a concept that developed later in Church history. The bishop of Rome was a bishop among bishops. He had nothing other than the power of personality and prominence of position. But he had no authority over any other bishop. That would be an ecclesiastical construct that would come later as the Church of Rome pushed its influence beyond the city and its regional influence.

The Church's increasing authority coincided with the fall of the Western Roman Empire in 476. With the Empire's decline, the papacy seized upon its newfound power, becoming the *de facto* ruler of the West. It filled the void left by the fall of the empire and took on an administrative role akin to that of the Roman Emperor, with Pope Gregory I (Gregory the Great) leading the charge in consolidating papal authority. Gregory used administrative reforms, liturgy (*e.g.*, Gregorian Chant), and monastic missions to institutionalize papal authority.

Gregory the Great and the Spread of Papal Power

Pope Gregory I played a critical role in disseminating the theological ideas formalized at Carthage across Europe. In particular, his missions to Britain were pivotal in establishing the Church's dominance. In 597, Gregory sent Augustine of Canterbury—a missionary—into Britain to convert the Anglo-Saxons to Christianity.

Gregory's impact was profound. Though not the intellectual equal of figures like Ambrose, Jerome, and Augustine, Gregory's administrative genius ensured the spread of Augustinian thought far beyond the Mediterranean. While he is often linked with the "Latin Fathers" of the Church, his true legacy lies in how he institutionalized their ideas and centralized the papacy. Gregory's teachings and reforms would shape the Catholic Church for the next millennium, solidifying his position as one of the true founders of the modern papacy. This centralization of power was crucial for the formation of a hierarchical structure in the Church, a model that would come to define the Catholic Church as we know it today.

This serves to reinforce the idea of power consolidation. Augustine's influence, combined with the rise of papal authority, would set the stage for a religious and political shift that would dominate the Western world. This wasn't just about who was "right" or "wrong" theologically—it was about who could shape and control the narrative.

The Conversion of Clovis and the Rise of Christian Kingdoms

The conversion of Clovis, king of the Franks, was another critical moment in the spread of Augustinian theology. Clovis's adoption of Nicene Christianity didn't just convert him—it set a precedent for the conversion of his entire tribe. This had profound theological implications, as it made Christianity the religion of the state. The Frankish Kingdom would eventually form the core of the

267

Holy Roman Empire, a political entity that aligned itself with papal authority.

Clovis' conversion not only consolidated power for the Franks but also laid the groundwork for the rise of Christian monarchies throughout Europe. His successors would continue the Augustinian legacy, eventually culminating in the reign of Charlemagne, who was crowned Emperor of the Holy Roman Empire by Pope Leo III on Christmas Day, 800 AD.

Charlemagne's reign represented the political and religious unification of much of Western Europe under the banner of Augustinian Christianity and papal authority. This moment, when Charlemagne was crowned by the Pope, marked a crucial step in the creation of the Holy Roman Empire—a polity that would endure for centuries and serve as a major vehicle for spreading the Augustinian vision of sin, baptism, and salvation.

The Crusades and the Expansion of Papal Power
By the late 11th century, the Crusades began. The Papal States—a collection of territories in central Italy—became directly involved in the military campaigns to reclaim Jerusalem from Muslim control. But as the Crusades progressed, it became evident that the papacy wasn't just concerned with reclaiming the Holy Land—it was also deeply invested in expanding its power.

The Crusades became a tool for the papacy to extend its political and economic influence across Europe and the Mediterranean. The wealth and land captured during the Crusades helped build the papal treasury, and the military endeavors solidified the Pope's political authority.

The Reconquista and the Rise of Catholic Monarchies
In the 8th century, the Moors, a Muslim population from North Africa, had taken control of large parts of the Iberian Peninsula.

This posed a challenge not just to the political order of Europe but also to the religious authority of the Church. King Ferdinand and Queen Isabella, both staunch Catholics, led the Reconquista to reclaim Spain from Muslim control. Their campaign wasn't just about territory; it was about religious identity, and the papacy played a key role in supporting them, spiritually and materially.

The papacy's backing of the Reconquista ensured the Christianization of Spain. The monarchs of Spain, influenced by papal authority, reasserted the Church of Rome's power in the region. They were granted the right to appoint bishops and control religious matters, further extending the Church's influence.

The Reformation: The Breaking Point of Papal Authority

The influence of the Church reached its zenith during the late medieval period, but as Lord Acton famously said, "Power tends to corrupt, and absolute power corrupts absolutely." It was the hubris of papal authority—the belief that the Pope held ultimate power over salvation—that ultimately led to the Reformation.

In 1517, Martin Luther famously nailed his 95 Theses to the door of the Castle Church in Wittenberg, protesting the sale of indulgences and questioning the authority of the papacy. Luther's stance was rooted in the doctrine of *sola Scriptura*, or the belief that Scripture alone should be the authority on matters of faith and salvation. In doing so, Luther challenged the theological and institutional framework that had been constructed centuries earlier—at Carthage and beyond.

The Reformation would eventually lead to massive theological and political upheaval, breaking apart the unified Christian Church and giving rise to Protestantism. But the ripple effects of the decisions made at Carthage—particularly the dogma of *original* sin and the necessity of infant baptism—remained at the heart of the theological debates that fueled the Reformation.

Conclusion: The Legacy of Carthage

As we look back through the annals of history, the Council of Carthage stands as a pivotal moment in shaping the future of Christianity—and, by extension, the world. The ripple effects of this decision still echo today, shaping the theological and political structures that govern much of the Western world.

From the rise of the papacy to the Crusades to the Reformation, the decisions made at Carthage were far more than theological—they were world-shaping. The theological struggle over sin and salvation gave rise to powerful institutions that would control kings and kingdoms, influence the outcome of wars, and shape the very cultural fabric of Europe and beyond.

As we walk through this journey of history, we realize the true power of ideas. What began as a debate over doctrine would ultimately shape the course of human history, forever changing the world as we know it. And just like a great detective story, the truth is revealed piece by piece, each event unraveling the deeper mysteries of how the initial "crime"—a theological decision—would become the force that shaped the destiny of the world.

Notes and Observations

Investigative Journal Entry: Date: _____ / _____ / _____

The Ripple Effect of Carthage: The chapter compares the ripple effects of the decisions made at the Council of Carthage to a chain of events triggered by a seemingly minor crime in Agatha Christie's *Murder on the Orient Express*. How did the theological decision regarding *original* sin and infant baptism evolve from a religious matter into one that reshaped Europe's political and social structures? In what ways did this transformation affect the Church's relationship with secular rulers?

270

30

From Spiritual to Temporal Dominion

The transformation of the Church of Rome from a purely spiritual institution into a dominant political and economic power is a central story in the history of Christianity. This shift, which occurred over centuries, redefined the role of the Roman Catholic Church, intertwining it with the secular governance of Europe and elevating it from a humble religious movement to a sprawling, powerful empire.

The Church's journey from spiritual leadership to temporal dominion was driven by a combination of doctrinal innovations, strategic political decisions, and an ever-expanding reach into the economic and political spheres of Europe. By the time the Church reached the height of its power, it was no longer merely a spiritual authority but a colossal institution that controlled vast lands, immense wealth, and the direction of European politics. But how did this transformation occur—and at what cost to the Church's original mission?

The Gradual Shift: When Did the Church Cross the Line?
Understanding when the Church of Rome crossed the line from being a purely spiritual institution to becoming a secular power is key to comprehending its transformation. The Church's shift from spiritual mission to political ambition can be traced to several key moments in history that gradually blurred the lines between the sacred and the temporal:

Constantine's Edict
The first major turning point came in the early 4th century when Emperor Constantine legalized Christianity with the Edict of Milan

271

in AD 313, and later made it the state religion of the Roman Empire. This was the moment when Christianity began to be recognized as not just a faith but a political force. With this newfound legitimacy, the Church was granted the right to own land, opening the door to its increasing entanglement with the imperial structure.

Competition for Primacy

As the Church of Rome began to gain power, it also began competing for primacy with other major Christian sees, such as Alexandria and Constantinople. Ambition for political influence signaled a shift in focus from purely spiritual matters to institutional control. The desire for primacy over other Christian centers was not merely about religious doctrine but also about secular dominance, as the Church began to vie for power both in spiritual and political arenas.

The Conversion of the Empire

In 380, Emperor Theodosius I declared Christianity the official state religion of the Roman Empire, making it the foundation of the imperial religious system. From this point, the Church of Rome was no longer a marginal entity—it became institutionally intertwined with the structure of imperial power. As Christianity became the state religion, the Church grew in political influence, gaining control over not only spiritual matters but also societal governance.

The Donation of Constantine

One of the more famous and controversial documents in the Church's history, the *Donation of Constantine*, a forgery created in the 8th century but attributed to Constantine himself, further solidified the Church's claim to both spiritual and temporal authority. The document, purportedly written by Constantine, allegedly granted the pope control over vast territories in the Western Roman Empire. Though the document was later exposed as a forgery, it played a critical role in bolstering the papacy's claim to both religious and political supremacy. Its long-lasting influence extended even into

272

the age of exploration, when papal authority was invoked to divide the New World between Spain and Portugal.

Pepin and the Papal States
In the 8th century, Pepin the Short, the King of the Franks, made a decisive move by granting the papacy control over the Papal States—territories in central Italy. This not only made the pope a spiritual leader but also a temporal ruler with land, wealth, and a political agenda. The donation of land to the Church transformed the papacy into a feudal lord, further intertwining the Church's spiritual mission with the business of secular rule.

Ecclesiastical Constructs
With the increasing wealth and power of the Church of Rome, new doctrinal constructs were developed to further consolidate its authority over both kings and peasants. Innovations like indulgences (remission of punishment for sins), auricular confession (private confession to a priest), and the concept of purgatory gave the Church increasing control over adherents. These constructs not only deepened the Church's spiritual authority but also allowed it to manipulate individuals and rulers, political alliances, and social behavior.

Clerical Careers and Nepotism
As the Church expanded, it became a vocational path for second sons of noble families, offering a means of social mobility. Ecclesiastical positions became tools for acquiring wealth and power, as families used the Church to further their own political agendas. Nepotism and the use of Church offices for familial advancement deepened the secularization of the institution, further distancing it from its original spiritual mission.

From Organism to Organization
The Church's transformation from a living body of believers, as originally envisioned by early Christians, to a hierarchical organiza-

273

tion is one of the most significant shifts in Christian history. The Church, once led by the guiding influence of the Holy Spirit, became increasingly dominated by human leaders who sought to consolidate power and control. This transformation laid the foundation for the Church's eventual role as a secular institution, deeply embedded in the political, economic, and social fabric of Europe.

The Church as a Secular Power: Economic and Political Dominance

By the time of Pope Innocent III in the early 13th century, the Church of Rome had amassed unparalleled temporal power. The papacy controlled vast estates across Europe, held sway over kings, and dictated the direction of European politics. The Church had become a transnational entity with the ability to influence regions from England to Italy and beyond. This shift from spiritual to temporal power was visible in several key areas:

Land Ownership

By the 12th century, the Church of Rome controlled extensive land holdings throughout Europe, including large portions of land in Britain, France, and Bohemia. In some areas, the Church's land holdings exceeded 50% of the total land in the region. This wealth in land provided the Church not only with material resources but also with immense political leverage. It could influence local rulers, dictate the terms of land distribution, and even control key strategic regions across the continent.

Revenue Streams

The Church developed numerous economic mechanisms to maintain its wealth and power, including tithes, taxes, and donations from peasants and kings alike. Pilgrimages and the sale of relics brought in substantial revenue, while indulgences—paying for the remission of sins—became a significant source of income. The Church also profited from auricular confession and penances, turning spiritual

274

practices into financial transactions. The Crusades, which were heavily promoted and funded by the Church, provided another source of income, as soldiers paid taxes to support the holy wars. Additionally, the Church's power over marriage allowed it to impact the wealth and political alliances of noble families, further solidifying its role in shaping the socio-political landscape.

The Church as a Business
Ekelund, Hébert, and Tollison, in their analysis of the political economy of the medieval Church, argue that by the 12th century, the Church of Rome had essentially become an economic firm. With a hierarchical structure, a vast network of administrators, and a consistent product—salvation—the Church operated much like a corporation, blending religious authority with economic and political goals. Its ability to extract wealth from the faithful through various economic mechanisms made it a powerful and enduring institution, wielding both spiritual and temporal authority.

Monopolistic Power and the Medieval Church
By the time of the Reformation, the Church's monopoly over the supernatural was deeply entrenched in European society. The Church not only controlled religious life but also had its hand in political decisions, the governance of kingdoms, and the moral direction of citizens. The papacy's influence was felt across all levels of society, from kings to peasants, and it played a critical role in shaping the political and economic structures of Europe.

The work of scholars like Ekelund et al. highlights the Church's monopolistic grip on Christianity. By 1100, the Church of Rome was no longer merely a spiritual entity—it was a political power that dictated the course of European affairs. The papacy had become a dominant force, with the ability to influence monarchs, shape religious doctrine, and control the economic systems of vast regions.

The Rise of Secularism in the Church

The Church of Rome's shift from a spiritual mission to temporal power was gradual, but inevitable. It began as a small religious movement, but over time, it morphed into an institution that blended religious, economic, and political authority. Through land ownership, the development of new revenue-generating practices, and the creation of doctrinal constructs that further cemented its control, the Church became a secular institution of immense power.

This transformation from an organism to an organization—one focused on wealth, influence, and control—set the stage for the Reformation. In that era, the Church's monopolistic control would face its greatest challenge, as reformers sought to break the Church's grip on both the spiritual and temporal realms.

Notes and Observations

Investigative Journal Entry: Date: _____ / _____ / _____

How did the Church's shift from spiritual leadership to political power shape the way it interacted with secular rulers and the general populace? Consider the influence of documents like the Donation of Constantine, the papacy's land holdings, and the growing economic power of the Church. How did these changes affect the relationship between the Church and European monarchs?

The Church's increasing wealth and political power led to its transformation into an economic and political "firm." How does this comparison help us understand the broader societal role of the Church during the medieval period? Reflect on the Church's ability to generate wealth through mechanisms like indulgences, tithes, and land ownership. How did these activities influence the political landscape of Europe?

31

The Basis of Church Power
Inherited Sin and Infant Baptism

The Church of Rome's monopoly on spiritual and temporal power was built upon two critical dogmas: inherited sin and the practice of infant baptism. These dogmas were not just theological positions; they were the very foundation upon which the Church's control over salvation—and by extension, society—was based.

According to Augustine's dogma of *original* sin, all humanity inherited the stain of sin from Adam and Eve. That meant all humans were born guilty and spiritually dead, separated from God. In this framework, baptism became the essential act required to cleanse the individual of this sin, and because sin was inherited at birth, infant baptism became the means by which even the youngest could escape the eternal consequences of *original* sin.

Through this lens, the Church of Rome positioned itself as the only mediator of God's grace. It was the Church, not the individual, that held the keys to salvation, and baptism was the sacrament that initiated the individual into this salvation. By controlling baptism, the Church controlled the very salvation of its adherents, and through the mandate of infant baptism, it ensured that every citizen would be born into the fold of the Church—whether they understood it or not. This concept established a perpetual link between the individual and the institution, securing the Church's monopoly over spiritual and secular life.

As history unfolded, this doctrine became a powerful tool of control. Kings, queens, and rulers may have wielded political and military power, but the Church controlled the eternal fate of souls—

277

an influence that transcended earthly dominion. Anyone who questioned or rejected these dogmas, such as Pelagius or later Protestant Reformers, was quickly branded a heretic and cast out, underscoring the threat to Church authority that any challenge to its foundational beliefs posed. For centuries, the Church's monopoly on salvation silenced any dissent, branding those who questioned its dogmas as heretics.

Yet the Reformers, far from seeking mere reform, sought to free believers from a system that had enslaved both body and soul in a distorted view of grace. The Reformation was not merely a call for change within the Catholic Church, but rather an attempt to return to the faith once delivered to the saints—the faith of the New Testament that called for a personal, individual faith in Christ and a return to the Scriptures as the sole authority.

Developing Your Own Doctrine of Sin and Salvation

As we conclude our discussion on the Church's rise to power, it's important to pause and reflect on how doctrines like sin and salvation have shaped history—and how they continue to shape our lives today. The medieval Church might have wielded immense power through its doctrinal monopoly, but the ultimate question remains: *What does the Bible really teach about sin and salvation? How can we, as modern believers, develop our own understanding of these central theological concepts?*

Now, it's time for you, the reader, to begin thinking about your own doctrine of sin and salvation—not as dictated by any institution or tradition, but as revealed in the Scriptures. This is a crucial moment in your spiritual journey, one that invites you to reflect on the original message of the New Testament—the once-for-all-delivered-to-the-saints-faith.

As you reflect on these questions, consider how the Church's historical monopoly on salvation continues to affect contemporary Christian belief. How much of your faith is shaped by tradition, and

278

how much by personal engagement with Scripture? This is not merely an academic exercise; it is a life-altering exploration that invites you to recover the pure, unadulterated gospel—the faith that was once for all delivered to the saints.

To help guide this process, consider the following questions—a few texts from the Bible will assist you as you formulate your response:

1. What does the Bible say about sin? How does the New Testament describe the origin and nature of sin, and what is its effect on humanity? *"But each one is tempted when by his own evil desires he is lured away and enticed. Then after desire has conceived, it gives birth to sin; and sin, when it is full-grown, gives birth to death"* (James 1:14-15).

2. What is the role of baptism? What does Scripture say about the purpose and practice of baptism, and how does it relate to salvation? *"Baptism, which corresponds to this, now saves you (not the removal of the filth of the flesh, but the pledge of a good conscience toward God) through the resurrection of Jesus Christ"* (1 Peter 3:21, Holman Christian Standard Bible).

3. What is salvation? According to the Bible, what does it mean to be saved? Is salvation something we earn, or is it a gift from God? *"For at just the right time, while we were still powerless, Christ died for the ungodly. Very rarely will anyone die for a righteous man, though for a good man someone might possibly dare to die. But God proves His love for us in this: While we were still sinners, Christ died for us. Therefore, since we have now been justified by His blood, how much more shall we be saved from wrath through Him! For if, when we were enemies of God, we were reconciled to Him through the death of His Son, how much more, having been reconciled, shall we be saved through His life!"* (Romans 5:6-11). *"For Christ is the end of the law, to bring righteousness to everyone*

279

who believes... But what does it say? 'The word is near you; it is in your mouth and in your heart,' that is, the word of faith we are proclaiming: that if you confess with your mouth, 'Jesus is Lord,' and believe in your heart that God raised Him from the dead, you will be saved. For with your heart you believe and are justified, and with your mouth you confess and are saved" (Romans 10:4, 8-13).

"For it is by grace you have been saved through faith, and this not from yourselves; it is the gift of God, not by works, so that no one can boast." (Ephesians 2:8-9).

"Therefore, if anyone is in Christ, he is a new creation. The old has passed away. Behold, the new has come! All this is from God, who reconciled us to Himself through Christ and gave us the ministry of reconciliation: that God was reconciling the world to Himself in Christ, not counting men's trespasses against them. And He has committed to us the message of reconciliation. Therefore we are ambassadors for Christ, as though God were making His appeal through us. We implore you on behalf of Christ: Be reconciled to God. God made Him who knew no sin to be sin on our behalf, so that in Him we might become the righteousness of God" (2 Corinthians 5:17-21).

But to all who did receive Him, to those who believed in His name, He gave the right to become children of God—children born not of blood, nor of the desire or will of man, but born of God (Jn. 1:12-13).

Your answers to these questions will shape your understanding of the gospel and determine the foundation of your personal faith. This is more than a theological reflection—it is a transformative journey into the truth that sets us free.

A Bold Challenge

This is the moment to not only reflect on the doctrines that have shaped history but to boldly anchor your life in the truth of Scripture. Will you allow the traditions of men to shape your understanding of sin and salvation, or will you return to the word of God, where the truth of salvation has been revealed for all time? The choice is yours—and it is the choice that will define the trajectory of your life and your faith.

Now is the time to reclaim your faith. The ultimate question remains: *Are you ready to step away from the traditions of men and embrace the true, liberating gospel as revealed in God's Word?*

Use this space to write your statement of belief about sin and salvation. This will clarify and solidify your thinking and your faith and will give you confidence as you share your view on sin and salvation—on your freedom in Christ. As Peter urged those believers two millennia ago—*Have no fear of them, nor be troubled, but in your hearts honor Christ the Lord as holy, always being prepared to make a defense to anyone who asks you for a reason for the hope that is in you; yet do it with gentleness and respect* (1 Peter 3:14-15).

I believe...

281

Notes and Observations

Investigative Journal Entry: Date: _____ / _____ / _____

Doctrine and Power: How did the Church of Rome use the dogmas of inherited sin and infant baptism to establish and maintain its monopoly on spiritual and temporal authority? Can you identify other moments in history where belief systems have been used to control or consolidate power in society?

***Original* Sin:** Reflect on Augustine's dogma of *original* sin. How does this teaching shape the church's view of human nature? Do you agree with the idea that all people are born spiritually dead and require baptism for salvation? Why or why not?

Infant Baptism: The Church of Rome regarded infant baptism as essential for salvation. What are the theological implications of baptizing infants without their personal consent or understanding?

The Role of the Church in Salvation: The Catholic Church positioned itself as the sole mediator of God's grace. What does this suggest about the relationship between institutional authority and individual faith? How does this position align—or conflict—with the New Testament emphasis on a personal relationship with God?

Scriptural Authority: What does the Bible teach about salvation and the role of baptism in that process? How do your beliefs align with key passages such as Romans 5:6–11 and Ephesians 2:8–9?

Tradition vs. Scripture: Reflect on the central question posed in this chapter: Will you allow human tradition to shape your understanding of salvation, or will you rely on the authority of Scripture? Do you believe salvation must be earned—or do you affirm, with Paul, that it is a gift from God, *"not by works, so that no one can boast"* (Ephesians 2:8–9)?

32

A Reflection on Reclaiming Truth

As we reach the end of this journey, it's crucial to take a step back and reflect on the deeper implications of what has been discussed in these pages. This book has sought to challenge the foundations of the dogma of inherited sin and the attendant constructs that have become institutionalized over centuries—wielded as instruments of both spiritual and temporal power. We have examined the doctrines that shaped the church and, by extension, the faith of millions—doctrines like sin, salvation, and the role of the church—and questioned their validity as historically and currently held.

The heart of this book is a call for reformation—not merely institutional, but a reformation of the heart, mind, and soul. It is a call to reclaim the faith as it was first delivered to the saints, as presented in Scripture, and to break free from the ecclesiastical constructs that have distorted the true essence of the Christian faith.

This is not just a historical critique; it is a theological challenge. It invites you to rethink your understanding of sin, salvation, and the role of the church. It calls for a return to biblical truth—untainted by the power structures of the church or the traditions of men. The ultimate question is whether we are willing—individually and collectively—

- to reclaim our faith,
- to return to the truth of the New Testament,
- to embrace a personal, unmediated relationship with Christ.

We need a faith rooted in the teachings of Scripture and a faithful, accurate use of the biblical text—rather than in the authority of any institution.

The historical examination in this book provides a critical lens through which to view the development of dogmas that were not purely theological, but also deeply political. The dogma of inherited or *original* sin and the corresponding practice of infant baptism are central to understanding how the Church of Rome—and later ecclesiastical powers—established and maintained their grip on both spiritual and political life.

By focusing on these two core constructs, we see how the Church of Rome positioned itself as the sole mediator of grace and salvation—asserting exclusive authority to direct souls toward eternal life. This gave the Church a monopoly on salvation itself, which in turn granted it sweeping influence over the lives of billions.

We have traced the evolution of these dogmas and their role in consolidating ecclesiastical power. And while the Protestant Reformation was a bold attempt to correct many abuses of the Catholic Church, it did not entirely free the Christian world from these deeply entrenched beliefs. The concept of inherited sin, for instance, was retained in many Protestant traditions—despite the Reformation's rejection of other Catholic doctrines. This raises a sobering question: Have we truly left behind those institutional frameworks, or have we simply carried their dogmas forward under a new name?

But this book does not merely critique the past—it offers a path forward. It is a personal invitation to reflect on your own theology. Are your beliefs about sin and salvation based on tradition—or are they grounded in Scripture? The goal is not rebellion for its own sake, but reformation for the sake of truth: a return to the pure, unfiltered gospel delivered once for all to the saints.

Through historical investigation, biblical engagement, and theological challenge, you've been invited to take personal responsibility for your faith. The call to reflect on sin, salvation, and baptism is also a call to reclaim personal engagement with Scripture—to let the word of God be your final authority. It is an invitation to step away from institutional dependency and step into the freedom Christ offers to those who walk with Him.

As we conclude this journey, the task now is to articulate your own understanding of the gospel—to create a personal confession of faith that reflects not institutional tradition, but your own encounter with Christ and Scripture. In doing so, we fulfill Peter's charge: to *be prepared to give an answer to anyone who asks about the hope within us.*

We have, in effect, become detectives—uncovering the evidence hidden in history and Scripture. We've exposed distortions, followed the trail of truth, and now stand at the crossroads between tradition and revelation. The questions that remain are these:

Will we let the truth we've uncovered shape how we live and believe?

Will we embrace a gospel rooted in Scripture and free from distortion?

Or will we continue to carry the weight of dogmas imposed long ago?

This is a bold challenge: to choose freedom.

Will your faith be shaped by the traditions of men—or by the truth of God's word?

Will you cling to inherited dogmas—or will you step into the light of the gospel, unfiltered and free?

The choice is yours—and it will define the trajectory of your life and your faith.

This is not merely a mental or theological exercise. It is a life-altering invitation to reclaim biblical faith, to embrace a personal relationship with Christ, and to allow that relationship to reshape your entire understanding of salvation, grace, and the role of the church.

Now is the time. Reject the dogmas that cloud your understanding. Embrace the truth of Scripture. Take ownership of your faith.

We are sinners because we choose to sin.
It's NOT Adam's fault!
God's grace, however, remains abundantly available to all,
offering the opportunity for restoration and reconciliation.

"Invitation of Grace"
We are sinners, each by choice,
Not by Adam's fall or voice.
Yet grace extends its healing hand,
Restoring all who heed the call.
So come, ye sinners, to the cross,
Where mercy flows, bearing loss.
Embrace the love that sets you free,
In Christ alone, find liberty.

Beyond Expectations
The Kingdom No One Expected

What kind of Kingdom begins with a cross?

Jesus came preaching the Kingdom of God—but not the one anyone expected.

Beyond Expectations: The Kingdom No One Expected invites you into 55 vivid vignettes—each a devotional window into the life of Jesus and the surprising nature of His reign. From the wedding at Cana to the cry from the cross, these reflections trace the arc of a Kingdom not built on conquest, but on compassion; not rooted in might, but in mercy.

Blending pastoral warmth, poetic insight, and biblical depth, this is **devotional theology**—Scripture brought to life in ways both reverent and real.

Whether read alone or used a guide for Bible study groups, *Beyond Expectations* will draw you deeper into the story of the King who came to save…
Not the way we imagined—but just as God had planned.

Step into the Kingdom.
Let it turn your expectations upside down.

Available at Amazon, Barnes & Noble, and retailers across the nation.

Get the companion to *Beyond Expectations*...

Profiles from Paul
A Life Poured Out for the Kingdom

What Jesus began, Paul explained and extended—through a Spirit-empowered life of mission, message, and ministry. *Profiles from Paul* explores the story of the early church through the eyes of the man who gave structure to the gospel and insight to the Kingdom. A devotional theology rooted in Acts and the Epistles.

In 75 short, reflective vignettes, the Apostle Paul's life is traced from conversion to calling, from mission to imprisonment. Each vignette includes biblical narrative, historical insight, original poetry, and questions for personal or group reflection.

Written for everyday Christians, this book brings Paul's letters and legacy into focus with warmth, clarity, and conviction. Ideal for personal devotion, small group study, or leadership training, this resource invites readers to walk the path of faith with Paul as their guide.

Available at Amazon, Barnes & Noble, and retailers across the nation.

www.ingramcontent.com/pod-product-compliance
Lightning Source LLC
Chambersburg PA
CBHW070548130626
46556CB00001B/59